T 0200 2700041 1

D0758397

RANDOLPH BOURNE AND THE POLITICS OF CULTURAL RADICALISM

American Political Thought

edited by

Wilson Carey McWilliams and Lance Banning

RANDOLPH BOURNE AND THE POLITICS OF CULTURAL RADICALISM

LESLIE J. VAUGHAN

UNIVERSITY PRESS OF KANSAS

Published by the University Press of Kansas (Lawrence, Kansas 66049), which was organized by the Kansas Board of Regents and is operated and funded by Emporia State University, Fort Hays State University, Kansas State University, Pittsburg State University, the University of Kansas, and Wichita State University

Library of Congress Cataloging-in-Publication Data

Vaughan, Leslie J.
Randolph Bourne and the politics of cultural radicalism / Leslie J. Vaughan.
p. cm.—(American political thought)
Includes bibliographical references and index.
ISBN 0-7006-0821-4 (alk. paper)
1. Bourne, Randolph Silliman, 1886–1918. 2. Radicalism—United States—History—20th century. 3. Criticism—United States—History—20th century. 4. United States—Intellectual life—1865–1918. 5. United States—Politics and government—1865–1933. 6. World War, 1914–1918—Social aspects—United States. I. Title. II. Series.
E664.B74V38 1997
973.91'092—dc21 96-48218

British Library Cataloguing in Publication Data is available.

Printed in the United States of America

10 9 8 7 6 5 4 3 2 1

The paper used in this publication meets the minimum requirements of the American National Standard for Permanence of Paper for Printed Library Materials Z39.48-1984.

For all malcontents

CONTENTS

ACKNOWLEDGMENTS

With every book, many obligations are incurred, and its publication offers the welcome opportunity to express one's gratitude to the people who have made it possible. In my case, the debts extend back to the days when this book was a dissertation. To Michael P. Rogin I owe my first debt of gratitude, for bringing Bourne's work to my attention and for encouraging me to continue to research his political thought during my graduate years at the University of California, Berkeley. Mike Rogin makes the study of political theory an intensely personal and politically challenging experience, as much by his example as by what he teaches. Other teachers at the University of California, Berkeley, particularly Norman Jacobson, Hannah Pitkin, and D. Paul Thomas also transmitted their enthusiasm for and knowledge of political theory that continues to inspire me.

My adviser at the University of Chicago, the late J. David Greenstone, encouraged me to write a master's thesis on pragmatism. His intelligence, deep humanity, and democratic sensibilities continue to light the way for all of us who were fortunate to have known or worked with him. David Tracy also brought new insight into the philosophy of William James and helped me draw out its connections to modern and postmodern thought. My dissertation advisers—Mike Rogin, Norman Jacobson, and Carolyn Porter—advised me through the stages of research and writing with patience and encouragement. Berkeley graduate student colleagues, including

Patricia Boling, Nancy Haggard-Gilson, Penelope Hanan-Dahmen, Sheryl Lutjens, and George Shulman, assisted with revisions of several portions of the dissertation. I also wish to thank the members of the West Coast editorial collective of the *New Political Science* who took seriously the Bourneian critique of the role of intellectuals in modern war during the "Vietnamization" of our own war, including Sheryl Lutjens, Michael W. McCann, Michael MacDonald, Jonas Pontusson, George Shulman, Sven Steinmo, and D. Paul Thomas.

My colleagues at Macalester College have been a source of strength and encouragement. My deepest gratitude goes to Norman L. Rosenberg, who is in every sense a mentor, an adviser, and an invaluable friend, not only for his many suggestions for the work as a whole but also for his support throughout its long gestation. Without him, this book would not have been written. I am grateful to Donald R. Culverson, Roxanne Gudeman, Michal M. McCall, Darrell Moore, Norman Rosenberg, Sanford Schram, and Joelle Vitiello for reading earlier versions of Chapters 6 and 7 and gave sound and critical advice. Members of the faculty writing group at Macalester College, including Adrienne Christiansen, Beth Cleary, Ruthanne Godellei, Roxanne Gudeman, Michal M. McCall, Darrell Moore, Rhona Leibel, Clay Steinman, and Joelle Vitiello, created a genuine intellectual community, a difficult accomplishment at best in a climate of competing obligations for faculty. Charles R. Green and Rhona Leibel were forgiving of my lapses as a teacher and colleague as I made the final revisions of this manuscript. Michal M. McCall, my dear and devoted friend and adviser, and Paul L. Murphy deserve special thanks for their support and assistance, and I am grateful for and strengthened by their confidence.

For research assistance, I wish to thank Alejandro Aguilera, Katherine Eckland, Amanda Humpage, Hideo Kobata, Mpho Leseka, and Genevieve Warwick. Roxanne Fisher in the Department of Political Science at Macalester College guided us through our tasks with tireless patience, humor, and sound advice. I would also like to acknowledge the students in my American political thought class of 1995, especially Christopher Teske, for interrogating Bourne's ideas about transnationalism and his critique of pragmatism, and I am grateful for the privilege of working with students at Macalester College and the University of Minnesota, Duluth.

Thomas Bender of New York University generously read the entire manuscript and offered critical suggestions on an earlier version of Chapter 7, as did members of his 1989 NEH seminar Cities, Biographies, and Texts, including Janet Noever, Jennifer Bradley, Donald Marti, and Ted Wolner. From different disciplines, we managed to form a cohesive and imaginative group of scholars with a common interest in the cultural politics of cities. Their intelligence and energy have sustained me in my continuing exploration of American progressivism.

I would also like to thank Donald R. Culverson, Tom Bender, Donald Marti, R. Jeffrey Lustig, Norman Rosenberg, Sanford Schram, and Michael Weinstein for reading and offering incisive and detailed comments on portions of the manuscript. Benedetto Fontana and Susan Abrams Beck provided steady encouragement and specific suggestions on the writing process.

I extend my enduring, loving, but inadequate thanks to my father, Sam Vaughan, who is an editor and publisher. His position was the most difficult of all, as I insisted that he read the manuscript as my father and not as my editor. Fortunately, he did not listen, and his impeccable editorial judgment remained uncompromised. My family gave me steady and uncompromised support, offering encouragement and presumptive confidence at every turn. My mother, Josephine LoBiondo Vaughan, always asked *the* penetrating question about the book, usually the one I could not answer or did not think to ask. Jeffrey M. Vaughan, David S. Vaughan, and Dana A. Vaughan provided the needed perspectives on how to approach this project and generously advised me on ways to navigate the competing demands made of a junior faculty member. David Vaughan's sensitive photography reminds me that one's work is never solitary but always a collaborative, indeed, a family affair. I am also grateful to Leonard LoBiondo for his constant and intelligent advice and support. My thanks and deep affection for Mike go beyond his providing me with an anchor and his understanding and patience.

I have been privileged to have Wilson Carey McWilliams and Lance Banning as my editors in the American Political Thought series at the University Press of Kansas as they could not have been more demanding, more knowledgeable, or more generous in their meticulous reading of the manuscript. Fred M. Woodward, director of the University

Press of Kansas, has been a constant and gentle guiding force from the very beginning of this project, answering innumerable and bothersome questions with grace, clarity, and patience. The staff at the press offered expert assistance at every stage.

A different version of Chapter 6 was presented at the annual convention of the American Political Science Association in 1992 as "A Post-Liberal Pragmatism? The Case of Randolph Bourne and World War I." Earlier versions of Chapter 7 were given at the annual convention of the American Culture Association in 1990 as "'Trans-National America': Another Look at Cultural Pluralism" and published in 1991 in the *Journal of American Studies* as "Cosmopolitanism, Ethnicity, and American Identity: Randolph Bourne's 'Trans-National America'" (25[3]: 443–59). I would also like to acknowledge the helpful suggestions of anonymous readers of the *Journal of Politics* and *American Quarterly* for their contributions to revised versions of Chapters 6 and 7, respectively.

The New Jersey Historical Commission, the National Endowment for the Humanities, and the University of Minnesota's Faculty Grant Program provided partial funding for my research, and Macalester College's junior-faculty leave program afforded me the opportunity to concentrate on scholarly pursuits free from the obligations of teaching. Kenneth Lohf and the staff at the Rare Books and Manuscripts Library, Butler Library, Columbia University, were helpful in making Bourne's papers available and for granting permission to quote from archival material. I would also like to thank Neda Westlake at the Van Pelt Library, University of Pennsylvania; Amy Stark of the Center for Creative Photography, University of Arizona; and Edward C. Carter II and his staff at the American Philosophical Society Library, Philadelphia, for access to Bourne's letters and permission to quote from them. I am grateful to all of them for their ready assistance and courtesies.

For the inevitable omissions and errors, I am, of course, fully responsible.

1
INTRODUCTION

Randolph Bourne was a leading figure in the pre–World War I rebellion of the twentieth century, a time of political activism, cultural experimentation, and youthful optimism, when, in the words of the visiting Irish painter John Butler Yeats, "the fiddles were tuning up all over America." As a member of the first generation to inherit a corporate capitalist order, Bourne became its spokesman and also one of its deepest critics. He advocated a broad-based cultural renaissance to rescue the "personal point of view," invoked by William James, and to institute a "culture of feeling," to offset the growing emphasis on technology, bureaucratic administration, and social control through the application of reason. He encouraged a youth revolt, generational in consciousness and concerned with freeing personal relations and social roles. He advanced the idea of a "trans-national" American culture, a cosmopolitan "federation of cultures" that would include America's newest immigrants as equal partners in the social compact.

He is remembered primarily for his opposition to military intervention in World War I. "War is the health of the state," he warned in an unfinished essay published after his death. Woodrow Wilson's war policies had centralized state power, rationalized the economy, Americanized the schools, and criminalized dissent, permanently altering the nature of liberal politics. Bourne reserved his harshest criticism for the "younger intelligentsia" of his own generation who, like Walter Lippmann, became publicists for the war, working for the Creel Committee on Public Information; or who mobilized consensus as journalists and educators in support of the war; or who, like John Dewey, the nation's leading philosopher, replaced the creative pragmatism of William James with an instrumentalist approach, its "vision" subsumed by "technique."

When he died at the age of thirty-two, six weeks after Armistice, Bourne was remembered in scores of testimonials and tributes. To many people, his death signified the end of an era and the martyrdom of a certain spirit of youthful innocence. To others, his was a voice of singular courage and political independence. Out of his public opposition to the war, a persistent legend emerged. He was the haunting figure of Dos Passos's *U.S.A.:*

> This little sparrowlike man,
> tiny twisted bit of flesh in a black cape,
> always in pain and ailing,
> put a pebble in his sling
> and hit Goliath in the forehead with it.
> *War,* he wrote, *is the health of the state.*

A crucial part of the legend fastened on Bourne's radical difference:

> If any man has a ghost
> Bourne has a ghost,
> a tiny twisted unscared ghost in a black cloak
> hopping along the grimy old brick and brownstone streets
> still left in downtown New York,
> crying out in a shrill soundless giggle:
> *War is the health of the state.*[1]

As with many writers, the corporeal image was an important part of the myth. Bourne's hunched back and crooked frame, in contrast to his moral rectitude, were recounted in a dozen memoirs, poetry, and at least two novels that since have become a part of the cultural fabric of the literary and political left. In the 1920s, legend had it that Bourne spent the last year in silence and disrepute, his manuscripts seized by federal agents and refused by publishers. It was said that he died poor and alone, abandoned by friends and persecuted by the government. His writings went unread, and Bourne himself became a text to be interpreted.[2]

In the 1930s, the legend was reinvented, this time by American Marxists, among them Michael Gold, who searched for indigenous sources of political radicalism. They heralded Bourne as the "Great American" literary critic who prized the virtues of proletarian art and literature.[3] In the 1940s, antifascists interpreted his solitary opposition to the state and to corporate impersonality as an exemplary resistance to democratic totalitarianism.[4] Again in the 1960s, his writings were reprinted and his ideas reconsidered by a New Left interested in "personal politics" and by student activists protesting the "multiversity's" role in state-sponsored research, education, and administration.[5] Not surprisingly, perhaps, during the 1980s, a time of reaction, Bourne's writings went out of print,[6] and his importance came to rest primarily on his failures as a "forgotten prophet," the last of a dying breed of visionaries or rebels whose failed and perhaps impossibilist mission to restore youthful virtues to an aging America has been relegated to the detritus of history.[7]

"The text finally disappeared under the interpretation," Nietzsche wrote of the French Revolution, a fate affecting Bourne's life and work as well. The legend mediates every reading, even in some examples of Bourne scholarship, telling us more, perhaps, about the generation that invented it than about the subject itself.[8] Legends are, after all, part of a culture's conversation with itself, reflecting and refracting its own anxieties about and aspirations for its common condition. They can reinspire a culture, as Nietzsche maintained. But they can obscure an intimate knowledge of their subjects or distract (and sometimes depoliticize) their inventors. The Bourne legend has obscured in this double sense. Yet it has also obscured unexpectedly, ignoring the role Bourne himself played in creating his own myth. We know Bourne by his shadowy, ghostlike presence in Dos Passos's text, not by his own words. We know him as other people have constructed him, not as he constructed himself.

In this book I return to a study of Bourne's life and work by offering an analysis from categories derived immanently, that is, from within his work itself. I do not try to demystify the Bourne legend or separate the "man from the myth"; rather, I seek to explore the particular role Bourne played in the creation of his own myth or "epic" (his word) and to evaluate the significance of that effort for his political thought. Through the epic nature of autobiography, I suggest, Bourne revealed a Nietzschean disposition to shape his own fate, to intensify his experience and make more of his being, in stories that others of his generation might read.

The Nietzschean influence I have chosen to highlight is consistent with the terms Bourne used to frame his own role as a radical critic and to construct the forces he saw as shaping modern culture. According to Nietzsche, every culture can be characterized by a particular combination of the moral and spiritual impulse of the apollonian and the physical and emotional energies of the dionysian. Nietzsche's apollonianism stood for art and the organizing capacity to create order, illusion, and form. The dionysiac pertained to the deeper recesses of passion and chaos, which often gave rise to communal revelry and frenzied bursts of energy but which could also inform and vitalize an apollonian construct. For Nietzsche, as for Bourne, it was in the balance between order and artful creation and the vitalism and energy of the pagan that a culture could regenerate itself.

Bourne theorized American political culture in similar terms. He found the apollonian will-to-form in Victorian counsels of self-control as well as in the progressives' fascination with scientific management. He saw the dionysian impulse in the crowds and lights of the city streets as modern-day carnivals and in the personal expressivity of neighborhood pageantry and artists' cooperatives. His attention to both sides of the modern experience—its rationality and irrationality, its order and disorder, the "puritan" and the "pagan"—and his unwillingness to choose between them or resolve them into some higher synthesis was unique among the progressives and radicals of the early century. For him, contradiction was creative, anticipating Herbert Marcuse, and the stance of "intellectual suspense" was a creative impulse, restlessly moving between dream and reality, following Nietzsche. It is this perspective—as a confirmed modernist who anticipated the "post-modern" (his word)—or, as he wrote of himself, as a social reformer with aesthetic aspirations—that makes him a pivotal figure in the history of American political thought.[9]

This book is informed by the recognition that Bourne's thought is valuable precisely because it offered a new political discourse and a set of cultural possibilities for American society at the height of the modern age.[10] Influenced by and responding to the romanticism of Nietzsche, the irrationalism of Henri Bergson and Georges Sorel, the idealism of Walt Whitman, the pragmatism of James and Dewey, and the democratic socialism of Graham Wallas, G. B. Shaw, and Henry George, his political and cultural criticism kept alive the competing tensions of this contradictory legacy. His writings, amounting to over 1,500 articles, several volumes of essays, hundreds of letters, and a dozen unpublished essays, written in only seven years, reveal a vision that was generous and democratic and a mind that was corrosive and increasingly impatient with liberal politics.

In this book I try to reposition Bourne's thought at the center of debates about the nature and limits of American liberalism.[11] Writing in what Antonio Gramsci calls the "national-popular" language, Bourne participated in public debates about war preparedness, immigration, educational reform, and feminism, but, I argue, his analysis was framed in terms other than those that were ordinarily given. Writing from a position "below the battle," he rejected the political options offered at the time—that one must be either prowar or antiwar, an American or an immigrant, a poet or critic—as choices constructed within the terms of liberalism itself. This stance, I suggest, created a contradictory situation for him: in repudiating politics, he did not repudiate the political. In my view, however, redefining politics and the outlines of political agency, the public space was opened to outside voices and alternative sites of engagement, creating the prospects of a more inclusive, more democratic politics.

It was a position that involved risks and limitations. It risked political isolation, as it was clearly oppositional. It was unpalatable to the intellectual who "craved certainty." It was difficult to sustain as a form of democratic politics. And, perhaps most significantly, it was a concession to one's ineffectiveness in shaping current policies. Nevertheless, when political alternatives were foreclosed, Bourne argued, his position "below the battle" was the most advantageous place from which to generate alternatives to liberal consensus.

This interpretation challenges the more familiar one initially offered by Lewis Mumford and more recently recalled by Casey

Blake in his formidable study, *Beloved Community;* that Bourne's politics were a form of romantic defeatism, or even worse, a retreat into political passivity.[12] It is my contention that Bourne's position "below the battle" was neither a retreat from politics nor a place taken outside the line of fire, as the phrase might suggest; rather, it was another form of political engagement, a way to free oneself from hegemonic certainties that block genuine debate, preclude alternatives to politics-as-usual, and prevent democratic change. Indeed, I argue that it is precisely from this "third space," borrowing Jacques Lacan's term, that Bourne was able to participate in practical, ongoing, grassroots efforts to reorganize relations among and between family, work, and community. As alternative forms of political organizing and education, these activities were practical—not utopian—expressions of politics, based in the neighborhoods of modern cities, that effectively reconstructed social relations among workers, students, writers, and activists that anticipated the kind of democratic politics Bourne wanted to see instituted in the nation as a whole.

In historicizing his thought within the debates about American liberalism, I seek to accomplish several objectives. My first goal is to uncover the historical roots of American political thought, and in particular, to locate the roots of twentieth-century radical thought. My primary focus is on the contradictions of progressive liberalism, especially with regard to the role of science and expertise in shaping the social and political order, the importance of nationalism in building a common culture, and the nature and role of the liberal state in a democratic society. Because Bourne shared many of the intellectual assumptions of the pragmatic progressives at the *New Republic,* the aesthetic commitments of the cultural nationalists at the *Seven Arts,* and the political convictions of the radical critics at the *Masses,* his thought can best be understood as a chronicle and critique of modern twentieth-century American political thought.

Second, I hope to clarify the relation of intellectuals to institutional politics, or what Norman Birnbaum has termed the "excessive integration of intellect and power," which first emerged during World War I. The support of progressive intellectuals for an administrative state and a centralized economy, indeed their integration with the state, marked a turning point in the political role of intellectuals and revealed a crisis within that class, and within the middle class generally, about the nature of political responsibility and involvement, which became a legacy of the war.[13]

Finally, I seek to offer an understanding of the ideas and experiences of a particular political generation and of the influence of generationalism on Bourne's thought. I regard his generational affiliations both as a context for his radical dissent and a vehicle for its construction. Part of my inquiry addresses the question of Bourne's representativeness, or his ability to represent the views of his generation, and by extension the experiences of young moderns. In his view, his experiences of personal struggles to deal with physical disability and exclusion represented the experiences of America's outsiders—the immigrant, the activist, the urban poor—and his own generation, discontent with Victorianism, politically powerless, and diffident toward corporate capitalism. In theorizing the nature of his representativeness, I also hope to explore the relationship between the modern intellectual and the public culture.

The chapters are organized conceptually. In Chapter 2, I provide the theoretical background to Bourne's political thought and to that of his generation and examine the nature of his representativeness as a young radical and modern intellectual. Chapter 3 analyzes his first autobiographical essay as a conversion narrative, or the spiritual journey, in Michael Rogin's words, of a "unique, and therefore, representative" American. Taking the form of an "auto–American-biography," in the fine phrase of Sacvan Bercovitch, it was offered as the story of a representative individual whose destiny was understood to be tied to that of his community.[14] In Chapter 4, I examine the "trans-valuation" of Bourne's (given) marginality to his (chosen) stance of purposeful discontent, a position that, I argue, was an effort to disembody his radical difference into a philosophical stance. Ironic criticism combined the poetical (dionysian) and the analytical (apollonian) approaches to critical judgment, detached and yet committed simultaneously.[15]

In Chapter 5, I analyze Bourne's advocacy of the idea of a youth rebellion, encompassing feminism, educational reform, and pragmatism, which were constructed as several means of "trans-valuing" personal relations and, through the artful creation of "personality," preserving the dionysian spirit of youth. His idea of a youth revolt was a challenge to the twin apollonian impulses of the age: the Victorian emphasis on the building of character and the progressives' fascination with scientific expertise. I try to make clear the connection between a fading Victorianism and an emergent progressivism by contrasting his idea of a youthful rebellion with Walter Lippmann's plea for "mastery" to rescue their generation from "drift," through professionalism and management skills, a move that Bourne regarded as a sign of premature aging.

Chapter 6 focuses on his wartime critique of the purely instrumental moment in social reform, the deceptions of the progressives' preoccupation with social control, and the risks of the integration of intellectuals with the state. Bourne's ambivalent relation to progressivism before the war was crystallized in his critique of Dewey's wartime pragmatism and led to Bourne's unyielding antistatist political theory in his essay on the state.

I outline Bourne's search for conditions that would fulfill America's "promise" in Chapter 7, analyzing his support of an ethnic and national cosmopolitanism as a counternarrative to the dominant discourse of "Americanization" and the melting pot ideal in the early twentieth century. A transnational American culture was based on the prefiguration of a more democratic form of politics and a new conception of national identity, taking account of individuals' cultural, ethnic, and political affiliations in the idea of a dual citizenship. Although Bourne did not fully work out the relation between political and cultural citizenship, the idea of multiple memberships remains a central issue in debates about the nature of contemporary democratic theory.

In Chapter 8, I investigate Bourne's literary and cultural theory, his theory of the role of art in society, and the prospects of a revitalized (dionysian) culture in America, supported in part by "beloved communities" (using Josiah Royce's phrase) of cultural workers acting collectively to bring art to all classes. I argue that his theory of the role of art—as a tool of social reform and as a means of reinspiring a culture—reflects the progressivist and Nietzschean influences on his thought, respectively. His literary criticism similarly combined a modern appreciation of the importance of creating a national literature and a postmodern sensibility in reading texts, tracing the thread of desire in the novels of Theodore Dreiser, Fyodor Dostoyevsky, and Willa Cather.

In the Epilogue I return to the Bourne myth and the significance of his critical theory. Against the scholarship of the last three decades, I evaluate his work within Nietzsche's three metamorphoses of the spirit, where, it has been said, Bourne was caught in the role of Nietzsche's lion—the position of always saying no—unable to offer an affirmative politics for radical work in the future. This interpretation, although persuasive in light of the broad sweep of his dissent, does not take into account his concession to the *limits* of dissent against the "inexorables" of war or his prefigurative politics of transnationalism and efforts to free the aesthetic impulse. In taking a position "below the battle," I suggest, he found an unmapped space to keep the "intellectual currents" flowing and pursue creative alternatives to impersonal bureaucratic politics, in an effort to fulfill America's "promise."

2
A POLITICAL GENEALOGY

> The country is . . . dotted with young men and women, in full possession of their minds, faculties and virtue, who feel themselves profoundly alien to the work which is going on around them. . . . They are genuine pragmatists and they fear any kind of absolute, even when bearing gifts.
>
> —*Randolph S. Bourne, "A War Diary"*

In the first decade of the twentieth century, America underwent a dramatic revolution in all aspects of cultural life: in taste and manners, in morals and philosophy, in institutional arrangements and personal relations. Social conventions regarding gender roles, women's "nature," workers' rights, immigration policy, internationalism, and artistic freedom were contested openly in a brief experiment in America's political culture that has come to be known as the "little rebellion." The young progressives, feminists, socialists, and bohemians who participated tried to break free from prevailing norms in political consensus, sexual conformity, and cultural formalism. They formed themselves into a highly self-conscious if somewhat disorganized group, certain of their historical role and their ideas for the future.[1]

The prewar rebellion was national in scope, but its primary centers of activity were in many of the nation's cities, including New

York, Boston, Chicago, San Francisco, Milwaukee, Madison, and Portland. In New York City, the "little renaissance" was based in Greenwich Village, its compressed spatial geography contrasting sharply with its cultural internationalism. Social reformers and political revolutionaries, writers and artists, socialists and anarchists, suffragists and settlement workers lived and worked together, often side by side. Their public culture took place in literary salons, armories, eating clubs, and art galleries where they displayed their paintings, performed experimental theater, and held literary readings. They formed political organizations to secure suffrage rights, educate children of the working class, protest labor conditions, and resist war preparedness. In their private lives they experimented as well, forming themselves into alternative families, bound together by friendship and shared ideals. And they made a deliberate effort to bridge the class barriers between themselves and the new immigrants from southern and eastern Europe, college students, and the urban poor, often living in the same neighborhoods.

In 1913 Alfred Stieglitz founded the Photo-Secession Gallery at 291 Fifth Avenue, a gallery-workshop-meetingplace for artists and their friends. The gallery exhibited the works of a new group of American artists and photographers—Georgia O'Keeffe, Marsden Hartley, Max Weber, Arthur Dove, and other modernists—and became an intimate and informally organized community space for social gatherings and discussions. In the same year Mabel Dodge formed her famous salon, where the likes of Walter Lippmann, Max Eastman, Lucy Claire Mitchell, and others convened to discuss current ideas in Freudianism, feminism, imagist poetry, and labor radicalism. Dodge captured the flavor of those evenings in her memoirs, describing the crowd that gathered as a mingling of "Socialists, Trade-Unionists, Anarchists, Suffragists, Poets, Relations, Lawyers, Murderers, 'Old Friends,' Psychoanalysts, IWWs, Single Taxers, Birth Controlists, Newspapermen, Artists, Modern-Artists, Club Women, Woman's-place-is-in-the-home Women, Clergymen, and just plain men."[2]

A number of little theaters sprang up, such as the Provincetown Players and the Washington Square Players in Greenwich Village, to perform contemporary material, including one another's work.

Neighborhood theater companies were formed, companies of non-professionals (and neighbors) who participated in the performances. Group pageants were also a popular form of experimental theater. The famous Paterson Pageant of 1913, re-creating the Paterson garment workers' strike of 1912, produced a kind of performance art on a massive scale, attracting 15,000 audience members, according to one historian, most of whom were working class and many of whom walked from New Jersey to Madison Square Garden in order to participate in the event. The pageant was a success in its own terms: it publicized the strike, drew support for the strikers, and, in broader cultural terms, broke the barriers between audience and performers in a staged rally/performance that spanned two days. In the dance world, Isadora Duncan scandalized genteel critics with her free-form modern dance. Among immigrant workers, Emma Goldman, among others, held public meetings to advocate free love, birth control, and women's health education, where she was frequently arrested, often before she even began to speak.[3]

Perhaps the archetypal event of the time was the Armory Show of 1913. An immense exhibition of 1,600 paintings, prints, drawings, and pieces of sculpture, the show introduced many Americans to the work of the European cubists and futurists. The bold colors and shapes of Matisse, Kandinsky, Duchamp, Brancusi, Rouault, Lehmbruck, and other artists shocked members of New York's art community. After spending "an appalling morning" at the show, the staid art critic Kenyon Cox wrote that he had witnessed the "total destruction of the art of painting." "To have looked at it is to have passed through a pathological museum where the layman has no right to go. One feels that one has seen not an exhibition, but an exposure."[4]

Exposing the pretenses of literary respectability was one of the objectives of the "little magazines." Based in Chicago, New York, and Boston, these small-circulation journals, some frankly socialist, others merely rebellious, aimed to break down the boundaries between high culture and popular culture and the modernist divide between art and politics. Among the little magazines founded in the prewar years were the irreverent *Masses* in 1911, edited by Max Eastman and Floyd Dell, prosecuted in 1918 by the U.S. government for sedition during the war; Harriet Monroe's journal *Poetry* in Chicago in 1912, a forum for the avant-garde; and the *New Republic* in 1914, edited by Herbert Croly, Walter Lippmann, and Walter Weyl, progressive intellectuals with an interest in the possibilities of a democratic socialism. Croly's opening editorial suggested the journal's slightly incendiary purpose; its aim, he wrote, was "less to inform or entertain its readers than to start little insurrections in the realm of their convictions." The lively and sophisticated *Seven Arts* was founded in 1916 by Waldo Frank, James Oppenheim, and Floyd Dell as a forum for American art and culture. In its two short years, the *Seven Arts* managed to publish noteworthy, new American authors, among them, Robert Frost, Amy Lowell, Sherwood Anderson, Stephen Vincent Benét, Theodore Dreiser, Max Eastman, Carl Sandburg, Eugene O'Neill, Vachel Lindsay, John Reed, H. L. Mencken, Harold Stearns, Paul Rosenfeld, and Van Wyck Brooks, some of them reaching fame decades later. Committed to cultural nationalism, it also welcomed European contributors, including Romaine Rolland, Kahlil Gibran, Bertrand Russell, D. H. Lawrence, John Butler Yeats, and writers issuing manifestos for a Young India, a Young Ireland, and a Young Italy, whose efforts were considered a part of a growing spirit of internationalism in an ever-shrinking world.[5]

It is important to understand the genealogy of the little rebellion and to locate Bourne's place in it. According to Nietzsche, a genealogy is not a chronological tracing of origins but a logical inquiry into the consequences and practices of a concept or an idea. It is not interested in the thing-in-itself (the nature or essence of an idea) but in the conditions of its expression and the ways in which it is constituted and constrained by institutions and practices. A genealogy, therefore, reverses conventional historical logic, which, as Nietzsche showed, imposes an artificial unity on its subject, after the fact. A genealogy shows, as Judith Butler suggests, what is at stake in labeling something as a cause rather than as an effect.[6]

At stake, therefore, in the genealogy of the little rebellion is another understanding of the "lost promise" of progressivism recently studied by Eldon Eisenach. I explore the cultural causes of that failure rather than the internal contradictions within progressivism itself. The circumstances that Eisenach understandably viewed as progressivism's failure as a "political regime"—its failure to construct a national unity based on nationalism, the idea of a common American identity, and democracy as a civic religion—can be seen as a success in the creation of a little rebellion, a significant moment of cultural renaissance whose cultural ideals were often at odds with those of liberal progressivism. Ideas and events that might be considered a failure from a political perspective can from a cultural perspective be recovered as a triumph. This genealogy turns our attention to some of the critics of progressivism and some of its disillusioned followers rather than to the architects of progressivism itself.[7] It offers a framework for understanding the "lost promise" of progressivism as less of a failure and more of a brief triumph in the creation of an alternative cultural politics.

To establish a genealogy of the little rebellion, it is necessary to return to the influences that shaped it and to understand the ways in which it created its own unity, despite its many internal divisions. Paradoxically, the movement—perhaps it was an outburst—was both a revolt against the past and a continuation of a revolution already under way in the universities and in the public culture generally. Rejecting a fading Victorianism, still influential in the public culture, middle-class progressives and radicals rebelled against its standards of morality, its Anglophilia in literature and art, and its romanticism. As a continuation of a "revolt against formalism," as Morton White termed it, begun by progressive intellectuals and activists in the 1880s, it expanded the challenge to the moral, scientific, and epistemological standards of late nineteenth-century realism and absolutism in philosophy, law, and the social sciences.[8]

Among the many significant intellectual developments of this knowledge revolution was Charles Beard's economic determinism, which looked into the private interests that shaped public choices; O. W. Holmes's legal theory, which maintained that law was, in great measure, "experience," hence pragmatic and inductive and not deduced from timeless principles or abstract rules;[9] James Harvey Robinson's history, which offered a pragmatic tool for explaining the present and controlling the future; Thorstein Veblen's institutionalism, which studied empirically the connections between economic institutions and other aspects of culture; and William James's pragmatism, which maintained that truth "happened to an idea" or that truth was a process, not residing in pure intellect alone but in its application, and that the pragmatic truth of an idea could be judged by the practical difference it made in one's life. These rebel fathers, as a group, abandoned the nineteenth-century preference for rationalism and positivism and the distinctions between fact and value, knowledge and morality. They rejected abstractions such as history or reason to explain social or historical change and looked to experience and empirical evidence—of economic interests or political motivations—to uncover human purposes in history. They were interested in concentrating on techniques of research, investigation, and experimentation rather than on developing grand theory. Antiformalism toppled the universalizing tendencies of Western philosophy and social science prevalent during the 1860s to the 1880s in a way that was distinctively modern.

For many children of the prewar generation, James's influence was especially important. In addition to the anti-Platonism of his philosophy, denying the idea of an essence residing in persons or things, James's pragmatism offered an inducement to practical involvement in the social world. It emphasized action as revealed meaning, according to John Diggins, which in turn encouraged young activists and intellectuals to apply their ideas in practical, political involvement in the real world.[10]

Moreover, James was the most sympathetic of contemporary philosophers to the politics of the subaltern and held the most idealist views among the American pragmatists, taking seriously the role of subjectivity in creating meaning. The emphasis on subjectivity as a constitutive force in the construction of culture had captivated the European public in the thought of Bergson, Sorel, and Nietzsche and had inspired French and Italian syndicalists.[11] Young socialists and pragmatists in America in turn took the ideas of European idealists, refocused through the lens of James, and turned their attention to the role of individual creativity and imagination as a stimulus to action and to the idea of authoritative freedom in the individual as a force for social change. Further, James's therapeutic philosophy held great attraction for middle-class youth who, whether caught in spiritual crises, having rejected their Protestant upbringing, or in personal uncertainty over how to contribute constructively to social change, could resolve personal crisis and spiritual doubt through a philosophy that looked beyond questions of ontology or metaphysics to one that emphasized the practical consequences of one's ideas.

In addition to James, American moderns were enthralled with Nietzsche. To them, he was arch-rebel and unregenerate. As Bourne put it, "The pagan, liberating, audacious message of Nietzsche touches the old puritan ideals to the quick."[12] His psychology of power became a tool for a corrosive critique of the genteel tradition and Protestant moralism in general. According to Alfred Kazin, Nietzsche had become the philosopher in vogue at the turn of the century, attracting older writers and public figures, including Theodore Dreiser, Jack London, Frank Norris, and Theodore Roosevelt, who were fascinated by his analysis of force and his emphasis on vitality. The new, tough, muscular men of the new century took Nietzsche as the architect of the vitalist ideal and the proponent of an ethic of magnetic energy.[13] Socialists in Bourne's generation, including Max Eastman and John Reed, moreover, saw no contradiction in combining Nietzsche's rhetoric of the idea of a super race with plans for a democratic socialism, arguing against Nietzsche that the idea could be universalized for the majority. Along with Nietzsche, European socialists such as Graham Wallas, Bertrand Russell, and G. D. H. Cole, who made the case for guild socialism, emphasized direct action and social engagement; and Walt Whitman became the apostle of democratic camaraderie.

Popular culture reinforced the emphasis of progressive intellectuals on action and practical success. Roosevelt's idea of the "strenuous life" appealed to the young rebels of the 1910s, some of them prizing the outdoor life, others the rise of the New Woman, and yet others the vitalism and activism of the muscular spirit. Youth itself became a virtue, an escape from the archaic moralism of the old century and a release from "drift," in Walter Lippmann's terms. The New Woman was described as bold and courageous, qualities formerly ascribed to men. As women became more assertive, John Higham has suggested, men became more martial. As progressives sought social influence, they reached for political power. The link between progressivism and imperialism was common by the end of the nineteenth century.[14]

The shift from a producer culture to a consumer culture that historians have described was experienced by middle-class progressives and radicals, as evident in their writings, as economic dislocation.[15] The emphasis in the colleges and universities was on the new scientific disciplines. College students were being trained for the new professions in economics, political science, and sociology and for participation in an increasingly corporatized society as technicians. Bureaucratic institutions required scientific managers and administrative experts. Accordingly, their discourse reflected an awareness of the new conceptions of economic rationality and the importance of scientific expertise and professionalism for working men and women.

Some intellectuals, like Walter Lippmann, were convinced that a new, rationalized order, embodied by the manager, the engineer, the professional bureaucrat, and the technician, was the welcome harbinger of the modern age. Science, management, and technology could make the society hum with efficiency and render scarcity obsolete. Other critics, however, including Bourne, opposed the rationalization of society by either the Puritan fathers or their technocratic sons, rejecting the impersonality within the corporate enterprise, the routinization of professional employment, and standardization (of knowledge and time). The bureaucratic "Moloch," quoting Bourne, threatened to "swallow" individual personality and creativity, and he and his compeers gravitated toward the presumably freer forces of irrationality and disorder, following a Nietzschean or Bergsonian inspiration.[16]

Historians have also characterized the "age of transition" as a shift from a culture that emphasized character and self-control to one of personality and self-expression.[17] In these terms, the children of the middle classes experienced the clash among cultural expectations of individual responsibility, social obligation, and personal desire as occurring within the family and often constructed it in familial terms. Their discourse consequently signified a rejection of the fathers and the rigid, life-denying ethic of a Puritan self-denial and a pursuit of their own values of youthful spontaneity and self-gratification and, alternatively, a pull toward collective responsibility, social work, or political involvement. As Bourne put it, "We feel social injustice as our fathers felt personal sin."[18] Their discourse was remarkably similar, whether as social reformers or poets, and it emphasized the importance of cultivating a public personality as its own resource. They rejected the requirements of the genteel culture, with its expectations of marital fidelity, personal character, and public honor as obsolete and as insufficient preparation for their participation in an economic order that now required marketing skills and job adaptability.

The link that joined these different and often competing discourses—the languages of the family and of the market, or in Michael Rogin's words, the languages of love and of contract, which are protean in American literature—was the idea of generationalism and generational change.[19] Generationalism marked a new effort in America and Europe to periodize history and to acknowledge lines of affiliation outside traditional economic classes and outside the family. Generations signified political divisions that could bring together like-minded individuals, regardless of class or educational background, to form new forces for social change. The idea of a generational revolt represented an important boundary breakdown for American generationalists, among them Jane Addams, Lippmann, and Bourne, as a way, as Addams explained, to create a unity between an unprepared middle class and a displaced working class while at the same time finding common cause with all rebels of the age. The unity of the younger generation was a constructed unity, to borrow Eisenach's phrase about progressivism's created unity, but it was a unity constitutive of its political identity. The discourse of generationalism broke down the divide between the language of the market and that of the family and created a symbolic unity that crossed class, gender, and ideological divides.

The younger generation shared concretely three sets of attitudes and goals captured in the idea of youth: a common set of assumptions about past grievances, a common agenda for personal and social change, and a highly developed consciousness about their collective destiny and historic role. Thus, despite the many and significant differences between the progressives, anarchists, and other radicals in the first decade of the twentieth century, the idea of a generational revolt captured their doubled-edged rebellion and the basis of their common cause: a revolt against the rigidity of the Puritan fathers and a resistance to the impersonality of the new corporate order. For the younger generation, the enemy was less the institutions of capitalism or socialism; it was the older people of the world who stood in the way of change. Social change would take place in the battle between the old and the young.

Ironically, the younger generation was never so united as when it abolished itself as a political generation. Its disarray, evident in the patchwork of clubs and organizations and public activities that proliferated before the war, was quieted when wartime preparedness began in earnest. Political activities were consolidated, narrowed, and became one-dimensional. Feminist issues and issues regarding educational reform became secondary. When the United States entered World War I, as Bourne explained, "This motley crew of ex-socialists, and labor radicals, and liberals, and pragmatist philosophers . . . united for the prosecution of the war."[20] As a distinctive political force, the younger generation became invisible by 1918.[21]

For Bourne, however, generationalism had a personal meaning as well. As a disabled child from an old-line Protestant family, his experiences were in many respects uncharacteristic of his middle-class generation—his physical challenges, a disabled father, six years of intermittent employment and a few years of factory experience, and an ambivalence toward institutions both as alternative families and as forces that suppressed the Jamesian "personal point of view." These differences between himself and his peers he thought generationalism could elide, given the common identity of youth. Generationalism became a means of affiliating with others who also had been marginalized or excluded (young and old), a figurative unity that was instantiated in the generational narratives he wrote. Bourne's identification with America's outsiders—its immigrants, public women, and the poor—linked the idea of difference (from the fathers) and marginalization (from the market) to his own experience of exclusion. It became constitutive of his public identity as a cultural radical before the war and as an "irreconcilable" during it. His autobiographical essays, in particular, were written in terms that were meant to capture the experience of growing up outside the dominant cultural norms.

To present Bourne's life and work as representative of a particular generation and a particular cultural crisis, therefore, is to present a paradox: he was representative precisely in his difference. Although generations are always based on their difference (from other generations), representatives are similar to those groups they represent. Just what is meant by characterizing Bourne's work as representative? By that term I mean an individual who has the capacity to organize meaning in such a way as to make sense of a cultural moment and its contradictions. A representative figure therefore "speaks" for him- or herself, but also for others. A representative's personal journey is linked to the struggles of his or her community. A representative is, or can be, an exemplary individual, as Emerson would have it, but the elitist implications of the Emersonian conception are undercut, in my view, when a representative speaks to the "common sense" of a culture. Representatives in this sense are thus constitutive of the conditions they seek to explain or signify in their work. They represent, not by mirroring that common experience, but in translating it into terms that are shared and instantiating it in their narratives.[22]

This signifying function of the representative is meant to contrast with political theories of representation that locate representation in relations with a subject already presumed to exist. Political theorists have identified three types of representatives—the formal representative (Hobbes), the descriptive representative (Burke), and the symbolic representative—each of which infers a certain relationship with constituents and a corresponding obligation of accountability. None of these conceptions, however, acknowledges the constitutive capacity of representatives. In Hannah Pitkin's pivotal study of theories of representation, for instance, the authority of the representative is derivative; it follows from his relation with his constituents.[23] A representative that creates a constituency, by contrast, acts as a political agent, constructing a public, or the idea of a public, where there was none. It is in this sense, I suggest, that Bourne's representativeness can best be understood.

3
ISHMAEL

> I can almost see now that my path in life will be on the outside of things, poking holes in the holy, criticizing the established, satirizing the self-respecting and contented. Never being competent to direct and manage any of the affairs of the world myself, I will be forced to sit off by myself in the wilderness, howling like a coyote that everything is being run wrong. I think I have a real genius for making trouble, for getting under people's skin. . . . Between an Ezekiel and an Ishmael, it is a little hard to draw the line; I mean, one can start out to be the first, and end only by becoming the latter.
>
> —*Randolph S. Bourne to Prudence Winterrowd,*
> *March 2, 1913*

At the improbable age of thirty-two, Bourne wrote an autobiography. It was the story of an education, a self-education of a culture critic, who, having been raised on the literary classics, spent the better part of his youth overthrowing them. If initially he found inspiration in the "dead classics" as a welcome relief from reading the Bible and popular adventure stories in his childhood home, he wrote in "History of a Literary Radical," his "apostacy" really began when he encountered the "cultural 'Modernists,' " who "vandalized the Church from within." Even these American naturalists and realists began to pale, however, in contrast to the imagists and psychological novelists, like Dostoyevsky, and America's literary giants, Twain, Thoreau, and Whitman. He felt in 1918 as if he were "standing at the end of an era," beginning to emerge as a "new classicist," mining the past for voices that could regenerate American culture.[1]

The essay, a synecdoche of the transition to modernism at the turn of the century, was also a commentary on the generational divide, a constant theme in Bourne's writing. In autobiographical form, he disclosed what he considered to be the failure of middle-class institutions—the patriarchal family, the Protestant church, the schools—to educate its youth. Underscoring the sentiments of Jane Addams and Walter Lippmann, among others, he maintained that his generation had "practically to bring itself up." In a move typical for him, however, he turned disadvantage into advantage. The neglect of these institutions, he maintained, gave him a chance to educate himself.[2]

The essay also combined thematically the personal and the social in a narrative about spiritual (and cultural) rebirth and renewal familiar to his predominantly middle-class readers. In the tradition of Christian conversion narratives, his essay traced the journey of a searching soul through its progressive stages to salvation: from the initial stage of ignorance and false consciousness, to a confrontation with the truth, to a period of crisis and confusion culminating in a moment of liberatory revelation. In a deliberately modernist variant, however, Bourne presented his conversion as culminating in uncertainty rather than certainty, his encounters with an international literature opening up a new search for new tastes, texts, and standards. In the version he told, he was saved, not in obedience or submission to a former truth, but in restless searching for the new literature for a "young world."[3]

The story of his literary education was not his first autobiography. Like others of his generation, including Waldo Frank, Van Wyck Brooks, and Addams, Bourne wrote his first autobiography while he was in his twenties. In "The Handicapped: By One of Them," written when he was twenty-five, he recounted another conversion story, this time of a young Ishmael, physically disabled, born to a long line of chosen Protestant gentry, who was misunderstood by his family and shunned in public. Convinced he was a "misfit" and a failure, this child of multiple disabilities rejected middle-class norms and institutions, preferring to remain outside, unassimilated and unrepentant. In the language of religious faith, he chose to remain cast out as Abraham's child of nature and unregenerate, at least in Calvinist terms. This Ishmael aspired to become an Ezekiel, the prophet of exiles, prophesying a "new religion" for other outsiders.[4]

In terms of both structure and function, however, his autobiographies were remarkably similar. Both essays recapitulated, however strictly, the journeys of the Puritan settlers and their Emersonian inheritors to create a new self in a chosen land. In particular, like their Puritan models, his autobiographies ("auto-bios," or self-life) taught by example, providing a practical, working guide to living out spiritual commitment. Like them as well, they functioned as a form of historiography, a literary form of factual allegory, tracing the path of one soul who had a vocation in the social world. Within that tradition, Bourne's autobiographies offered a guide to reformulating one's internal moral system by its encounter with the Word and an acceptance of responsibility for sin.

Moreover, as comparisons with other autobiographies of the prewar generation show, Bourne represented his personal dilemmas as one aspect of a larger social crisis affecting his generation at a time when, in Henry May's words, the "cracks in the surface" of the genteel culture had begun to show. In this sense his essays functioned as life stories of a particular generation of Americans coming of age. The generational subtext of his autobiographies suggests that they belong to the tradition of "auto-American-biography," in Sacvan Bercovitch's fine phrase, a discursive tradition that recreated the experience of a "representative" individual whose life stood for an American experience and a personality that expressed an American character.[5] Such life stories become collective histories, as the personal journey of one individual was linked to that of the community (or generation), a people, or a nation. In this sense, they were as much about his own past as about America's.

Yet parallels with the Puritan and Emersonian past can be taken only so far, for Bourne clearly elected to remain outside the

Protestant community and often in opposition to its expectations for social and personal conduct. Instead he offered a redefinition of the relation between the self and the social. He located sin in the world, not in the individual soul or one's character. He placed responsibility for social injustice onto a collective agent rather than in individual conscience or obedience to established norms. Unlike traditional Christian conversion narratives, his spiritual journey—his self-education—did not require submission as a necessary part of agency. Thus, despite his reliance on the language of religious fervor, a discourse common to American autobiographies from the seventeenth century to the present day, Bourne's work was disruptive of that tradition. The aspiring "preacher" of "stern new truths" offered a new religion distinctly subversive of middle-class norms. Using the dominant discourse of religious faith and spiritual uplift, he turned it back on itself, writing what might be seen as the confessions of an ex-convert.

His efforts, on another level, can be seen to be inspired from a Nietzschean standpoint as an effort not to re-create his own experiences but to reinvent them for his generation. The task of the moral man, Nietzsche wrote, was not to rediscover another's myth but to create his own. His ability to discharge (dionysian) insight into (apollonian) images revealed his capacity to outstrip himself, to *act* rather than merely contemplate, to *become* rather than merely be. From a Nietzschean perspective, Bourne's autobiographies thus can be seen as different instantiations of his own myth or epic, the variations as different performances of a self-in-becoming. Self-creation was an ongoing process, a pathos, in Nietzsche's terms, or an effort that was "not a being (*Sein*), not a becoming," but a process always happening. The particular state of the self at any given time was epiphenomenal. Self-invention constantly gave form to the self.[6] In the process of inventing and reinventing his story, Bourne can be seen as reinventing himself, creating not a different self for every occasion (as the therapeutic culture required), but a self that was constantly becoming, a social process in formation. If the different versions of his life-time autobiography seem inconsistent, as they frequently do, it may be that we as readers have misunderstood the pathos.

I interpret Bourne's work as (a part of) the product of the creative intelligence actively engaged in reinventing the self. "Every man should realize that his life is an epic," Bourne wrote. "We should oftener read our own epics—and write them. The world is in need of true autobiographies, told in terms of the adventure that life is." Autobiography was a form of self-invention through story.

> The best autobiographers are still the masters of fiction, those wizards of imaginative sympathy, who create souls and then write their spiritual history, as those souls themselves, were they alive, could perhaps never write them.[7]

These mythmakers relied on artistic imagination and self-detachment, an ironic stance of introspection and self-distancing. "Look at yourself as an interesting stranger to be interpreted."[8] They turned their lives into works of art, following Nietzsche, a move Bourne often invoked as a guide for his own work. Following him, I have interpreted his autobiographies and his work in general as works of art, grounded in experience but not as literally "factual." They are inventions meant to be of pedagogical value for his own generation and for Americans, generally. Autobiography was an act of the apollonian, a form of self-invention for himself and for others, redeeming a culture divided against itself by class privileges and by generational values. In this sense, it was all myth, that is, as Nietzsche meant it, as a means of healing a culture by restoring to it an act of creativity.[9]

In this chapter I return to the work as an aspect of his life. Bourne's life and work are understood as texts to be interpreted within the political economy and psychosocial history of their time. The value of these texts lies in their interaction, not in their correspondence with experience. Autobiography, social history, and myth are intermingled in this perspective as part of a dialogue about creating a "personality," re/forming a culture of the self in the way that self-invention might take place. His canvas was his personality, an imaginary terrain for the artistic will to form an epic story.[10]

"The Philosophy of Handicap" was written at the suggestion of Ellery Sedgwick, editor of the *Atlantic Monthly,* after Bourne's essay on the generational revolt, "The Two Generations," received considerable response. Sedgwick proposed it as a form of therapy for Bourne—although perhaps it was more so for Sedgwick, who was preoccupied with Bourne's deformity and with his radical politics. He suggested it as an opportunity for Bourne to write about the relation between his physical disability and his political philosophy. (He also thought it would cure Bourne of his socialism.) As therapy it failed; Bourne wrote a manifesto for other "unpresentables" in a transvalued politics of marginality. As a conversion narrative it also failed; Bourne did not counsel recovery from the abyss through spiritual rebirth but a reaffirmation of the divided self and its philosophy of multiple truths, caught between two worlds.

As a traditional Christian conversion story, it dealt little with his family, suggesting by their absence from the text that he had been exiled almost from the start. Born on May 30, 1886, in Bloomfield, New Jersey, to a family of solid bourgeois credentials, he was the first son of Sarah Barrett and Charles Rogers Bourne. His mother's lineage was "relentlessly aristocratic," tracing back to the arrival in 1628 of Edward Fitz-Randolph and Elizabeth Blossom in America.[11] His father's ancestors came from upstate New York, of predominantly Protestant clergymen and teachers. His paternal grandfather was the longtime pastor of Sleepy Hollow Congregational Church and his great-grandfather an abolitionist and acquaintance of Ralph Waldo Emerson and William Lloyd Garrison. Despite its pedigree, the family's status was precarious, as Charles Bourne had no clear prospects for employment when his first son was born and for a decade seemed to subsist on his debonair charm.[12]

Randolph managed to survive his birth, but just barely. The elderly attending physician ineptly used forceps during the delivery, twisting and scarring the baby's face and mangling one ear. Bourne was reported to have commented, in considerable understatement, it was a "terribly messy birth." The "second blast" came four years later when he contracted spinal tuberculosis,[13] leaving him permanently stunted in size, hunchbacked, and barrel-chested.[14] At his full adult height, he was no more than five feet tall, according to his passport.[15] His friend, James Oppenheim, editor of the *Seven Arts,* wrote of "the humped back, the longish almost medieval face, with a sewed up mouth, an ear gone awry." Theodore Dreiser decided that on first meeting Bourne he had just laid eyes on "as frightening a dwarf as I had ever seen . . . the legs thin, the chest large, the arms long, the head sunk deep between the bony shoulders." Sedgwick himself concluded that Bourne's appearance was "without a redeeming feature." To friends and acquaintances, his disabilities signified disorder, a condition reflecting the fragmentation of the modern age.[16]

In his autobiography Bourne wrote of his marked difference in biblical terms. "Bearing simply a crooked back and an unsightly face," he wrote without elaboration, he carried his disabilities as "a real, even though usually dim, background of consciousness." In this repositioning of the sign of the body to the plane of subjectivity, he disembodied his original sin, a strategic move within the grammar of a conversion narrative that enabled him to identify with all other marginals living in "darkness" or "ignorance" or outside the community. Nevertheless, his body was marked with a sign, a sign of nativity, like the dark-skinned Ishmael of the Bible, that signified to his predominantly Protestant neighbors God's disfavor and his unchosen status as an Ishmael.

As he described it, people responded to his difference in two ways: either they treated him as if he did not exist, or they treated him as a child. In respectable circles, he was often pushed aside. When he ventured to Sedgwick's club in Manhattan, for instance, he was ushered to the servants' entrance; when he became involved in a discussion at a library with another patron in a wheelchair, they were both asked to leave. Relatives and friends, on the other hand, patronized him. He recalled one humiliating incident where an aunt "inspected" him before going to a concert. His mother, Sarah, in contrast to the biblical Sarah, and his sisters "coddled" him and catered to his wishes.[17] He was not a full member of the community, either of the family or of the larger society. His outsider status was an effect, as he described it, of a culture that defined him as other. "The deformed man is always conscious that the world does not expect very much from him. . . he is discounted from the start. . . . as a result, he does not expect very much of himself."

In the discourse of a Christian conversion experience, his self-doubt moved him to the second stage of his journey, a readiness to come to terms with his unregeneracy. As a Calvinist, he was certain of his own weakness but uncertain of where the truth (his responsibility) lay. If as a child he openly rebelled against the "inevitable," by adolescence he had become increasingly resigned and had internalized his failures. The transition from childhood ignorance and false consciousness to a confrontation with truth was told in strict adherence to the conventions of the Christian narrative. He reported that he "grew up with a deepening sense of failure, and a lack of pride in what I really excelled at." Individual responsibility was instilled in him as a necessary path toward grace. He became his own worst critic. "It never used to occur to me that my failures and lack of skill were due to circumstances beyond my control, but I would always impute them, in consequence of my rigid Calvinist bringing-up, to some moral weakness of my own."[18] This self-doubt, which extended also to his successes—musical talents, high grades—was appropriate to a guilt culture, according to Philip Slater, that reinforced the development of internalized restraints and required "almost permanently" postponed gratification.[19]

In these terms he described childhood as "the worst time of all," because he felt like "a strange creature in a strange world." In adolescence, though attracted to "the world of admiration and gayety and smiles and favors and quick interest and companionship," he was made to feel an outsider by the "silent, unconscious, gentle oblivion" of his peers, "as if a ragged urchin had been asked to come and look through the window at the light and warmth of the glittering party."[20] He felt his isolation most profoundly in his adult relationships with women. Writing to a friend after college, he confessed:

> You make me feel suddenly very old and bitterly handicapped and foolish to have any dream left of the perfect comrade who is, I suppose, the deepest craving of my soul. It is her I write to, meet casually in strange faces on the street, touch in novels, feel beside me in serene landscapes and city vistas, grasp in my dream. She wears a thousand different masks, and eludes me ever.[21]

Even though he was a frequent guest at Patchin Place, a feminist eating club in New York's Greenwich Village, he feared he was for them merely an amusement or a "dull vaudeville act."[22] In the

Lutheran phrase of marginality, he confirmed, "I was truly in but not of the world."[23]

The text is again silent about the decline of his family's fortune, a silence appropriate for a culture of privatized guilt. When Randolph was about nine years old, his father's absence became more literal when Charles was disabled himself, struck by a passing trolley car in New York City, which caught his coat and dragged him down the street. Thereafter, he walked with crutches or two canes. Work, always difficult to obtain, became even more so. Whether drink led to failure or failure to drink is unclear, but as Charles's health deteriorated, the family's fragile unity dissolved. They moved into Sarah's mother's house on Belleville Street, but within a few months Charles was asked to leave by the Barrett family. Halsey Barrett, Sarah's brother, agreed to support her and the four children on the condition that Charles never return.[24]

Having lost his father to drink, Bourne almost lost his mother to religion. Retreating into the great house, she suffered silently, "dominated by Puritanism." In their "semi-fatherless" state, the great house grew "doleful," and the family's attendance at Old First Presbyterian Church became more regular. Bourne himself was "united" with the church at the age of fifteen, despite his grandmother's misgivings about his readiness to receive grace. She may have been right, because "left alone to follow his own desires," he underwent a conversion experience that affirmed rather than renounced the standpoint of the (Protestant) sinner.[25]

Outwardly, however, he had become Abraham's chosen son, Isaac: editor of the school newspaper, a debater, senior class president, valedictorian—a success in worldly affairs. He was admitted to Princeton in 1903, the college for sons of Presbyterian elites. Yet Sarah's brother told Bourne he would not finance his education. Halsey Barrett, a Morristown lawyer, informed him it was inappropriate for someone "like you," with obvious physical disabilities in an age of marketing and appearance, to think of attending university or to hope to succeed as a middle-class professional. He made it clear that Bourne should earn a living in a trade or industry and support his mother.[26]

Bourne spent the next six years in frustrating and mostly futile efforts to find employment. For two years, he found no work at all.

He then worked for two years as a "factory hand," as he described it, in a relative's office in Morristown. He next worked in a factory in New Jersey, turning out music rolls for player pianos, until his wages were cut by the employer, Frederick Hoschke, in an effort at labor intensification. Bourne quit, writing of it later in "What Is Exploitation?"[27] Drifting from one factory to another for another year or more, his situation began to resemble his father's all too clearly. He decided to fall back on his musical talents and began playing piano for minstrel shows and vaudeville acts and accompanying silent movies with a live sound track from a theater piano. He also gave music lessons in his grandmother's home in Bloomfield and worked as an accompanist in the Carnegie Hall rehearsal halls. Of these dispiriting years, Bourne later wrote,

> There is the poignant mental torture that comes with such an experience—the urgent need, the repeated failure, or rather the repeated failure even to obtain a chance to fail, the realization that those at home can ill afford to have you idle, the growing dread of encountering people.[28]

Bourne's descriptions of the requirements of a corporate liberal world provide a clue to the degree of its success in standardizing work, time, and profit margins. In the corporate world, he wrote, one must be "all things to all men," and he was unable to "counteract that fatal first impression." Often turned away at the reception desk, his experience confirmed to him that "the hasty and superficial impression is everything." Like his father, he was coded as "unfitted for any kind of work." "The attitude toward me ranged from 'You can't expect us to create a place for you,' to 'How could it enter your head that we should find any use for a man like you?' " He was told, "It is not business to make allowances for anybody." Large corporate bureaucracies required employees who were readily exchangeable. "All this talk of natural talents or bents or interests . . . have no commercial value in themselves." Individuals were tailored to the requirements of the job, not the job to the individual.[29]

He claimed his "Calvinism began to crack" when its tenets of individual responsibility, good character, and hard work did not produce the promised dividend of success. Both he and his father had tried to provide for their family, and they both failed. He may have had his father in mind, the family's first rebel and its first failure, when he wrote:

> It makes me wince to hear a man spoken of as a failure, or to have it said of one that "he doesn't amount to much." Instantly I want to know why he has not succeeded, and what have been the forces working against him.

In the name of the many who had "failed," he began to rebel against the doctrine of the elect.

> I . . . experienced a revulsion against the rigid Presbyterianism in which I had been brought up . . . a sort of disgust at the arrogance of damning so great a proportion of the human race. For some time there was considerable bitterness in my heart at the narrowness of the people who could still find comfort in the old faith.[30]

Turning to other philosophies, principally those of Henry George (after reading his *Progress and Poverty*), Thomas Buckle, and Oliver Wendell Holmes, Bourne found a new skepticism toward convention and explanations for "why men were miserable and overworked, and why there was on the whole so little joy and gladness among us—and which fixed the blame" that allowed him to abandon Puritan counsels of judging individual worth. Yet even George's more promising philosophy, in Bourne's view, merely shifted the blame from the individual to society, arguing that an injection of upper-class philanthropy could improve the lot of the poor and uneducated. George's response was still fundamentally Christian, Bourne thought, simplifying it considerably, personifying good and evil rather than locating it systemically "by throwing the burden for the misery of the world on these same good neighbors."[31] It did not appease his hunger, and his crisis of faith found no solution. "My sensitiveness to social misery . . . a sense of social guilt quite analogous to my Puritan ancestors' personal guilt . . . cannot be wiped out by the simple operation of being personally 'saved.'" Moreover, spiritual conversion was too high a price to pay. "The cure for this spiritual dyspepsia is called conversion, but it is a question of whether the cure is not often worse than the disease." He preferred to have no morals at all rather than to be "forced to digest . . . by spiritual operation" the morals of a former generation. "Obviously, the thing is then to renounce salvation."[32]

His decision to reject Calvinist patriarchy and its cartography of regeneration represented Bourne's unwillingness to abandon his own past and former (unregenerate) self. From William James's *Varieties of Religious Experience* and his own personal experience with revivalism, Bourne understood that a traditional Christian conversion required a killing off of one's past. In other words, the twice-born "sick soul" required two births to make it whole, but that unity came at the expense of a former self.[33] He did not want to "digest" his former self but to retain it, and so he became a "divided self," in James's terms, caught between two worlds: the anhedonia of the sick soul and the mind-cure of the twice born. He understood that the price of remaining a divided self would be to be caught in a certain soul sickness or exaggerated sensitivity to social misery and injustice that prevented pleasure. Yet, as James had found, the sick soul came closer to the center of religious insight than the "healthy-minded," because in its deepest distress, it had a deeper understanding of the nature of man's conflicted existence.[34]

In Bourne's words, "This widening, which has meant the possibility of living the contemplative and imaginative life on an infinitely higher plane . . . has meant also a soul-sickness to the more sensitive. . . . It has . . . opened a nerve the pain of which no opiate has been able to soothe."[35] To renounce that pain, the anhedonia of which James wrote, would be to cut himself off from the single most important source of understanding others.

> When he has been through the neglect and struggles of a handicapped and ill-favored man himself, he will begin to understand the feelings of all the horde of the unpresentable and the unemployable, the incompetent and the ugly, the queer and crotchety people who make up so large a proportion of human folk.[36]

Bourne's decision to remain a divided self and to reject spiritual conversion meant that he would struggle against anhedonia and evil in the world.

> I can almost see now that my path in life will be on the outside of things, poking holes in the holy, criticizing the established, satirizing the self-respecting and contented. Never being competent to direct and manage any of the affairs of the world myself, I will be forced to sit off by myself in the wilderness, howling like a coyote that everything is being run wrong. I think I have a real genius for making trouble, for getting under people's skin. . . . Between an Ezekiel and an Ishmael, it is a little hard to draw the line; I mean, one can start out to be the first, and end only by becoming the latter.[37]

The biblical Ezekiel had promised "a new heart and a new spirit" if the exiles set aside their old ways.[38] Bourne, adopting the prophetic role, suggested that a collective renewal could come through an audacious paganism for other exiles. His new religion clearly inverted the Protestant ethic of individual grace into one of soul-sickness and psychic fragmentation. It subverted the doctrine of original sin, locating sin in social arrangements rather than in human nature. It was an ambiguous position he was negotiating: not precisely the status of an outsider (an Ishmael) but of one who inhabits both worlds (also an Ezekiel). It described an alienation that would not resolve itself, unlike the Hegelian split-consciousness or the Rousseauean version of internal self-division. Where Rousseau tried to heal the split, Bourne's theory affirmed it. Its contradiction was an asset, the basis of his unregenerate, unre/(de)formed personality, a modern response to dislocation in contemporary society.

As a divided self, Bourne reapplied to college in 1909 and was admitted to Columbia University on full academic scholarship. Columbia was a burgeoning cosmopolitan university with a young, insurgent faculty and an international student body, where Bourne claimed he found his first taste of "beloved community." Its revisionist scholarship was headed by Charles Beard, John Dewey, Franz Boas, Edward Thorndike, Brander Matthews, and other scholars, who provided a more appropriate climate for him than either Princeton or Harvard to push beyond studies of classical literature to the "new disciplines" of political science, history, and anthropology. "We are all instrumentalists here at Columbia," he wrote in 1913, a position he considered fully consistent with his socialist and his syndicalist sentiments.

By all accounts he was a brilliant student, or, as he put it, his self-esteem began to "grow like a weed." By his second year, he had become something of a "minor celebrity on campus," due to the publication of his article, "The Two Generations" in the *Atlantic Monthly* and his editorship of the *Columbia Monthly*.[39] He was a vocal and active leader in university activities, a member of the Intercollegiate Socialist Society (ISS), the Boar's Head and Philolexian (student literary societies), and a campus radical, protesting, in one instance, the administration's policy of underpaying its "scrubwomen" who daily cleaned the lecture halls and student dormitories. His editorial, excerpted in the *New York Times,* engendered considerable red-baiting in the college newspaper. By the time he had graduated, in a four-year master's program in political science, he had written a prizewinning essay on Thomas Paine, several reviews for scholarly journals, including a new journal of pragmatist philosophy, and seven articles for the *Atlantic Monthly*. His master's thesis, written under John Dewey's direction, was a study of the economic and cultural changes of suburbanization in the northeastern corridor, later excerpted for *Atlantic Monthly*.[40]

The first conversion narrative ended here. His spiritual conversion was complete; his political transformation would occur later. After being graduated from Columbia University, he went to Western Europe on a traveling fellowship in 1913–1914, where he spent an extended time in London and Paris. He came to love French imagism, developed a respect for German city planning, and admired Italian labor radicalism. In France, he saw that the intellectual's role in modern society could be integral to the public culture. As a delegate to the international conference of the ISS, however, he had to leave Europe in haste; the conference was canceled abruptly when war broke out in August 1914.

Back in New York, with the help of his former teacher Charles Beard, he secured a position at the *New Republic* as a contributing editor, reporting on educational reform and the youth culture.[41]

Under the arrangement, Bourne produced approximately 30,000 words in less than two years for the new journal of opinion, writing more than half his essays on John Dewey's new educationism. He began to frequent New York's radical, bohemian, and feminist clubs and associations, joining the then-bohemian Liberal Club, the Heretics, a radical feminist group, and the Civil Club, among others. During debates over preparedness, he joined the influential American Union Against Militarism, and along with Winthrop Jordan, Amos Pinchot, Roger Baldwin, and Crystal and Max Eastman, formed the Committee for Democratic Control, to call for a referendum on the war, a group that collaborated with the New York chapter of the Women's Peace Party.

When President Woodrow Wilson asked for a declaration of war from Congress in April 1917, the *New Republic* came out unequivocably for intervention. Bourne objected to it from the start, during preparedness talks in 1915. He was able to get a few articles published by the journal in that year, but his status there became increasingly precarious. He turned to the *Masses,* the *Dial,* the *Seven Arts,* and, his "good angel," the *Atlantic Monthly,* which continued to publish his articles. But he became increasingly preoccupied with the war and wrote about it whenever he could. Indeed, it was his antiwar writings that made his reputation, and for some readers, his notoriety. He was a "venomous German viper," according to one, a resolute pacifist to others, and an annoyance to his editors.

His suite of antiwar articles published in the *Seven Arts* in 1917–1918 are among the great essays of American dissent, in my view, showing Bourne's critical powers at their best. Yet at a time when charges of sedition were used to close editorial offices and suspend mailing privileges, when writers were put under surveillance, and public support for the war was "advertised" from Washington by George Creel's Committee on Public Information, there were real consequences to political dissent.

Bourne was himself put under surveillance by the U.S. Navy Department in 1918. The Office of Naval Intelligence listed him as a named "suspect" on a Confidential List of Aliens and Suspects: List A, which included the names and addresses, when available, of "persons and firms in the United States and abroad suspected of pro-German sympathy and activity." A copy of his essay "War and the Intellectuals," reprinted in Emma Goldman's *Mother Earth,* was included in a Bureau of Investigation file concerning the political activities of Goldman and Alexander Berkman.

Moreover, Bourne and his fiancée, the actress Esther Cornell, of the New York family, reported that in summer 1918 they were followed by a young naval officer while they were walking along the beach in Cos Cob, Connecticut. Apparently it was Cornell's "rhythm dancing" on the edge of the shore that caught the attention of the officer who, Bourne warned her, might think she was signaling to a gunboat waiting offshore. A week later, they were approached in Martha's Vineyard by an officer who inquired about their reasons for being there and inspected Bourne's notebook of vacation expenses. Over Bourne's objections, Cornell invited the officer to join them for coffee. He later phoned his superiors to report that they were just "a coupla nuts."[42]

The war had militarized all aspects of American culture. The wealthy sponsor of the *Seven Arts,* anxious about reactions to Bourne's articles and government reprisals, withdrew her funding from the journal, forcing it, in Robert Frost's words, to "die a-Bourneing." In 1918, at Dewey's insistence, the *Dial* fired Bourne as an editor, a notorious episode in the history of intellectual responsibility. The *New Republic* continued to close him out, although it still published his book reviews. During the last two years of his life, however, he managed to publish two books on education, including one on the Gary school system; edited a volume on international cooperation; translated a French novel, *Vagabonds at Sea* by Maurice Lauroy; began an ambitious essay on the state, left unfinished at his death ("Fragment on the State"); and started an autobiographical novel, also left incomplete. He became engaged to Cornell, but he died before the war became memory, six weeks after armistice, a victim of the influenza epidemic of 1918. The young pastor Norman Thomas presided at his funeral, attended by fifty or more friends and admirers on a rainy day in December in New York.[43]

He was immediately martyred to America's involvement in the Great War. "We may rejoice that as England had her Bertrand Russell, France her Barbusse and Rolland, Germany her Liebknecht [*sic*] and Nicolai, so America had her Randolph Bourne."[44] The personality Bourne had worked to create—the young Ishmael and aspiring Ezekiel of other exiles—was rewritten and the particularly American nature of his dissent forgotten. Oppenheim's tribute suggested that Bourne's sacrifice had become universal, the fate of every innocent in a wicked world. But Bourne's self-invention was distinctively American, tied to its liberal past but designed for a modern, pagan America emerging from the confines of an established, old-line liberal Protestantism.

To recover that personality from historical memory, it is necessary to return to the original impulse behind its creation. The importance of creating a personality had been for Bourne, typically, more than a personal concern. Warren Susman has traced the development of the "culture of personality" that Bourne preached as the "new idealism" in 1913. As a cultural ideal, it replaced the earlier conception of "character" in the opening decades of the twentieth century in popular culture, self-help literature, and mass-circulation journals. Each cultural conception was a product of a particular era, an ideal of the self that was responsive to changing social needs and conditions.[45] The nineteenth-century notion of character prescribed a moral and spiritual ideal to which a man (and its application was exclusively male) might aspire to achieve his "highest" self. Character was conceived in terms of spirituality and moral perfection, through which the baser parts of man's nature were bred out of him. Over the course of a man's life, a certain respectability and breeding of the soul could be attained, often corresponding to his material and social status. Character was often a man's very salvation from the degradations and democratization of an imperfect society. Paradoxically, character was also the product of civilization, an artificial self, created rather than given. Thus, in order to become a self, one must sacrifice personal needs and desires to a higher duty or law. Character came by denying one's "nature," through self-denial and self-control. In short, self-mastery was the means of building character; it was also the means of denying the self.

By contrast, personality was a conception proposed by popular therapists and members of the progressive literary elite of an alternative idea of self, no more "natural" than the older ideal but one that emphasized man's ability to stand out from the crowd and display his uniqueness and individuality. Personality was achieved in self-expressiveness, self-assertion, in admirable magnetism and vitality. It was therefore possible to assert that a man did not "have a personality," in the private, possessive sense of ownership of certain qualities or skills. But the notion of personality also entailed its own contradiction, for one could not be well-liked and admired while expressing one's needs fully and achieving personal satisfaction. "Personality is the quality of being Somebody," a popular advice manual declared in 1915. Associated with its usage were terms evoking dynamism and charisma, such as "fascinating, stunning, attractive, magnetic, glowing, masterful, creative, dominant, forceful." These qualities signified a marked change from those associated with character, which was associated with qualities of nobility, wisdom, duty, honor, golden deeds, integrity, manliness, citizenship. One volume devoted to the subject of character explained "How to Strengthen It"; another, on personality, described "How to Build It." Character, this author implied, was something to be preserved; a personality, by contrast, could be created.[46]

Moreover, the original meaning of personality, with its roots in *persona,* was maintained in the modern version of the term, in that the mask used by a player or character in a play became part of what it meant to be a human being in the modern world. The individual who performed life's many social roles—that of producer and consumer, of man, woman, and citizen—required a *persona* or mask for every social encounter he or she undertook. As Erving Goffman and other scholars have shown, the self as performer reached its apotheosis in the latter half of the twentieth century.

The formation of personality then was a modern response to the alienation brought by the new era. In the shift from a class to a mass society, the question for individuals was how to distinguish oneself from others. A personality was a bulwark against the leveling forces of society, a form of power in its own right. Thus, Bourne saw it as a political obligation of his generation. "Let personality be the chief value in life . . . let us be ends in ourselves." To social radicals in particular, he advised, "Self cultivation becomes almost a duty, if one wants to be effective towards the great end." Armed with a "vital" and "glowing" personality, a self-confidence and pride in one's self, one could not help but be effective in one's vocation, whether in the law, or in journalism, or in social work, or in the university. "By allowing our free personality to develop, do we contribute most to the common good." One's own personality was a tool to help transform an individualist and competitive society into a progressive and cooperative one.[47]

The "younger generation" of the prewar years knew the value of self-cultivation. "We have come with a rush to the realization that personality and values, are, after all, the important things in a living world."[48] Traditional definitions would give way to the new. "We classify people by new categories. We look for personality, for sincerity, for social sympathy, for democratic feeling, for social productiveness, and we interpret success in terms of these attainments."[49] Personality was such an important concept that Bourne used it as the yardstick to measure social progress and as a criterion to evaluate social institutions and organizations. Their value rested on the degree to which they encouraged diversity and individuality.

> The aim of the group must be to cultivate personality, leaving open the road for each to follow his own. The bond of cohesion will be the common direction in which those roads point, but this is far from saying that all the travelers must be alike. It is enough that there be a common aim and a common ideal.[50]

Personality was as much a product of its environment as an inner quality. Thus, in contrast to the older ideal of individual character, it was a psychosocial entity, not strictly spiritual. A personality in Bourne's understanding was a quality displayed or expressed, realized fully only in association, not possessed privately or understood subjectively. In view of this conception of personality as a social product, one's personality was essentially a relationship both subjective and objective, reconciled neither with "nature" nor with "society" but with the self.

> It is exactly the discovery of this younger generation that . . . the intelligent, veritably humanistic, personal plane can only be reached by transcending both the animal and the institutional. In other words, personality was a struggle against both raw "Nature," and . . . organized society.[51]

Personality was a practical myth, as Nietzsche might suggest, that is, a myth that had effects. A personality was the means whereby one acquired the authority of a creator, a text created in the midst of a contextual frame.

Sharing oneself was the first step toward broadening one's world and the first chance to see the world from outside the prison of one's own inner subjectivity. "There are adventures of personality in studying and delighting in the ideas and folkways of people that hold much in store for those who will only seek them." Bourne urged other radicals to encourage the same freedom for others. "Let us live so as to stimulate others, so that we call out the best powers and traits in them, and make them better than they are, because of our comprehension and inspiration." Through cooperative social relations, everyone would benefit, and much more so than if locked into a liberal ethic of competitive individualism. "It is not true that by examining ourselves and coming to an understanding of the way we behave we understand other people, *but* . . . by . . . our friends we learn to interpret ourselves."[52]

The key to freeing personality, in short, lay in cultivating a breadth of experience beginning with one's earliest educational encounters. "The earlier the education is begun, the higher will be the type of personality achieved and the greater the development of individualities." One need only look at other societies to demonstrate the importance of a "variety of stimuli." "Men are most alike in illiterate societies, or in groups such as the separate professions,—in groups where there is no culture at all, or in groups where each member received the same training." The distinction was not between primitive and advanced cultures; it was between those that were varied and heterogeneous and those that were conformist and homogeneous. The solution was obvious. "The greater the variety of stimuli present, and the more constant their play, the richer, both in quality and quantity, will be the personality achieved."

It was surely an American personality Bourne intended to create, dependent more on routes rather than on roots in Paul Gilroy's artful distinction,[53] or shaped by the variety of one's experience rather than by one's origins. With it, one could live in multiple worlds, constructed by different cultures, ideologies, and faiths, as the America of increased immigration and accelerated urban growth, of the power of the New Woman and the religious zeal of the progressive reformer required. In the autobiographical essay written during summer 1918, the summer in which Bourne decided to turn his attention to the "values of which the war has no part," he joined the debate on the relevance of the canon in the university. His position suggested that the education of a young cosmopolitan would depend less on where one came from than where one had been. If proponents of a literary education took seriously the idea of multiculturalism, he argued, they would contribute to the building of that modern personality who was at home with all literature, a literary radical of cosmopolitan tastes and standards interested in classical and contemporary literature, different national literatures, and different regional literatures in America. Thus he was anticipating "the revolutionary world is coming into the classic."

The metaphors of sin and conversion in "The History of a Literary Radical" were familiar. He argued he had undergone two conversions—a rebirth from the "orthodoxies" of dusty Anglophilia to the "propaganda" of Socialist realism—literary conversions that, in a genealogy inspired by Nietzsche, were beyond good and evil. The aspiring "man of letters" had become a "cultural revolutionist." He did not want to become another "cultural vandal." He urged other "devout and progressing pagans" to stand ready for another conversion. In his last autobiography, he would reinvent himself again. The self-in-becoming anticipated America's self-becoming, its pathos, a process always in formation.[54]

4
IRONY AND RADICALISM

> The world is no stage, with the ironist as audience. . . . He is as much part and parcel of the human show as any of the people he studies. . . . If the ironist is destructive, it is his own world he is destroying; if he is critical, it is his own world that he is criticizing. And his irony is his critique of life.
>
> —*Randolph S. Bourne, "The Life of Irony"*

"The real trouble with middleclass radicalism in this country today," Bourne wrote before the war, "is that it is too easy." His concern was with the romantic anticapitalism of middle-class intellectuals, which often seemed to turn American radicalism into a spectator sport. Progressive and socialist intellectuals spent their energies in easy sympathy with fashionable causes—in support for the Industrial Workers of the World (IWW) or anarchist groups—as their members were deported or their strikes were broken by the government or corporate security forces, instead of doing the hard work of formulating a theory of radical democracy on which to form an alliance of the middle classes and the labor movement. Ignoring the struggles of "the oppressed masses and excluded races at home," they waited to see what the Russians would "do for the world."

Yet there was work to be done in formulating a radical philosophy that linked democratic strivings at home with those abroad, for the war had revealed that class allegiances cut across national boundaries. "The real arena lies in the international class-struggle, rather than in the competition of artificial national units."[1] An American radicalism that had conformed to a narrowly conceived nationalism would miss the opportunity to build a radical philosophy for an international alliance. Bourne called the young radicals back to the social movement and back to their origins as intellectuals. "The only way middle-class radicalism can serve is by being fiercely and concentratedly intellectual." They must resist the temptation to "put aside their university knowledge" and "disguise" their intellectualism; they must not be reluctant to debate ideas or to risk offending the labor movement. "The young radical today is not asked to be a martyr, but he is asked to be a thinker, an intellectual leader."[2]

If the idea of intellectual leadership still had appeal for Bourne in 1916 it was because it spoke to the sense of possibility that he and other progressive, pragmatist, and socialist intellectuals shared about the role of ideas in effecting social change. In those years they believed that the application of intelligence to social problems could remove the social ills of poverty and illiteracy. Some progressives argued that a philosophy of social democracy would restore a sense of individualism to counter the corrupt influence of large corporations and trusts. The culture critics of the *Masses* and the *Seven Arts,* including Bourne, were convinced that discourse, specifically cultural criticism, would revitalize cultural sensibilities and invigorate political knowledge. These middle-class intellectuals held stock in the power of discourse to shape consciousness and to influence social practices. The purpose of the intellectual vocation was to make a practical difference in social struggle.

In particular, the new class of culture critics, according to Alan Trachtenberg, carved out a new social role for themselves as nonacademic, generalist intellectuals whose point of view was shaped by the role they created.[3] They lived and worked as William James had predicted American intellectuals would in the twentieth century, that is, most of them gave up comfortable middle-class careers, separated themselves from universities, and opted for the public culture of cafes and literary societies. James had welcomed the shift of the center of power from the university to the cosmopolitan collective because, he argued, it would free the individual to express the "personal point of view."[4]

Bourne's own antiorganizational sentiments mirrored James's. Fearful of the conformist influence of organized groups and institutions on individual expression, he encouraged the idea of leadership as a form of engagement or political commitment working outside the "centripetal" force of institutions. Calling young intellectuals to a "restless, controversial criticism of current ideas," he used the concept of the intellectual as a counterweight to the "martyr-complex" of the middle-class radical. For him intellectual vanguardism was explicitly a Sorelian myth to inspire political involvement. "Most of us have given up looking on ourselves as heroes and martyrs," he wrote to dispel the romanticism in the idea of the radical as social outlaw. The idea of intellectual leadership was at best a "vital myth," an impossibility that could point to no tangible results. It was a symbol to discourage delusions of independence (detachment) and the martyrdom of a misunderstood truth-bearer.[5]

Despite his effort to discourage a modernist romance around the idea of intellectual leadership, Bourne's wartime writings about the role of an "irreconcilable" critic carried some of the symbolic weight of the individual speaking truth to power. Even so, in examining his writings both before and during the war, it is clear that he understood not only the limits of criticism but also that every theory of intellectual leadership privileged the voices of intellectuals over those of the majority. In this sense, it was an ironic stance that he proposed for the radical intellectual: to be at once inside the society of which he was, at the same time, a critic.

In another sense, his conception of the role of the intellectual can be seen to stand at the cusp between modernity and postmodernity. As Ross Posnock has argued, Bourne's conception was cast in terms that went beyond the antinomies of the role of intellectuals as either dégagé or engagé, detached or committed, involved concretely in the material world or retreating to the high abstraction of political philosophy. He wrote as Theodor Adorno has suggested of the immanent critic, "in and through contradiction," coming from a divided society (between the Brahmin elite and a new transnational majority), unwilling to resolve contradictions in a transcendentalist philosophy.[6]

Bourne himself came from a fractured genealogy that had an enduring effect, in the double-sided pressure to be both insider and outsider. As a radical critic, I argue, he developed a double-sided sensibility, comfortable with "intellectual suspense" that not only worked its way into his political imagination but also became an integral part of his radicalism, distinctive for its doubled meanings, anticipating what M. M. Bakhtin calls internal dialogization. Bourne's ironic radicalism was a political strategy for dealing with opposition and contradiction in modern consciousness.[7]

The title of this chapter, borrowing from the final chapter of Thomas Mann's *Reflections of a Non-Political Man,* ironically inverts Mann's prescription for the apolitical intellectual and scholar. The stance Bourne assumed was the opposite of Mann's: a stance of political engagement, skepticism, and commitment to radical dissent. Irony was a basis for critical judgment based in contradiction that allowed both detachment and commitment for the radical critic. Put simply, Bourne developed a discursive response—within language itself and as part of particular genres (critical philosophy, autobiography, political polemic)—that complemented his personal marginality. As an unregenerate or "irreconcilable" critic, he engaged in the free play of genres and discursive strategies, strategies anticipating Bakhtin's conception of carnivalization—with radical content. The strategic use of irony, in particular, reflected Bourne's unwillingness to resolve contradictions that were unresolvable and his preference that they remain in a doubled-over relation to the other.[8]

In a college essay examining classical irony, Bourne admired it as the "science of comparison," a philosophical method used by Plato that contrasted the "is and the ought" in order to generate an ideal of justice that was complex, individuated, and grounded in contemporary reality. The Platonic "gift of living analogy" used examples from daily life persuasively to illustrate and make more relevant the more abstract ideal. Bourne particularly admired the dialogic use of divergent perspectives to give *The Republic,* in his reading, a pluralist and ironically a relativist perspective, combining the aesthetic sensibility of the "poet" with the "critical realism" of the "economist," "educator," "historian," and "psychologist," "welded together in one living tissue of thought." In contrast to the "matter of fact . . . materialis[m]" of the time, Plato's idealism showed that "all is not what it appears to be" and that real disagreements over meaning could be traceable to a lived subjectivity; yet his idealism was also tempered and informed by those various and contentious points of view representing the multiple nature of experience. The dialogue looked at experience(s) from many sides, the apparent as well as the latent, and expressed Plato's own perceptions in alternating voices—scientific, aesthetic, metaphysical.[9]

Clearly a revisionist, almost Jamesian reading of classical Platonism, Bourne's interpretation moved away from the dialogue's central distinction between theory and practice to one between the is and the ought, a move James would have endorsed to release American philosophy from debates over metaphysics and determinism. Bourne's interpretation of Socratic irony was equally revisionist and equally Jamesian, appreciating the artful deception used as an investigative tool to uncover hidden meanings and to draw out the inner, unrealized knowledge of his interlocutors, which could be tested in dialogue and interaction. From this interpretive interchange, social truths were constructed. Socratic irony, like James's radical empiricism, helped create truth in the intersubjective exchange of perceptions and observations to be weighed, evaluated, and judged by a community of interpreters.[10] Moreover, the Socratic veil, a charade to demystify and destroy false idols, became a kind of second nature to Socrates; in Bourne's words, it was not simply a "method" but a "life," a way of seeing and making sense of experience in practice. Socrates' irony was "no mere by-product but the very root and soul of his character," an inseparable feature of his "autobiography."

As he did in his own autobiography, Bourne focused on the interaction between personality and social structure. Irony was realized in social interaction, not in the solitary remove of the contemplative scholar. "The daily fabric of the life of irony is woven out of our critical communing with ourselves and the personalities of our friends, and the people with whom we come in contact."[11]

It used the benefits of both science and art in its judgments: as the science of comparison, it measured contemporary realities against one's ideals; as the art of analogy it tapped the human capacity to create, through the apollonian art of interpretation and imagination, restoring consciousness to its proper role as the stimulus to action. It also suggested a philosophical independence, in form as well as content. Somewhere between the passionate commitment of an ideologue and the dispassionate stance of the scientist, the ironic critic might combine both virtues. Socratic irony showed how irony could be both radical and engaged. In Bourne's construction, Socrates was not Nietzsche's disinterested scholar, the theoretical man and archdemystifier, the enemy of enchantment. He was a partisan who brought values to bear. He spoke not from logic only, or from tradition, but from the inspiration of discovery and invention, creating a "city of words." Bourne's reading of Socratic irony was, thus, more ironical than Mann's, and even Nietzsche's at times, resting on the belief in the imaginative potential of the very intellectual act of demystification. In his view irony was creative, but so was radicalism.

"The Life of Irony," published in 1913, counterbalanced the intimate, intensely personal "philosophy of handicap" of his 1911 essay with its abstraction and theorization of political agency, distancing Bourne from his personal genealogy to an intellectual one that could be useful for other young radicals of the middle class. Daniel Aaron recognized the importance of the essay to Bourne's work as a whole. "Much of Bourne's philosophy of life is contained in 'The Life of Irony'—the detached probings of the ironist, the search for the measurable stuff of personality, the agile putting on and off of masks and characters."[12] The essay theorized the self-masking Bourne employed in his writing and the unstable position he occupied as a critic "who cannot yet crystallize, who does not dread suspense."[13] The shifting identities and roles—first as author, then as friend of protagonist, then as narrator and interlocutor—signified the disembodiment of his corporeal marginality, a way of "making over the body," in Bourne's phrase, by taking on the personality of another and making it his own. As a form of self-distancing, irony was also a means of joining that democratic community of interpreters, following Charles Peirce, creating democratic truths.

Bourne's central argument in the essay was that irony was best understood not as a trope but as a lived experience that comes in accepting contradiction. "Things as they are, thrown against the background of things as they ought to be,—this is the ironist's vision." The ability to endure contradiction, to live in the gap between the is and the ought, resulted from living a doubled existence, the common condition in modern society. Early modern theorists had sought to heal the split—that is, to restore a unity to the alienated self (Rousseau), or to reaffirm a species essence to class-identified individuals (Marx), or to transcend it in a universalist state (Hegel). Bourne, however, saw the contradictions of modernity as important to sustain. The gap between the is and the ought opened a space for a regulative ideal to guide social transformation.[14] Anticipating Marcuse's critical theory, Bourne's embrace of absurdity and contradiction in the modern experience was an acknowledgment that negation had creative value in that the competition between opposites was understood as the agent of change and of individual release. On these grounds Bourne argued for the retention of contradictions in society and in the self.

"The ironist is born and not made," an ironic claim for a student of pragmatism who understood the natural as a product of one's experience. One's nature, in this sense, was created, not acquired. Yet his naturalizing of irony underscored his thesis that the ironic disposition was "not a pose or an amusement" but an integral part of one's life. Because "a life cannot be taken off and put on again at will . . . as if it were some portable commodity, or some exchangeable garment," the life of irony was more than a guise or a mask; it was experiential and thus, on one level, constitutive of the self. The ironist understood the appearance/reality opposition and would play with the signifiers. Yet if irony were not a cloak to be taken on and off but a part of oneself, the ironist could step outside the self—could take the self on and off, as it were—first as an observer, then as a participant, then to step in the shoes of another, in an expression of *amour de soi*. In this sense irony was superior to introspection because it has "no [fixed] perspective or contrast" so that the ironist could get outside himself and "view himself objectively." The self-distancing and deliberate alienation maximized the critical sense. It unsettled one's certainty; it challenged one's complacency.

Most important for his political philosophy, irony was the basis of solidarity with others. "It is not true that by examining ourselves and coming to an understanding of how we behave we understand other people, but that by the contrasts and little revelations of our friends we learn to interpret ourselves." The presumed detachment of an ironic observer was its opposite: a means of getting out of oneself (*amour propre*) to bond with others. "Many of our cherished ideals would lose half their validity were they put bodily in the mouths of the less fortunate." By "putting himself in another's place" and adopting "another's point of view," he "lost his egotism completely." Irony was a vehicle for democratic camaraderie, a political tool of personal affiliation.

> The most illuminating experience that we can have is a sudden realization that had we been in the other person's place we should have acted precisely as he did. To the ironist this is no mere intellectual conviction that, after all, none of us are perfect, but a vivid emotional experience which has knit him with that other person in one moment in a bond of sympathy that could have been acquired in no other way.[15]

Therefore, ironic detachment, often misunderstood as a barrier, was not destructive to identity; it affirmed one's humanity. "Irony is . . . the truest sympathy," drawing one into sympathetic understanding of the experiences of others. Its skepticism did not deaden one's sensitivity; it leavened it. It became "a necessary relief from the tension of too much caring. It is his salvation from unutterable despair." Here Bourne drew on his personal genealogy, the anhedonia of the sick soul and the uncertainty of his unresolved status as a divided self. Through a shift in perspective, an inclusivity of points of view, and a "sense of proportion," irony permitted one to lose one's self-absorption. "He acquires a more tolerant, half-amused, half-earnest attitude towards himself." Irony's "critical attitude" gave one a "temporary escape, a slight momentary reconciliation, a chance to draw a deep breath of resolve before plunging into the fight. It is not a palliative so much as a perspective."[16]

With the ironic sensibility as a political stance, Bourne found the discursive stance from which he could gain some distance from his own position of being "in but not of the world." It meant he could understand himself, his society, and the role he might play in it as an "unintegrated self," using irony as the alternative to both "bad conscience" (guilt) and *ressentiment* (rancor), responses of the self-defeated in Nietzsche's terms. The ironic mind recognized contradiction in personal and social experience and mirrored it. "Absurdity is such an intrinsic part of the nature of things that the ironist has only to touch it to reveal it." If modern social life were fundamentally contradictory, the absurdity of the ironic mind was part of it.

"To the ironist it seems that irony is in the things themselves, not in the speaking,"[17] in the doubled meaning in the gaps between signifiers. In recognizing the distinction between the represented and its representation, Bourne also problematized it, anticipating the postmodern understanding but in a way that did not collapse the boundaries between "things" and their "speaking." The world maintained its own boundaries, but under an ironic gaze, it became a text. His analysis opened up the possibility of blurring conventional boundaries—between the normal and the deviant, the sane and the insane—but without destroying them. From the perspective of the radical critic, the deviant—the discontented voices of the "forgotten masses and excluded races at home"—became the norm. As Olaf Hansen notes, "Truth is thus established in the process of gradually eliminating the balance between the normal and the exception, shifting it around until we look at the normal as the exception."[18]

The political premise of the argument was made more apparent through the aesthetic analogy of modern photographic technology that Bourne used to illustrate irony's critical, demystifying technique. "The ironical method might be compared to the acid that develops a photographic plate," highlighting what is already there. It did not "distort the image but merely brings to light all that was implicit in the plate before." Similarly irony, "the photography of the soul," revealed elements of the subject that would be otherwise overlooked in a literal (representational) reading. "The picture goes through certain changes in the hands of the ironist, but without these changes the truth would be simply a blank, unmeaning surface." As the crystals on the plate revealed various "values and beauty" when light fell upon it at different angles, so irony exposed the aspects of its subject to different light. While the photographic plate presented a reverse image of its subject, irony, in presenting the "photographic negative of the truth," reversed and inverted traditional valuations. "Irony revel[s] in a paradox . . . truth with the values reversed." Irony transvalued values and tested them against the standard of contemporary "social validity" and democratic interchangeability.[19]

Democratic truth, the political ground of Bourne's conception of modern irony, emerged in discourse. "The deadliest way to annihilate the unoriginal or the insincere is to let it speak for itself. Irony is this letting things speak for themselves and hang themselves by their own rope. Only it repeats the words after the speaker and adjusts the rope." The ironical outlook tested opinions by "transplanting" them to the "lips of another."

> If an idea is absurd, the slightest change of environment will show that absurdity. The mere transference of an idea to another's mouth will bring to light all its hidden meanings. . . . If a point of view cannot bear being adopted by another person, if it is not hardy enough to be transplanted, it has little right to exist at all.[20]

The modern ironist was thus "the great intellectual democrat in whose presence and before whose law all ideas and attitudes stand equal." His democracy extended to the final selection of truth. "If irony destroys some ideals, it builds up others. . . . Those it does leave standing are imperishably founded in the democratic experience of all men." In this sense the ironist was a pragmatist; he tested ideas "by their social validity, by their general interchangeability among all sorts of people and the world." Deriving his ideals from experience, he tested them against the same experience. He "compares things not with a fixed standard but with each other, and the values that slowly emerge from the process . . . are constantly revised, corrected, and refined by that same sense of contrast." If politics privileged speech, irony undercut the orthodox and the parochial, initiating a counternarrative to challenge the culture of the last Puritan.[21]

In several respects then, an ironic critique is similar to a dialectical one. Like the dialectic, it understood appearance as deceptive and contradiction to be in the "nature of things." Unlike the dialectic, however, it did not see contradiction as the dynamic by which men could be lifted to ever higher levels and eventual fulfillment. It did not rely on a transcendent telos to redeem humankind. It left contradiction alone, untranscended, expressing different possibilities and different experiences of social truth. The ironic for Bourne can be seen as similar to that of Bakhtin's conception of the parodic. Both irony and parody, unlike the dialectic, do not offer a new synthesis but remain in a doubled relation to the original. Thus Bourne was able to accept the fact that a belief and its opposite were both true, and both were possible to hold at the same time ("man is born free, but everywhere he is in chains"). Irony made it possible to endure contradictions critically, to acknowledge that contradictory truths could be held simultaneously, without resolving them. Irony allowed him to accept and even welcome "contradictory situations" and impossible results.

An ironic perspective was therefore not synonymous with cynicism or with satire. Mencken's cynicism, for instance, in Bourne's view, revealed a contempt for democracy without at the same time suggesting alternatives. Mencken found it easier to poke fun at the "booboisie" than to take a stand with the "demos" and work to improve society from within. Moreover, for the purely philosophic or literary applications of irony, Bourne had no use. "The kind of aesthetic irony that Pater and Omar display is a paralyzed, half-seeing, half-caring reflection on life—a tame, domesticated irony with its wings cut . . . the result not of exquisitely refined feelings, but of social anesthesia." Yet the political limitations of irony were equally clear. If the critic's role was to generate standards of judgment that could stimulate action, irony is not enough on its own. Coupled with radical convictions, however, it defended against mindlessness, lazy generalizations, and apathy. An ironic sensibility that was not at the same time political had no pragmatic value in the modern century. It was an indulgence that was unaffordable, an abdication of one's membership in the larger social community. The question was not whether the social movement could afford irony, but whether it could get along without it.

In 1914 Georg Lukács described irony as the quintessential stance of the modern novelist, critical at the same time it was descriptive, the vehicle most appropriate for modern literature, a literary disjuncture between bourgeois man and his society. The unity, now lost, between classical man and his world, reflected in the classical art form of the epic, was revealed in the life of the modern protagonist, who is shown to be an estranged seeker of the meaning of existence, retreating "into subjectivity as interiority and [who] strives to imprint the contents of [his] longing upon the alien world." For Lukács, irony was "the modern method of form-giving," a constituent part of the modern world and the novelist's own awareness of the subjective and objective alienation of his protagonist. It was "the highest freedom that can be achieved in a world without a god," Lukács wrote, showing men the best they could do, in a world out of joint. It signified a "self-correction of the world's fragility," both critical ("realist") and descriptive ("naturalist"). Irony attempted to transform inadequate relations even as it forced men to confront them.[22]

In a review of Dreiser's work, Bourne described his realism in terms that suggested substantial agreement with early Lukácsian aesthetics. Dreiser's technique illustrated a modern aesthetic that captured the alienation experienced by ordinary Americans and a variety of perspectives to describe their efforts to find meaning and attain self-determination in the chaos of the modern city. On the one hand, according to Bourne, Dreiser distanced himself from his characters, presenting them as "rather vacuous people, a little pathetic in their innocence of the possibilities of life and their optimistic truthfulness," "unconscious of their serfdom" to the "great barons of industry." The disjuncture between his awareness of the chaotic interplay of wills-to-power and their unconscious innocence buffeted about in the great cities of America illustrated the kind of ironic contrast Lukács had described. Further, Dreiser distanced himself from his characters without at the same time "convicting" them, in Bourne's words. He took their experiences of modern life's cruelty and beauty as a given, "neither praising nor blaming" his characters for their weaknesses and misfortunes but recognizing "how much more terrible and beautiful and incalculable life is than any of us are willing to admit." Although literary brokers found Dreiser's ethical standards shockingly nihilist or libertarian, Bourne saw them as refreshingly realistic and compassionate, the judgments of a "moral democrat."[23]

The role of the critic and intellectual suggested in Mann's *Reflections of a Non-Political Man* can be seen as the theoretical antithesis to Bourne's understanding of the political use of irony. The differences between Mann's conception of the political responsibility of intellectuals and Bourne's illustrate the fundamentally conservative and the profoundly radical interpretations of the role of the intellectual and the ironic mind in a modern, fragmenting society. Mann's *Reflections,* written five years after Bourne's essay, inveighed against the tendency of contemporary intellectuals to become involved in political controversies. The modern intellectual must choose art, not politics, as the only appropriate place for his creativity. Mann warned fellow intellectuals (including his politically active brother) and artists that they must choose between irony (as expressed in art) or radicalism (as evidenced in democratic activism and abstract intellectualism). Irony and radicalism, Mann held, are antitheses—an "Either-Or"—in sharp contrast to Bourne's fundamental integration of irony and radicalism, whether in art or in criticism.[24]

Mann, of course, like Nietzsche before him, wanted to rescue men from the recesses of science, religion, and philosophy and from the excessive intellectualism of the apollonian will. Irony returned man to the innocence of the dionysian, sustaining life and eros. Only irony was creative, Mann insisted, evoking the sublime and the spiritual from the abyss of tradition. But his reading of Nietzsche was also deeply conservative, associated with all that was sublime in the German character, nation, and tradition and distinctly not the tool of the new socialist or of democratic politics. His retranslation of Nietzsche ignored the fact that Nietzsche wanted to combine art and politics in a "gay science," to enable men to live an aesthetic life that had political consequences as well, as suggested in the idea of an "artistic Socrates." The question for the scholar, as for the poet, Nietzsche suggested, was not whether one was conservative or radical but whether one's activities were "life-affirming" or "life-denying." Life-affirming intellectual activity gave men (and women) standards for judgment and thereby helped them avoid nihilism. Although intellectuals could not *create* forms, they could generate values that gave meaning to forms created by artists and poets. The "hardest test of independence" for the intellectual was "not to remain stuck in one's own detachment, to that voluptuous remoteness and strangeness of the bird who flies ever higher to see ever more below him" but to learn to "conserve oneself" and remain connected to the stream of human experience.[25]

The dangers of excessive detachment and abstractness were clear to Bourne as well, even before the war, when political contingency dominated public discourse. "If irony is the virtue of philosophers, abstractness . . . is their vice." Specifically he meant to warn against becoming a "lonely Zarathustra," withdrawing to the "mountain top," avoiding human contact. With detachment, his vision would be lifeless. "Without people and opinions for his mind to play on, his irony withers and faints." His feet must be firmly planted in the empirical world. "Like the modern city, he is totally dependent on a steady flow of supplies from the outside world. . . . This world is his nourishment."[26] Using a feminine signified of the early twentieth century (the New Woman as associated with the chaos and disorder of the modern city), Bourne showed irony to be a part of the dionysian.

But Bourne's view of the role of the radical critic was also an implicit admission of the limits of criticism. In a 1912 letter, he acknowledged the embattled and often impossible premises of the critic's project, particularly in a society ambivalent about intellectualism.

> Criticism . . . constantly conscious . . . of its limitations . . . struggle[s] heroically and resolutely up a path to a goal that it knows it will never achieve. And yet somehow that march, predestined as it is to failure, aids countless wayfarers, whose eyes would be otherwise fixed stonily on the ground, to see the vision at the goal and be glad.[27]

The futility of criticism was ironically its raison d'être, the role of the critic possible only because it was an impossible one. The myth of intellectual leadership was even more necessary to inspire a "relentless criticism of everything existing." The combination of irony and radicalism began to suggest a political solution to Bourne's choice of vocation at the same time that it gave him a point of view that was shaped by that social role. Along with the other culture critics of his generation, he would go without institutional affiliation and without access to power but would try to create a new role, with new power, in which public criticism could contribute to what they called the "American promise."

Only war presented a unique situation, Bourne argued, because discourse became one-dimensional and political debate became polarized into either/or propositions: one must be prowar or antiwar; there was no in-between. The choice proved unacceptable to those intellectuals who "cannot yet crystallize" or to those who did not dread "intellectual suspense." During wartime and in times when a war economy was operating, the ironic critic became an outlaw, a radical by virtue of his "irreconcilability" to the positions offered. Writing "below the battle," he could retain his irony—and his radicalism. He could, inverting Mann's meaning, be both creative and radical.

5
YOUTH

> Youth's attitude is really the scientific attitude. Do not be afraid to make experiments, it says. You cannot tell anything will work until you have tried it.
>
> —*Randolph S. Bourne, "Youth"*

> We no longer make careful distinctions between the fit and the unfit, the successful and the unsuccessful, the effective and the ineffective, the presentable and the unpresentable. We are more interested in the influences that have produced these seeming differences than in the fact of the differences themselves. We classify people by new categories. We look for personality, for sincerity, for social sympathy, for democratic feeling, for social productiveness, and we interpret success in terms of these attainments.
>
> —*Randolph S. Bourne, "For Radicals"*

While in Europe in 1914, Bourne wrote his suffragist friend, Alyse Gregory:

> You cannot think how I envy you, with all your hustle and adventure of work, your crowds of interesting friends, your ostensibly . . . so easy command of life. . . . It would be so glorious to be "in" something, making something go, or at least connected up with something or somebody to whom you were important and even necessary.[1]

They agreed that "life was primarily action," but she had managed to "count for something in the world," he wrote, turning her beliefs into a "motive of action, a basis of behavior, a program rather than a creed." Yet if Bourne's admiration was personal, it was also political, for Gregory was "learning life by action," taking up the Jamesian challenge to experience life rather than merely to contemplate it.[2] She was the New Woman, and the suffragists in England and America signaled the end of a declining patriarchal order in Europe and America to his mind and the radical leadership of the modern generation. He decided Gregory exemplified youth itself, that spirit of adventure and experimentation that he offered to his own historical generation, what C. Wright Mills has called a moral optic, or a countersymbol to itself. The idea of youth was his means of appealing to a particular modern generation to fulfill its promise to humanize the scientific spirit, welcome the power of the New Woman, and move beyond moralism to pragmatism in politics.

By the time Bourne wrote Gregory, he had already formulated a philosophy of youth in *Youth and Life,* a collection of essays that had earned him a considerable audience for a writer of twenty-five and a position at the *New Republic* as a contributing editor on issues of education and the culture of youth. His ideas on the politics and experiences of youth were often phrased in terms of optimism and uplift. He praised the young adults he knew (and imagined) for their idealism, their involvement in political causes, and particularly their willingness to experiment in social relations. "The whole philosophy of youth is summed up in the word, Dare! Take chances and you will attain!"[3] Given their appetite for experimentation, he anticipated a disruption of the influence of the bourgeois family, its ethos of individualism, and the middle-class career patterns expected for his generation.

But the prewar generation in America was internally divided about itself and its collective mission. If opposition to the Victorian order gave them a collective grievance and a common identity to mark out its members as a generation, they differed in their diagnoses of the new order and in the remedies they proposed to deal with social and economic crises, including the growth of poverty, the centralization of public and private authority, the rapid rise of immigration, and the possibility of building a common culture in America.

The politics of the prewar generation and its internal divisions are seen in the writings of Bourne and Walter Lippmann, two of its prominent spokespersons, who represented two sides of the divided generational mind of the modern century. I have chosen them to illustrate this divide, not because they represent the extremes of political debate in prewar America but because their views highlight the multivocality of the political climate and within the progressivist coalition itself, which ruptured only a short time later when war preparedness became the salient public issue in 1915. Their differences, often papered over in the language of generationalism, were sometimes elusive even to the generationalists themselves, including Bourne and Lippmann, as they concentrated on their desire to break with the past. My emphasis is designed to illustrate what was at stake even before the war about the idea of progress, the nature and limits of liberal reform, and the kind of civic society they wanted to build.

I have isolated two historical narratives to clarify the complicated nature of the prewar debate. The first is centered on the role of science, technology, and professional expertise to shape social reform (and save souls). Lippmann's initial attraction to Bergsonian vitalism was supplanted by 1914 in *Drift and Mastery* with an unqualified endorsement of the leadership of the new technocrat, trained in the modern social sciences of economics, political science, and communications, who, he maintained, knew more about the public interest than the public itself. Bourne's similarly enthusiastic embrace of instrumentalism at college, as he studied under John Dewey, was replaced by the plea for more experimentation, his attempt to rescue the pragmatism of James from the instrumentalism of social bureaucrats and to restore personal authority or "the personal point of view" to decisions about social reconstruction.

Even in his instrumentalist days at college ("we are all instrumentalists here at Columbia"), Bourne tried to temper the fascination with science and expertise as a basis for political authority by arguing that it would lead to rigid thinking (the apollonian mind) if wrenched from its Jamesian roots. "Science brings us only to 'an area of our dwelling,' Whitman says," he frequently reminded his readers.[4] It could not address the meaning(s) of experience or offer principles of social philosophy. It could not deal with what it could not quantify or measure. The disagreement between Bourne and Lippmann over the limits of the "scientific attitude" therefore went beyond the question of the role (social) scientific expertise should take in modern reform; it extended to the very meaning of science and scientific knowledge itself.

The second narrative revealed in their writings is a related one about the gendered nature of public authority and its effect on personal liberties. Although the language of science and the language of gender did not overlap one another exactly, as templates lining up on every point, they revealed a common attention to the gendered implications of a society that was run by experts. To overstate their differences only slightly, Lippmann's feminism looked to the liberation of women within the home or as consumers and secondarily as individuals competing in the market, welcoming the advances that modern technology would bring to (middle-class) women to make their domestic labor more efficient. Bourne's feminism, by contrast, looked to the freedom of public women, acting outside the home, to "feminize" professionalism as well as to redistribute the responsibilities of domestic labor. He believed in the idea of a women's culture that contained a certain sensibility beneficial for society as a whole. He therefore expected professional women—the reformers, lawyers, teachers, and social workers he knew in New York—to live outside conventional roles and resist the norms of bourgeois professionalism. He castigated them when they turned him out after late evenings of talk so they could get a full night's sleep, and he implored them not to turn their circles of friends into tight little communities that did not tolerate difference. Through his romantic feminism he wanted, in short, the New Woman to "feminize" society and public authority or to "soften the crudities of this hard, hierarchal, over-organized, anarchic" society.[5]

Within these two narratives, I trace the politics of the generational mind before the war. My interpretation differs from those offered by other scholars, however, by characterizing the debate primarily in cultural terms rather than in purely political terms. I have chosen to interpret these two sensibilities in Nietzschean terms, that is, as a debate between the emphasis on the apollonian mind, or the desire to order society through social reform and expertise, and the faith in the dionysian spirit, to inform political action and encourage experimentation through critical inquiry and cultural adventure. Bourne proposed to combine these two subjectivities in a "post-scientific" philosophy, a remarkably postmodern alternative to scientism and ideology, which would restore to the scientific spirit the creativity of the poetic imagination.

My interpretation also differs from that of other scholars in that I consider Bourne's social criticism as an alternative to progressivism rather than as within its terms. Reading his essays closely, one finds that Bourne's support of progressive social reform was consistently qualified and ambiguous. He supported the idea of social reform when it was democratic, rather than as a program run by experts; he supported educational reform when it tried to break down class barriers rather than serve social utility; he supported the use of science and expertise when it was experimental, preserving the spirit of James. But he did not share the progressivist faith in progress, the idea of social reform as a means of social control, or its reliance on an activist state.

Moreover, Bourne was unambiguously critical of social reform experiments that created artificial environments that isolated their clients from the disorder of the larger society, such as Jane Addams's Hull House.[6] He was hostile to schools that educated with an eye to making students useful to society and corporate needs, such as the vocational technology education in New York public schools.[7] He split openly with his own university over its labor policies toward the "scrubwomen" who daily cleaned the steps and halls of the dormitories and classrooms and over its educational policy of teaching the English canon at the expense of contemporary American literature.[8] His support and criticism of progressive educational reform, the rise of social science and management expertise, or the development of progressive social programs were part and parcel of his broader cultural criticism in this sense. Thus in deference to his own insistence that education was inseparable from life, I have chosen not to analyze his educational theory separately but as part of his political and cultural criticism, to see it as encouraging youthful experimentation and the interplay between pragmatics and the imagination in cultural renewal.[9]

Before examining Bourne's and Lippmann's diagnoses of the modern generational crisis in America and Europe, it is worth noting that generational analysis first developed at the end of the nineteenth century, promoting—and reflecting—new categories of political agency and identity. Generational theorists writing at the turn of the century, such as Karl Mannheim, Antonio Gramsci, and José Ortega y Gasset, conceptualized generations as distinctive social groupings, similar to social classes but crossing over national, class, and even gender lines. If they agreed that generations were a workable sociological category and a potent political phenomenon, however, they differed in defining the exact nature of the generation that was the object of their study. Mannheim's examination, the "Problem of Generations," associated generations and the rise of generational consciousness with the formation of a dissident intelligentsia that, as a result of certain destabilizing experiences, begins to feel, articulate, and defend a core set of values and ideals against a society they perceived to be indifferent or hostile. For Mannheim, and for Francois Mentré as well, the character of a generation was therefore not marked by a common or majoritarian experience of individuals in an age-cohort group but by the experiences of its more distinctive and atypical members. Other generational theorists agreed that generational identity was fundamentally an elite phenomenon, with a clear separation of experiences between the mass and the elite that the concept did not reflect. Some scholars even argued that generationalism was a phenomenon unique to no one but the generationalists themselves.[10]

Though it may be accurate historically to associate the idea of generational identity and generational conflict with the rise of an independent literary intelligentsia, there is a question as to whether such an identifiable elite can be found in prewar America. Nevertheless, generational identity and generational consciousness was a common frame of reference for young socialists and progressives in the first decades of the twentieth century, as well as for Bourne and Lippmann, despite their ideological differences. Indeed, the prevalence of generationalism suggests that as a framework of analysis and a form of social consciousness, it had developed as a way to foster collective consciousness in a society in which class was often ignored. Thus generationalists, in positing a generational identity, actually helped create the phenomenon, despite forces that might have undermined it, adding a new twist to Mannheim's otherwise fruitful analysis.

The significance of generational thinking, particularly as it developed in the early twentieth century, lay in its political potential as an organizing concept and a source of identity. Generational theorists commonly agreed that generations as a social category referred to more than an age-cohort group of individuals coexisting at the same period of time. Rather, the term was used as an organizational concept and a frame of reference to conceptualize society and as a means of transforming it. Generationalists thus structured the world in terms of generational categories, using an approach in much the same fashion as did social-class analysts, as a form of collectivism and determinism. Unlike the concept of class, however, the idea of generation emphasized the temporal rather than the socioeconomic location of its members. According to Mannheim, what bound together members of a generation was not community and physical proximity but location in society or the objective facts of their existence. For him, therefore, generations were much like classes in their objective determination. American generationalists, specifically Bourne, Lippmann, and Addams, perceived themselves to be part of an entity that was facing for the first time problems of a decidedly modern nature.

In his study of the prewar generation in Europe, Robert Wohl argues that all generations believe themselves to be special, but the "generation of 1914" came to signify a particular "unity of experience, feeling, and fate," which led to a significant shift in the meaning of the idea of generation itself. All generational theorists agreed, among them Ortega and Mannheim, that membership in a generation implied, above all, the sharing of a common destiny.[11]

Peerage was neither a necessary nor sufficient characteristic of generational identity or of the sense of shared destiny, which explains why Bourne frequently pointed out that "pioneers" among the older generation—e.g., William James, Walt Whitman, and Henri Bergson—had managed to articulate the values and agenda of his own generation even before a majority of them had signed on. Put differently, generations are an argument, Sherman Paul has suggested, that nicely established the synthetic nature of their identity. They stand for certain ideas or hopes and against others, by way of constituting themselves. More than the factor of age, generational consciousness, and by implication generational identity, constitutes a necessary ingredient in the formation of a generation.[12]

The idea of generations in its modern form was tied frequently to that of generational conflict so that by the end of the nineteenth century, the idea of "youth in revolt" had emerged as a byproduct of generational theory in the association made between the world of the fathers and all that was corrupt and decadent, against which the younger generation stood in opposition.[13] Generational consciousness and the associated idea of generational conflict signified a discontinuity with the past and an opportunity to make the world over again. It stressed a similarity of perspective among members of a generation as well as a radical break with the thought and experiences of others and with the past itself.[14]

The theory of generational revolt produced a cluster of attitudes that has been termed "the ideology of youth," which reached its apotheosis in the 1920s, emphasizing in particular the sense that one's youth was a superior stage of life, marked by its purity and innocence.[15] As Laura Nash has pointed out, the association between the idea of generation and one's chronological youth became so automatic by the end of the nineteenth century that the idea of generation "came to mean not so much men who shared the same age, as men who shared youth," undercutting, to some extent, the emphasis on the importance of voluntary membership.[16] In identifying generation with youth, however, a generation in this sense offered its own unique lifestyle, in this instance the bohemian experience appropriate to an interclass group and its own form of political association, the youth movement based on the segregation of age and consciousness.[17] It became possible to refer to "youth" as a significant social group so that the generational tag was often dropped altogether, implying in the concept of "youth" the notion of the "younger generation."[18]

A key element of a generation's common frame of reference, in sum, was the identification of a certain event or set of experiences that constituted a definite rupture from the past. That rupture usually took the form of a great historical event or crisis, a famine, a war, a revolution, or the like. The generation of 1914 in Europe, according to Wohl, was subject to several dislocating experiences. Among them was a marked decline in parental authority that produced in them a rejection of the "fiercely competitive capitalist society" of their "stern" fathers as a locus of "unbearable tyranny," a deterioration of traditional forms of social identification, and at the same time, a challenge to the bourgeois ethic of competitive individualism, the latter two presenting them with the opportunity to create alternate forms of collective association that crossed class and geographical lines. The separation between the adult world of labor and marriage and the experiences of adolescence, a separation marked by increasing numbers of youth spending extended periods of time in universities and military service, according to Annie Kriegel, prolonged the dependency and increased the restlessness of young men and women. As their participation in activities of productive labor and the attainment of economic stability were postponed, the links that traditionally were forged in families and social classes began to break down even further, setting individuals free to redefine their social roles.[19]

The disaffection of people born between 1880 and 1910 in Europe was expressed in a quiet rage against a world that was seen to be relativistic, chaotic, and morally bankrupt. For European youth, World War I thus presented an invitation (that few resisted) to restore the world to a more spiritually pure, more orderly condition. Their historical mission, they believed, was to purify and renew their world, and many of them became feverishly nationalistic and even militarist, ultimately aligning against groups on the political left.[20] In America the chief source of generational grievance was against the society that they referred to collectively as the Puritan order: the pietistic, disciplinary culture of the middle class. They saw themselves uniting against the determinism and moralism of a staid Protestantism, even if they divided along the lines of science (order) among the reformers or the New Woman (disorder) among the radicals.

The fragmentation and alienation that were products of this historical rupture were paralleled not coincidentally in the "discovery" of adolescence, a unique stage between the child's identity and the adult's, which, according to G. Stanley Hall's 1904 treatise on adolescence, was a product of a rapidly industrializing world that delayed adulthood (primarily, for young men). Hall determined that adolescence (and by implication the younger generation) was characterized by an awareness of a radical alienation (separation) between one's self and the world around one, which, according to more recent literature, leads to an urgent need to develop an independent and autonomous identity, using ideals, rebellion, asociability, commitment to transient groups and identities, and ambivalence toward oneself and one's own power. Bourne, having read Hall, was confirmed in his conclusion that the adolescent experience of sensitivity to and estrangement from the perceptions of the external world was generational, that is, was peculiar to his generation, the one that was in fact studied by Hall.[21]

In "The Two Generations," his first published essay in the *Atlantic Monthly,* Bourne defended his generation against charges of laziness and self-indulgence. The "rising generation," especially the young men of good families, according to Cornelia Comer, a contributor to the *Atlantic Monthly,* had abandoned the ways of the fathers by celebrating the will (Shaw) and relying on "Whitmanesque Personality." Their lack of social accomplishment showed them to be "soft" and deformed by "*mental rickets and curvature of the soul.*"[22] Bourne may have found the metaphor too much to go uncontested. The "older generation," he wrote, turning the criticism on its head, had failed its children. "I doubt if any generation was thrown quite so completely on its own resources as ours is." Left to "bring itself up," the younger generation developed its own standards and contested the old divisions of the fathers:

> We no longer make careful distinctions between the fit and the unfit, the successful and the unsuccessful, the effective and the ineffective, the presentable and the unpresentable. We are more interested in the influences that have produced these seeming differences than in the fact of the differences themselves. We classify people by new categories. We look for personality, for sincerity, for social sympathy, for democratic feeling, for social productiveness, and we interpret success in terms of these attainments.[23]

It was their openness to experiences and ideas, their commitment to "the wildest radicalisms," their "thirst" for varied and new experiences that represented a reformulated will to power, a fluid and malleable concept rather than a rigid and domineering one. Their power lay in their dionysian exuberance and energy, as an antidote to the apollonian drive for control. With youthful ardor and a firm set of revitalizing goals, they would bypass the problem of acquiring mastery altogether.[24] Bourne therefore insisted that youth "must be not simply contemporaneous, but a generation ahead of its time." As ruling ideas were "always a generation behind our actual social conditions," it was necessary for youth to be "not less radical but even more radical than it would naturally" so that when the time came to take positions of power, it would be able to break the cycle of power and resistance that supported cultural consensus. In a shrewd understanding of the dialectic of consent and coercion that underlay the crust of hegemony, he looked to youth to redefine the nature of authority itself.[25]

Many historians have concluded understandably that Bourne eventually resorted "to a full-fledged cult of youth"[26] and an ideology of generational revolt led by an international band of insurgents or "league of youth." As James Hoopes has written, "Bourne staked his hopes on a league of youth so radical that it would live socialistically in the present and help to create thereby the 'communal life of the future.'"[27] In light of the criticisms of his own generation in America and the reservations he expressed over the feverish fanaticism of European youth, however, this conclusion seems untenable.[28] More often Bourne argued that the "constant guerilla warfare" between generations could be contained by solutions permitting cooperation and mutual understanding.

> I want to see independent, self-reliant, progressive generations, not eating each others' hearts out, but complementing each other and assuming a spiritual division of labor. I want the father and mother besides raising the children to lead independent lives of their own, to add their own life-works of art to the great picture gallery of personality of the past.[29]

He suggested an alliance—of status, on the one hand, and sensuality, on the other—an unlikely combination that could "conserve" the spirit of youth for society as a whole, coupled with the power of age. "Middle age has the prestige and the power," and "youth has the isolation, the independence, the disinterestedness so that it may attack any foe."[30]

Though his own generation was the exemplar of youth, privately he wrote its members were not so independent or certain of their goals as he declared in *Youth and Life.* He knew too many prematurely old young men, following their fathers into business or settling down into families.[31] Others seemed to be stuck in what he and his circle of friends at Columbia University referred to as Hamlet's "destiny," the paralysis of the apollonian mind, incapable of taking creative or heroic action. "Of course, we are all Hamlets," he wrote in 1913. "Our decadence is hateful to us; we struggle against it, and in so doing live to a far greater intensity than does the one who sits down and contemplates it."[32] Hamlet's dilemma, of course, was the dilemma of the brooding and introspective intellectual; his need was to find ways of acting in the face of (horrible) truth (or meaninglessness).

In several ways, the dilemma of middle-class youth mirrored that of the late nineteenth century, the paralysis facing the rebel fathers among the late Victorians as they confronted with terror both directions of the modern century, symbolized by Henry Adams's Dynamo and the Virgin. For Hamlet, the solution (to inaction) was in illusion; through self-enchantment he could act. Some of the rebel fathers, according to Michael Rogin, overcame their paralysis in an embrace of the irrational to salve the anxiety of seeming disorder (Sorel, Nietzsche, Bergson); others found the "personal point of view" as a way of recovering the self from excessive patriarchal control (William James); and still others moved to direct action itself, ultimately in war, to rescue themselves from anhedonia (melancholia), leading to suicide (Woodrow Wilson). In some sense, all who faced terrible truths used the veil and relied on therapeutic philosophies to free them.[33]

Through the enabling philosophies of James and Nietzsche, among others, the prewar generation in America relieved its anxiety over its social role through experiments in social and cultural renovation, as Jane Addams aptly prescribed.[34] Max Eastman, James Oppenheim, Waldo Frank, and Floyd Dell, for instance, wrote poetry and short stories for the little magazines and formed new, experimental publications in Greenwich Village or the Lower East Side. Some artists established galleries, such as Alfred Stieglitz's Gallery 291, displaying works of American and European modern art and photography, and some directed and produced new drama in "little theaters" or in group pageants.[35] Other individuals, such as Addams, Henrietta Rodman, Crystal Eastman, and Carl Zigrosser, were active in settlement houses, social welfare agencies, and the judicial system, working for improved public services to alleviate the desperate conditions of the poor and for better working conditions for labor. Some activists established experimental schools in Greenwich Village, such as the Ferrer Center for adults and the Little School House for children.[36] Others worked directly within the state—as did Walter Lippmann, then a socialist, securing the election of the first socialist mayor in the United States in Schenectady, New York, in 1912, or fighting city machines in local and state governments, or, by 1917, working for the Wilson administration's public information office.[37]

It was this group of politically involved and culturally active artists and writers who formed a generation and became the subject of Bourne's political philosophy. In a Foucaultian sense, they became an effect of his linguistic and political attempt to represent them in the abstract symbol of youth. But with all representation, a gap exists between the representation and the represented, rendering, to some extent, according to Anne Norton, the crucial political concept of representation a fiction—that which stands for that which is not.[38] The prewar generation outstripped its representation in Bourne's youth symbol and reinscribed its own cultural norms in Lippmann's idea of mastery, resignifying them. In Lippmann's symbolic order, in other words, aspirations to Promethean mastery and control were neither elusive nor undesirable to this particular historical generation, proving him to be an important counterweight to Bourne's more romantic notion of youthful experimentation.

One of the most articulate spokesmen of the young progressives was Walter Lippmann. In *Drift and Mastery,* subtitled "An Attempt to Diagnose the Current Unrest," he characterized the discontent of his generation. "All of us are immigrants spiritually," he wrote. They were dislocated and restless in the wake of rapid changes in social and personal roles and relations.

> We are unsettled to the very roots of our being. There isn't a human relation, whether of parent and child, husband and wife, worker and employer, that doesn't move in a strange situation. . . . There are no precedents to guide us, no wisdom that wasn't made for a simpler age.

Traditions had been demolished, the old shibboleths exposed. "The sanctity of property, the patriarchal family, the heredity caste, the dogma of sin, obedience to authority,—the rock of ages, in brief, has been blasted for us." The great problem of the age, Lippmann announced, was not securing individual freedom; it was deciding what to do with it. In assuming that Americans had been liberated, he turned to the rather perverse dilemma (of the middle class) of having too little direction and no clear vision of what they would like to become.[39]

This bold claim, which ignored the material unfreedom of many Americans, was startling, but it was even more so because it directly contradicted his own political philosophy outlined only two years earlier in *Preface to Politics.* In it Lippmann had argued that the problem of the modern age was the influence of too much tradition, which stifled imagination and quelled spontaneity. He drew upon the ideas of the European thinkers—Bergson, Nietzsche, Sorel, and also Freud—to challenge the rationalism of the nineteenth century, of which he was skeptical, and to encourage the freeing of the "will" as a force for change. Yet in *Drift and Mastery,* it seemed that the problem was too much "drift" and the elusiveness of "mastery." People were living passive lives, unrooted and directionless, uncontrolled either by principle, scientific rationality, or even, ironically, tradition. Their ineffectuality allowed industrial exploitation and corporate inefficiency to go unchecked, lingering on by "default" rather than from utility. It was a critique of the progressive reform movement as well as of the impasse in American public culture. "Reform produces its Don Quixotes who never deal with reality; it produces its Brands who are single-minded to the brink of ruin; and it produces its Hamlets and its Rudins who can never make up their minds."[40]

In place of routine, he proposed that "purpose" be substituted: "We can no longer treat life as something that is trickled down to us. We have to deal with it deliberately, devise its social organization, alter its tools, formulate its method, educate and control it." In practical terms, the solution was that the younger generation would need to forge new instruments of management and manipulation, placing the future in the hands of the "industrial statesmen," a new class of professionals, schooled in the science of business administration and expert in the rational organization of industrial production. "You have in a very literal sense to *educate* the industrial situation, to draw out its promise, to discipline and strengthen it."[41] The sort of education he had in mind, as evident in the discourse, emphasized discipline and control to shape social behavior, following the assumptions of the educator E. A. Ross, who argued that the conscious manipulation of behavior would produce a consequent alteration in moral character.[42] Lippmann and Addams, among others, viewed the expert as the policeman and redeemer of society in general, capable of producing that change in character. The results, Lippmann went so far as to add, would civilize the whole social conflict. With the new professional business administrators in charge of streamlining production and rationalizing employment practices, revolution would be unnecessary.[43]

If the shift in his position was not explicitly acknowledged, there was no doubt that *Drift and Mastery* urged a reassertion of control and discipline through scientific administration and technocratic expertise. Experts in the "art of society" could create the future consciously through the application of reason and science, designed to maximize efficiency. To be fair, it was not a call for scientism, for his notion of scientific management contained a sense that creativity, cooperation, and democracy were components of mastering one's environment. He appealed specifically to Jamesian pragmatism as the source of that collaborative effort among a community of peers. Nevertheless, the clear faith he and other progressive intellectuals placed in professional expertise and technocratic solutions illustrated strikingly their decision to subject free creativity to the tests of rationalism and efficiency. Lippmann's greatest fear, it seems, was of the "waste" that would come from the profit motive and the disorder that would result from too much rebellion. Science, in addition to denoting invention, fellowship, and creative experimentation, implied the discipline that was necessary to impose on capitalism in order to prevent social unrest.[44]

Bourne greatly admired *Drift and Mastery,* recommending it as "a book one would have given one's soul to have written."[45] It offered a diagnosis similar to his own, as outlined in his essays on the generational crisis in *Youth and Life* and in his articles on educational reform for the *New Republic.* Yet it is surprising that Bourne did not realize that their conceptions of mastery through science were ultimately incompatible or that the training of a new generation of experts would violate his own commitments to the idea of democratic education. If he were troubled by Lippmann's preoccupation with mastery, which he had decided to be an (unliberating) illusion, he did not say. These differences and their implications can be seen in the distinctive diagnosis Bourne offered of the nature of the economic and family crises his generation faced and of the kind of scientific spirit he recommended for the schools and (social welfare) institutions.

In Bourne's analysis, the unprecedented condition of his generation's freedom was primarily a consequence of the changing rules of the marketplace. "The economic situation in which we find ourselves, and to which *not only the free . . . but the unfree* of the rising generation are obliged to react, is perhaps the biggest factor in explaining our character." Whether working class or middle class, the choice seemed to be between immersing oneself in the "routine of a mammoth impersonal corporation . . . or . . . living by one's wits within the pale of honesty." Members of his generation were skeptical of all forms of discipline and control, he argued, and so they looked with ambivalence on the professions of public relations and business management that Lippmann outlined for the modern saint.[46] Though they wanted to "count for something in life," in looking at "the men who 'count' in the world today," they decided, as Bourne put it, that they "did not want to count in just that way."[47] His language suggested that their fears were of a physical threat to their very existence. Corporate domination appeared in menacing images of organic and corporeal consumption. The bureaucratic "Moloch" "devoured" its young; it "swallowed" or "consumed" or "smothered" or enveloped the new recruits, invoking images of maternal power.

By contrast, family discipline appeared in images of mechanical destruction. The family could "distort," "warp," and "mutilate" the child's individuality; it could "shrink" the soul and "stunt" one's personality. Its methods were direct, blunt, and clinical. It used ridicule and censure. Both the middle and working classes were threatened by the "sect-pressures" of hierarchical organizations that would (literally?) consume or destroy them.

In Bourne's analysis, the crisis of the family and of the new corporate economy became a crisis of education. The centrality of education to his political thought places him in the company of other democratic theorists, including Rousseau and Kant, as Joseph Featherstone points out, as well as James and Dewey.[48] The "helplessness of the modern parent" caused mothers and fathers to turn to "experts" in childrearing, a move that paralleled the turn by owners of corporations to experts in industrial engineering and scientific management.[49] Many of the responsibilities formerly left to the family and the community were charged to the schools, as the state was sometimes seen as unduly corrupted or partisan. Increasingly schools were regarded as the institution to eliminate abuse and injustice caused by larger social, economic, and political forces. "The school already overshadows the church. . . . [It] constantly encroaches on the home. It provides play and work opportunities that even well-to-do homes cannot provide." It was a change Bourne and many progressives welcomed. But he warned that educational reformers ought not to concentrate solely on reforming administration and professionalization, or they would risk creating "capable administrators faster than we create imaginative educators."[50]

The progressives' response was again divided over the kind of mastery that was desirable to shape the economic and social order. The more political of the educational reformers wanted to modernize and centralize the public education system, believing that schools could be run as efficiently as business corporations. They focused on improving administration and cultivating expertise, arguing that specialists must replace politicians and that teachers be trained as professionals and promoted on the basis of merit rather than through political cronyism. The social reformers, on the other hand, favored a change in curriculum and pedagogy, a more costly set of programs designed to meet the varying needs of children in different classes with diverse language skills and abilities. They stressed the need for schools to socialize children and to improve the living conditions of the city's immigrants and the poor, filling the gap left by the family and community. Their agenda was modeled along the lines of the social work idea that schools must take charge of children in all aspects of life, taking them off the streets and devising programs that would give them the incentive to remain in school and that would train them for productive work in society.

Both sectors of the education reform movement came together over the issue of pedagogy. They agreed that the traditional method of teaching through memorization must be replaced with a scientific pedagogy, based on an understanding of the nature of children and stressing psychology and ethics rather than the arbitrary authority of the teacher. As Diane Ravitch has noted, however, in New York City, there was a wide gap between the intellectual ferment of progressive educators and the practices of the schoolroom. Education remained traditional, with virtually a military discipline prevailing in the classroom, and teacher-centered, with the teacher demanding obedience and attention from students.[51] Indeed, during the first decades of the century in New York, educational reform amounted to little more than a temporary routing of Tammanist ward trustees, a standardization of curricula, a centralization of personnel decisions, and a streamlining of expenses in the quest for efficiency by rotating students in shifts day and night, actually reducing the educational budget per capita, despite the overcrowding and dilapidated physical plants.[52]

Dewey's proposal to turn the schools into "workshops" in democracy, teaching citizenship as well as practical skills for the world of work, seemed to Bourne to be a promising set of propositions to remove the factorylike environment of the traditional classroom and to attend to the real class differences in educational preparation.[53] As laboratories for practical experiments in a cooperative, intergenerational democracy, the schools could integrate "work-study-play," allowing students' interests to determine their studies.[54] But Bourne also read in Dewey's theories an encouragement of democratic socialism because of his emphasis on broadening the domain of culture to include the practical and industrial arts and on abolishing the distinction between people who worked with their hands and people who worked with their heads.[55] Dewey's form of education would turn children into little socialists, in Bourne's view, because it would be classless, rejecting the class-based divisions in education that serviced those divisions in society. "Democratic education does not . . . fasten class education upon us."[56] Anticipating the pedagogy of the Brazilian educator, Paolo Friere, Bourne's idea of democratic education involved preparation for a future society rather than a reflection and reinforcement of status quo hierarchies. Education as "preparation for life" involved preparation for a future life rather than for the life of the moment. If it were "self-conscious," it would determine the nature of society itself. "To decide what kind of a school we want is almost to decide what kind of a society we want."[57]

The new education held the promise of a new society because it would prepare the child to live as an integrated "worker-citizen-parent," possible only in a society that had abandoned bourgeois individualism. At the same time it would bring that new society into effect as it prepared children for the future: it would restructure the culture of public institutions, its authority structure, and its governing philosophy, as well as re-order social relations, constructing programs around children/citizens rather than children/citizens around programs; it would refrain from treating children as adults or from forcing them to conform to the needs of adult society; and it would remove invidious distinctions between kinds of learning. Put simply, democratic schools represented the theory and the practice of radical change in Bourne's view. They could actualize a pragmatist tenet that purposive action could shape one's environment and would bring into effect the new society. In this construction of the role of educational reform, Bourne was perhaps more pragmatist than Dewey himself.

More important perhaps in terms of his own political thought, Bourne's reliance on the schools suggested his belief that they were the mechanism of change to deal with social and economic dislocation. In contrast to his much more frequently voiced anti-institutionalism, his educationism revealed a willing and conscious reliance on practical, institutional responses to effect change. This openness to institutionalism as politics is a significant concession, for he often stood outside the state and outside the institutions of mass society in his radical criticism, which frequently left him with no place to stand and no basis on which to build a constructive political philosophy or practice. Despite his reservations about piecemeal reform, the schools were at the center of his theory of social transformation, understood as both prefigurative and practical sites for experiments in a cooperative learning experience.

Because the Gary schools emphasized "learning by doing" and student activities grew out of real-life situations and because the schools contributed to the local community, both Bourne and Dewey thought they were workshops in democracy and, to some extent, were inseparable from the public culture.[58] The university-extension aspect of the Gary schools made it literally a "people's university," in Bourne's phrase.[59]

When the Gary plan was imported to the New York City schools in 1916–1917, however, it became another means for progressivist administrators to streamline costs and turn overburdened classrooms into factories for education. A coalition of immigrant parents, Tammanists, and traditional teachers and principals routed the progressive reformers in 1917, rejecting "platoon schools" and the caste-education that immigrant parents feared would result.[60] For the first time, Bourne and Dewey disagreed over the direction of educational reform and the issue of the appropriateness of adopting the Gary-Wirt plan for the more heterogeneous New York City. Dewey supported the adoption of the plan on a trial basis; Bourne resisted it, recognizing the costs to working-class and immigrant students of tracking and part-time education.[61]

With this disagreement, Bourne's educational theory became less of an unreflective adoption of Dewey's educationism. Bourne's lack of critical distance is evident in many of the articles he wrote for the *New Republic* as education editor, reprinted in *Education as Living*. Dewey's own ambiguity over the ends of education may have contributed to Bourne's failure to appreciate the degree to which the new educationism could induce conformism. Though Dewey urged educators to be "guideposts" for students' interests by shaping children to be useful to society, as Richard Hofstadter indicated, he "had no criteria for discriminating where, when, and toward what" children ought to be guided.[62] Bourne assumed on the other hand that democratic education would thoroughly resocialize children rather than reinscribe and reinforce gender and class roles. The child-as-redeemer-of-society seemed to capture Bourne's own emphasis on releasing the forces of youth in society at large, prefiguring a modern, democratic society.

As a result, he simultaneously expected too much of educational reform (the breakdown of social classes) and not enough (schools could not teach morality and should not try). Moreover, his views were often inconsistent. Privately he regarded his own university as an environment that nourished "beloved community," but publicly he denounced it as an institution that reinforced the "sect-pressures" of organized institutions he tried to escape, most notably the bourgeois family and the corporation. "The issues of the modern university are not those of private property but of public welfare." His profiles of Nicholas Murray Butler, the president of Columbia University, and his sketch of a retired professor, an itinerant intellectual, reflected disillusionment with the professionalization of the academy and the modern university's inhospitality to thinkers.[63] In these conflicting expectations and reservations about the power of educational reform, Bourne's ambivalence about the power of institutionalized politics remained.

His solution to the drift of which Lippmann wrote in 1914 therefore was not mastery and not science, but freedom itself.

> The youth of to-day cannot rest on their liberation; they must see their freedom as simply the setting free of forces within themselves for . . . radical work in society. The road is cut out before them by pioneers; they have but to let themselves grow in that direction.[64]

The very circumstances that produced youthful drift and indecision were, in Bourne's analysis, those that held the greatest opportunity for a "trans-valuation of values." "It is the glory of the present age that one can be young. Our times give no check to the radical tendencies of youth." The experience of bringing themselves up reaffirmed the importance of staying young. "We believe in ourselves; and this fact, we think, is prophetic for the future." What was needed was not new instruments of control and domination but a further release of youthful energy. "The secret of life is . . . the spirit of perpetual youth."[65]

A scientific approach was a youthful attitude because it was experimental and flexible. "Youth's attitude is really the scientific attitude. Do not be afraid to make experiments, it says. You cannot tell anything will work until you have tried it."[66] In welcoming the scientific attitude, he put in a plea for science in its place. "The scientific philosophy"—by which he meant "dusty positivism" modeling itself on the natural sciences, the empirical social sciences, and the new sciences of business administration and social welfare—was no more than a substitute religion, "as much a matter of metaphysics, of theoretical conjecture, as the worst fanaticisms of religion." Where faith had served to give people a sense of place well into the nineteenth century, science provided the same for people at the turn of the century. As ideology, (social) science replaced the Victorian emphasis on moral perfection with a secular belief in the idea of human progress. Both science and religion were expressions of the will to power, under the guise of service to others and the disciplining of society. "We must resist the stern arrogances of science as vigorously as the scientist has resisted the allurements of religion."[67]

In short, his critique was not of science but of scientism as a mystical force assumed to solve problems of meaning, metaphysics, and social utility. Science had a role to play, one that was "relegated strictly to the practical sphere,"[68] used for the "tools" it provided "to control our environment." Its laws were "not visions of eternal truth, so much as rough-and-ready statements of the practical nature of things, in so far as they are useful to us for our grappling with our environment and somehow changing it."[69] Science and social science provided "a description simply of the machinery, the behavior of the world, not of its palpitating life." Science was "in no sense valid as an interpretation of life and life's meaning."[70] Different kinds of cognition were at stake between the rational and the experiential and different judgments. "The interpretation of the world lies not in its mechanism but in its meanings, and those meanings we find in our values and ideals." For these values, "we must trust our own feelings rather than any rational proof."[71] Even if practiced rigorously, science as a basis for understanding experience as it was lived was insufficient. "We must somehow comprehend a world where both the cold, mechanical facts of the physical plane exist and the warm emotional and conscious life of desires and ideals and hopes." Science, to be truly scientific, should be flexible, critical, and interested in human purposes as much as material accomplishments. "Relativity is thoroughly scientific; it is the absolutist way of thinking that is theological."[72]

Clearly Bourne's critique of science was a critique of ideology and reification rather than a rejection of science per se. He was skeptical of the promises of scientific rationalism and positivism because, ironically, they were not scientific enough. "In spite of his lip-service to science," the rationalist was "fundamentally unscientific." "By constantly attempting to disprove . . . the other world," he managed to keep it alive.[73] Bourne's critique of scientism and plea for the modesty of the scientific enterprise marked the beginnings of his critique of intellectuals who were invested in reproducing power/knowlege interests, connections that became more clear to him through the war's reliance on intellectual participation.

In place of the "Anglo-Saxon" emphasis on Promethean mastery and domination, exhibited in the fascination with science and technology, he proposed a "post-scientific ideology,"[74] combining the "wonder" and "imagination" in Whitman's poetry, Maurice Maeterlinck's mysticism, James's pragmatism, and the capacity for objectivity and abstraction found in the "new science" of primitive psychology. This ideology integrated instinct and intellect, D. H. Lawrence's blood and judgment, the "personal vibrations" of the artistic life with the "quiet sea of impersonality" of the scientific mind.[75] As Sherman Paul has suggested, it amounted to a "new idealism, scientific in method but mystical in scope."[76]

The solution Bourne proposed differed markedly from Lippmann's conclusion that Bergson's élan vital would fritter itself away unless it came under the control of scientific discipline. Unlike his *Preface to Politics,* in which he looked to intuition or creative myth as an escape from drift, in *Drift and Mastery* Lippmann aligned himself with the growth of the bureaucratic corporation, the centralized state, and the hegemony of professionals and managers promoting the "scientific spirit." Bourne, unmasking scientific expertise and the idea of rational control to remove social conflict as ideology, argued that the current fascination was a theological fascination with faith itself.[77] Although the scientific manager might exude charm and kindness, he warned, "his object in life is to make men efficient [and] to make them purr while doing it."[78] Again he recommended giving up on mastery altogether: "This belief in the power and the desirability of controlling things is illusion. Life works in a series of surprises. One's powers are given in order that one may be alert and ready, resourceful and keen."[79]

Rather, he turned to the feminist movement for the kind of "post-scientific philosophy" that he hoped would transform the Anglo-Saxon preoccupation with mastery and control. The frank rejection of masculine hierarchy and institutions exhibited by English and American feminists impressed him, as he wrote from Paris:

> The feminist movement is so inspiring, for it is going, I hope, to assert the feminine point of view,—the more personal, the social, emotional attitude towards things, and so soften the crudities of this hard, hierarchical, over-organized, anarchic—in the sense of split-up into uncomprehending groups—civilization, which masculine domination has created in Anglo-Saxondom.[80]

The identification of the feminine with the "unofficial" and "naturally human and sensitive" has been understood to reflect Bourne's appreciation of a women's culture.[81] That appreciation is also suggested by his frequent association with the feminist community in New York, the friends such as Elizabeth Irwin, Elizabeth Westwood, Mary Alden Hopkins, and Alyse Gregory and acquaintances such as Frances Perkins, Katherine Anthony, Crystal Eastman, and Helen Boardman. His admiration of their cultural politics is worth noting at some length:

> There is a most delightful group of young women here who constitute a real "salon." . . . They are decidedly emancipated and advanced, and so thoroughly healthy and zestful, or at least it seems so to my unsophisticated masculine sense. They shock you constantly. . . . They have an amazing combination of wisdom and youthfulness, or humor and ability, and innocence and self-reliance, which absolutely belies everything you will read in the story-books or any other descriptions of womankind. They are of course all self-supporting and independent, and they enjoy the adventure of life; the full, reliant, audacious way in which they go about makes you wonder if the new woman isn't to be a very splendid sort of person. . . . They talk much about the "Human Sex," which they claim to have invented, and which is simply a generic name for those whose masculine brutalities and egotisms and feminine pettinesses and stupidities have been purged away so that there is left stuff for a genuine comradeship and healthy frank regard and understanding.[82]

More than any other, this group of feminists symbolized to him the great hope of the modern revolution. Not only would a feminized/ist culture "soften" the "crudities" of masculine civilization, but it also would place personal relations on a different plane, more cooperative, more egalitarian, and more responsive to personal needs and differences. "Whether we could work the feminine into our spirit and life . . . the personal, the nonofficial, the naturally human and sensitive" was his mark of that revolution's success.[83] Accepting women as "an equally valid personality" would disrupt America's "chivalric attitude towards life," a "dread fear of life, sex, despair, and the depths of experience."[84] Since American culture associated the feminine with "effeminacy," it placed women in a "highly artificial position, adored and-despised, at once"[85] and "transform[ed] every feminine human being into a lady and then ma[de] her uncomfortable or illegitimately flattered by reverencing her." To the hardened masculine mind, a feminist revolution meant reformulating "too many codes, too many relations." To Bourne's mind, however, "it would make life an adventure rather than a ride in a suburban train."[86]

Although he welcomed the "feminine" qualities of the New Woman, he also admired the public involvement, activism, and autonomy of feminists and suffragists, qualities associated traditionally with masculinity. Their political activity was not cooperative but confrontational. They put themselves on the line; they risked arrest, went on hunger strikes, and endangered their personal safety. The British suffragists had developed "a model for all revolutionary parties the world over."[87] In addition to his admiration of a women's culture, then, it is clear that he was impressed by the direct political activism of the suffragists, probably because they reshaped political discourse and altered the exercise of power, despite fears of the (real and perceived) powers of (public) women. His feminism was therefore complicated, associating on the one hand femininity and the feminization of culture and consciousness with traditional female attributes, and on the other, conceiving of feminism more broadly, in terms of activism, independence, self-reliance, and energy, qualities that ranked among the highest cultural ideals he held. If these cultural values were traditionally associated with masculinity, he associated them with the dionysiac—that is, with youth itself.

Indeed, the association of feminists and youth and the dionysian was made from the start. "Youth" was "really more typical of the feminines I have known than the youths," he wrote in 1911 with reference to the feminists and suffragists he knew.[88] Feminist rebellion was a youth revolt because it frankly rejected traditional power relations and was thoroughly anticonventional. Like the youth of his generation—the activists, writers, radicals, and bohemians—feminists had little power or status and certainly no class privilege, but they were energetic, committed, cooperative, and courageous, terms of power and dionysian vitalism.[89] Suffragists also were demonstrating that power was not inimical to femininity; they offered "stunning proof that even the most constant participation in the melee of public life doesn't necessarily make women unwomanly. I think it rather tends to make them great."[90] Female power, associated with chaos and disorder, was feared with the appearance of the New Woman. Bourne may have agreed, but he welcomed it as he welcomed the dionysiac in an excessively apollonian culture.

Although he did not fully unmoor the traditional cultural understandings of gender and gender difference, he subverted the easy association of certain characteristics with certain gendered subjects. Citing the differences between men and women as erotic differences, he showed the importance of freeing individuals from the regulative fictions of sexual difference.

> So much of the cruelty in human relations seems to me to spring from the unequal endowment of desire and appreciation in men and women, and this arises largely from the inequalities of position and social milieu.[91]

If he positioned women conventionally, on the side of sensitivity and cultivation, he saw that difference as a contingent one, subject to an economic order that prized independence and autonomy. In offering a view of gender difference as a difference in desire, however, he anticipated the return to the theoretical exploration of the semiotic, the jouissance of the presymbolic order, to which feminist poststructuralists have turned in the latter part of this century.

Nothing may more clearly distinguish Bourne's social radicalism from Lippmann's progressivism than their views on the feminist movement, women's economic power, and the treatment of women's "roles" or "natures." Lippmann revealed a fundamental ambivalence to "the woman's movement" and the idea of women as politically active and an open hostility to the idea of women as full participants in the economic substructure.

> The first impulse of emancipation seems to be in the main that woman should model her career on man's. But she cannot do that for the simple reason that she is a woman. . . . She cannot taboo her own character in order to become suddenly an amateur male.

There were "plenty of men on this earth," he continued, setting to rest the thought of welcoming women into industry or the professions. "I, for one, should say that the presence of women in the labor market is an evil to be combatted by every means at our command."[92] For women to achieve mastery, they must learn to integrate the discipline of science into the home. By rationalizing marketing chores and organizing childcare, they could take advantage of scientific advances and alleviate some of the burdens of homemaking. Women could, and should, exercise their powers as consumers, Lippmann insisted, and in that capacity they might strengthen the consumer influence overall in politics. But mastery for women emphatically did not mean extending to them political rights or agency as producers, much less economic resources, other than those that pertained to their primary roles as housekeepers.[93]

Lippmann used mastery as the measure of social progress; Bourne used the liberation of women because women were more subject to institutional controls than even he, an outsider freed from many Protestant expectations. For women it was much more difficult to reject gendered conventions. In the final analysis, Bourne's youth revolution was conceived as much in terms of a sexual revolution as a generational rebellion. By feminizing culture, members of his generation would socialize it; by feminizing consciousness, they would restore the personal point of view into human relations. By feminizing politics, they would make it more active and confrontational. In short, in backing the feminist revolution, he was also reasserting the dionysian virtues of the younger generation.

The shift from youth to young intellectual began increasingly to carry the weight of his social agenda, and by 1915, he began referring to young intellectuals rather than to the more abstract youth as his historical agent, particularly as the youth of Europe and America began to turn toward nationalism and militarism during the course of the war. His reference to young intellectuals, as the vanguard not only of their generation but of intellectuals as a whole, implied that there were individuals of a certain age and type who could carry the cultural and social agenda forward. His attention to their role and responsibilities constituted his response to the increasing importance of intellectuals in the war effort. The progressives in particular saw the war as the "great integrative enterprise" they were looking for to turn their talents to practical effect. Bourne's criticism of their rush to war brought him to break openly with the pragmatic-progressive wing of the liberal intelligentsia. His most trenchant critique was the culmination of his effort to battle for the allegiance of his own generation.

6
INTELLECTUALS AT WAR

> The war has revealed a younger intelligentsia trained up in the pragmatic dispensation, immensely ready for the executive ordering of events, pitifully unprepared for the intellectual interpretation or the idealistic focussing of ends. . . . Practically all this element, one would say, is lined up in service of the war-technique. There seems to have been a peculiar congeniality between the war and these men. It is as if the war and they have been waiting for each other.
>
> —*Randolph S. Bourne, "Twilight of Idols"*
>
> What is the matter with the philosophy? One has the sense of having come to a sudden, short stop at the end of an intellectual era. In the crisis, this philosophy of intelligent control just does not measure up to our needs. What is the root of this inadequacy that is felt so keenly by our restless minds? Van Wyck Brooks has pointed out searchingly the lack of poetic vision in our pragmatist awakeners. Is there something in these realistic attitudes that works actually against poetic vision,

> against the concern for the quality of life as above machinery of life? Apparently there is.
> —*Randolph S. Bourne, "Twilight of Idols"*

During America's brief but traumatic involvement in World War I, Bourne's growing political reputation became linked inextricably to issues of war and nonintervention. By 1915 his name was associated in the public's mind with the voice of America's conscience, the war's most uncompromising enemy, and, ultimately, its martyr.[1] His opposition to the war was not based on pacifism or on principles of conscientious objection.[2] Rather, as Thomas Bender rightly notes, Bourne was concerned with the relation of war and culture;[3] in that sense, his position effectively redefined the terms of the debate over war and peace.

No other writer at the time offered a principled defense of academic freedom when Charles Dana and William Cattell were fired by Columbia University for "aiding and abetting the enemy."[4] No other critic linked American liberal politics to military absolutism. And no other writer recognized that something new had happened in the technical organization and management of modern war that made the collaboration of intellectuals crucial to its success. Modern war, Bourne determined, finding its apotheosis in the liberal state, had made patriotism obsolete and democratic support irrelevant. Depending, above all, on advanced technology, intensified industrialization, and the centralization of political and military authority, it was run by a cadre of bureaucrats, scientific experts, and policy advisers who managed and administered the militarization of society. "War is the health of the state," he wrote, appropriating Heinrich von Treitschke's phrase but rejecting his conclusions.[5] War was not a moral obligation but the state's raison d'être. Thus opposition to war and the policies of the modern warfare state entailed, at the same time, opposition to the profit and privilege of the intellectuals whose cooperation was essential to its success. By laying bare the relation between the modern liberal state and war and between elite support for war and a militant nationalism, Bourne challenged not only the hegemony of that association but also the ascendancy of his own class of young intellectuals.

The failure of America's intellectuals to stand outside the growing support for war was, in part, a failure of pragmatism, the philosophical form of progressive liberalism at the time. As originally formulated, pragmatism, according to John Diggins, was a theory of knowledge to Dewey, James, and Peirce; to James, it was also a theory of meaning. As a theory of knowledge, it maintained that the propositions of philosophy, history, morality, and politics could be validated by testing their operations and thus consequences in the daily world of experience. As a theory of meaning, it validated the subjective experience, restoring what James called the "personal point of view." James, Dewey, and Jane Addams turned to pragmatism rather than to closed systems of thought to create meaningful, personal connections to public life. To the young progressives who followed James and Dewey, pragmatism offered a way of healing the affliction Addams had diagnosed as the subjective alienation of middle-class youth overwhelmed by social forces and provided a means of relieving the objective misery of the urban poor. For its young proponents, pragmatism offered a way out of bureaucratic rationality and a way into a more personally fulfilled life.[6]

Yet in its first crucial test, pragmatism failed on both counts. As a theory of knowledge, it failed to test ideas and their consequences adequately (the idea of whether intervention was necessary—for peace?) or to generate alternatives (should economic production be centralized or the schools be militarized—for democracy?). More important, perhaps, it failed to restore the personal connection to public life that gave it such appeal to the children of the middle class in the first place. With preparation for war, personal connections were sacrificed for bureaucratic service. Social experimentation was replaced by instrumentalism, personal and political values by process. The desire of young progressives and pragmatists to become involved and to be effective—to have mastery, in Lippmann's terms—led them to serve the state and ignore other alternatives of engagement. In Bourne's analysis, war thus became more than a practical avenue to realize personal ambition and class power. It became a fantasy into which the intellectual class escaped to resolve the infantilization the state produced by denying them an authoritative role to play as citizen-rulers. The psychic damage that resulted from a nation at total war, he suggested, was just the kind of consequence that should be part of a pragmatic evaluation of the merits of intervention.

The identification of pragmatism with militarism is not a historical distortion. John Dewey made the connection repeatedly in the pages of the *New Republic* in 1917–1918 in an influential series of articles advocating and supporting U.S. entry into the war and justifying intervention in the name of pragmatism. The thrust of his argument was to show the compatibility of pragmatism and the war, offering pragmatism as the means that could turn the war into a great social experiment in democratic reconstruction. Unconvinced, Bourne called him to account. Invoking "the spirit of William James," Dewey's former student wrote his own series of essays in the *Seven Arts,* protesting the bureaucratic version of pragmatism as abandoning the emphasis on creative experimentation and contingent truths. His challenge addressed both sides of pragmatism's promise: it tried to rescue pragmatism's theory of truth (Dewey's reliance on science or "creative intelligence") and to recover James's attention to the "personal point of view" (and "creative desire"). In his *Seven Arts* articles, Bourne concluded that Dewey and other prowar liberals had "moved out their philosophy, bag and baggage from education to war," by abandoning "vision" for the fascination with "technique."[7]

Dewey never responded publicly to Bourne's charges. Instead he arranged to have him removed as editor of the *Dial,* one of the few journals willing to publish his antiwar essays by 1917–1918.[8] By then Bourne had become quite isolated, as the U.S. Justice Department had prosecuted the *Masses,* for which Bourne also wrote, under the Sedition Act of 1918, closing its offices and sending its editors to trial twice for sedition;[9] the prowar *New Republic* had stopped publishing all but his education articles by 1917; and the funding for the *Seven Arts* was withdrawn abruptly in 1917 as a direct consequence of its backer's fears of reprisals caused by Bourne's articles. "The magazines I write for die violent deaths, and all my thoughts seem unprintable," Bourne wrote a friend in 1918.[10] Within a few weeks after his removal from the *Dial,* Bourne was dead, a victim of the influenza epidemic of 1918 at the age of thirty-two.[11]

The conflict between Dewey and Bourne remains, on one level, a minor episode in American cultural history. On another, it represents a decisive turning point in the integration of intellectuals and power, a collaboration that is of interest to all intellectuals and activists who must grapple with questions of intellectual honesty, political accommodation, and the relation of theory and practice. The historic integration of liberal, progressive, and socialist intellectuals and power during World War I and the consequences for democratic politics is addressed here. If Bourne is right—that total war can be waged without democratic support, but only with the support of intellectuals, administrators, and experts—then the need for political theorists to reformulate the notion of human agency and examine the sites in which it can be effective becomes a crucial issue to confront.

In this chapter I also analyze the historic relation between pragmatism and war, and by extension, the relation between liberalism and war. It is important to be clear about what I wish to interrogate in this analysis. Although I do not mean to suggest that there is a necessary relation between pragmatism and war because of the historical alliance between pragmatism and militarism and pragmatism and liberalism in the early twentieth century, the still-pertinent question arises: what are the conditions under which a philosophy, grounded in a stance of flexibility, inquiry, and practical critique, can become accommodationist and support dominant or hegemonic political values or politics? In other words, it is clear that in light of the many significant revisions to pragmatism in the last two decades, ranging from Jurgen Habermas's analysis of the importance of attending to an interest-based knowledge in *Knowledge and Human Interests* to Richard Rorty's embrace of the free play of political commitments in *Irony, Solidarity and Commitment,* pragmatism(s) may be critical of dominant political values (as is often the case with the work of Habermas) or supportive of them (as is often the case with Rorty's). The question I wish to raise is under what conditions in which knowledge is produced and represented today can pragmatic inquiry be both flexible and critical? This issue is both political and pragmatic and remains pertinent today.

In Bourne's analysis, I suggest, pragmatism became associated with war as a result of two historical calamities: the *unpragmatic* distortion of a pragmatism divorced from guiding principles or "poetic vision," and the war itself, which created its own "inexorables" against which, ultimately, *any* pragmatism could not stand. His argument about the relation of war and pragmatism was thus a complex one. It combined an immanent critique, that is, a pragmatic challenge to the instrumentalism practiced during the war, and an external critique, outside the discourse of pragmatism, that investigated the nature of the modern state in which a pragmatic philosophy functioned. Although historians have suggested that the controversy between Dewey and Bourne was essentially a family affair, that is, one taking place between pragmatists and on "Deweyan terms,"[12] it was also by extension about the nature of liberalism and its political values, a relation that was central to C. Wright Mills's critique of Dewey's pragmatism.[13]

Although disillusioned with the wartime pragmatism in the face of the inexorables of total war, Bourne recommended that a reconstructed pragmatism be formulated to keep "intellectual suspense" alive and to prevent the "premature crystallization" of ideas.[14] It resembled his "post-scientific ideology," in many respects, in that social experimentation, like the old pragmatism, would be central to the testing of ideas. Unlike the old pragmatism, however, its theory of truth would recognize that values and interests were embedded in one's knowledge and that knowledge was shaped by one's socioeconomic position and relation to power. It was a stance that also recalled his earlier conception of irony, requiring both political engagement and intellectual skepticism but stubbornly refusing political oppositions: passive/active, prowar/antiwar. Encouraging "malcontents" to take a position "below the battle," a position of apparent powerlessness, Bourne argued that they could generate alternatives more freely, more critically, even if they had no effect on the course of military strategy or foreign policy. This difficult position, admittedly a stance only for the most radical of social critics, was not a position of acquiescence or political passivity, as many scholars have argued, but a stance of active undecideability, as Ross Posnock persuasively argues.

In Posnock's analysis, Bourne's "legacy" of flexible critique was continued in Dewey's postwar pragmatism in the idea of a "cultivated naivete," Max Horkheimer's "immanent critique," and the restless stance of Michel Foucault's "specific intellectual," who sought to avoid totalizing, closed systems of thought while remaining politically engaged. This unusual lineage, Posnock suggests, shows Bourne to be part of a "style of cultural and political inquiry, whose guiding value is nonidentity and whose philosophical orientation is a pragmatic emphasis on creative, experimental action produced by historically embedded subjects."[15] The pragmatism of the sort Bourne expounded, operating "below the battle," was not shielded from the realities of power but rooted in it. The "malcontented" intellectual did not transcend into the realm of ideas or retreat into paralysis, Bourne insisted, but remained embedded in the practical. "This does not mean any smug retreat from the world, with the belief that the truth is in us and can only be contaminated by contact."[16] It meant that the nature and terrain of political agency was redefined to account for the situated nature of knowledge and identity. Understood in this way, Bourne's construction of pragmatism and his critique of it can offer significant contributions to the continuing debate over pragmatism as critical theory and to the "politics of nonidentity."

From its beginning, World War I was a war of ideas in America. No physical territory was threatened, no diplomatic alliances were abridged, and none of the traditional indices of military interventionism was at stake. Accordingly, the war involved the mobilization of minds. It was advertised by the Wilson administration, debated in liberal journals, and promulgated in the schools as a "war to end all wars," a struggle between the forces of "light" and "darkness," democracy and "autocracy" and "civilization" and "barbarism," whose ultimate objective in order to "make the world safe for democracy" was "peace without victory."[17] This highly inflated rhetoric and abstract level of debate, according to one historian, was particularly congenial to the progressives and liberals of the *New Republic,*[18] who believed, as Croly explained, that "a certain amount of conscious patriotism in our critical standards is necessary in order to enable us to have the effect which we should like to have."[19] Although he later had doubts about continuing involvement in the war, as Edward Stettner shows,[20] at the outset Croly hoped that he and the other editors, Walter Weyl and Lippmann, as conscious patriots, could have an influence beyond New York's intellectual community; they hoped to shape the practical politics of Washington elites. As their opening editorial stated in 1914, their aim was to "bring sufficient enlightenment to the problems of the nation" in a way that was both "popular" and "serious."[21]

But more was at stake than high-minded rhetoric. Real economic benefits were an integral part of the foreign policies of the Roosevelt, Taft, and Wilson administrations, each designed to enhance and consolidate corporate wealth by stabilizing the social orders that supported it. As William Leuchtenberg shows, the link between progressivism and imperialism had been clearly established by 1912 with the Progressive party supporting imperialist ambitions in Cuba, Mexico, Santo Domingo, and the Far East.[22] Roosevelt's New Nationalism was based explicitly on Croly's synthesis of domestic reform and imperialism, as mutually compatible endeavors, outlined in *Promise of American Life* (1909). Moreover, when Croly, the foremost intellectual architect of liberal progressivism in the early twentieth century, undertook the editorship of the *New Republic* in summer 1914, it was on the understanding of its sponsor, Willard D. Straight, that the journal would be a platform "to explore and develop and apply the ideas of Theodore Roosevelt when he was the leader of the Progressive Party."

According to Leuchtenberg, it was Croly more than any other spokesperson who integrated rhetorical excess with the interest in practical politics.[23] In vague and often evangelical terms, Croly's *Promise* called for a national revival, including a new ascendancy for the American state imposing order domestically and internationally. In the area of international relations, Croly advised that to achieve a "more definite and a more responsible place in the international system," the "'old-fashioned democratic' scruples and prejudices" must not be permitted to stand in the way of developing a "stable American international system." The recent "pacification of Cuba" and "the attempt to introduce a little order into the affairs of the turbulent Central American republic" were necessary to put down "revolutionary upheavals" and to make South American countries "more stable and more wholesome." The national revival he advanced required a "policy of extra-territorial expansion" to give a "tremendous impulse to the world of national reform." Domestic reform and international expansion mutually reinforced each other in a single, sustained national program and philosophy.[24]

The belief that linked imperialism and progressivism and made possible the support of progressives and liberals for an American involvement in a European war was based on the underlying and shared conviction that action was valuable *in itself* and that the only legitimate test of a course of action was in its consequences or practical effects. The faith in action for its own sake was so strong among American liberals that at times it overshadowed a second, and equally strong, article of progressive faith, the belief that the American form of democracy was the only legitimate form of government for free nations. Many progressives and pragmatic liberals assumed that democratic results would be achieved regardless of the means employed—the logic being that, as the Spanish-American War had proved, not only were people freed from tyranny because of the war, but "since the United States was the land of free institutions, any extension of its domain was *per se* an extension of freedom and democracy."[25] But frequently there was no examination of the necessary link between means and ends, a cardinal tenet of pragmatism as James and Dewey had initially formulated it. The appreciation that means were a requisite determinant of ends was lost in the modified pragmatism of the preparedness debate.

In the first months of the war, the *New Republic* editors attempted to evaluate national policy options pragmatically, that is, in terms of their practical consequences or probable results. When the European war still seemed remote to American interests in 1914, their editorials inquired into the consequences of a policy of American neutrality as advocated by fellow progressives and President Wilson when he first assumed office. Especially concerned to deal with the arguments of the pacifists, with whom Wilson and many progressives had allied themselves before the war (on the shared belief that negotiation and arbitration were key in attaining world harmony and universal prosperity), the editors also questioned the results of the pacifists' urging of a peaceful negotiation of differences through international arbitration and treaties. In both cases, the editors asked if neutrality or arbitration would contribute to (total) victory. Indeed they might have asked if neutrality or arbitration would contribute to a swift cessation of hostilities. The argument for intervention, in other words, was virtually preselected on the basis of a shared consensus on ends, and the defense of U.S. involvement was made possible on the "pragmatic" grounds that it would speed along victory (rather than peace). Thus defined, it took little time before the editors advanced, on a pragmatic basis, the argument that intervention would also spread the cause of democracy.

Readers of the self-defined "journal of opinion" expressed concern with its vacillating editorial stands, which seemed to change with each turn in contemporary events.[26] The noted historian James Harvey Robinson blamed the editors for failing to define their governing philosophy or underlying principles. The *New Republic,* he wrote:

> appears to have no set convictions, no clearly defined political, religious, social, economic, or artistic principles, ancient or modern; it espouses no current issue. Nevertheless it seems to have no end in view. May it not be that the chief public distinction and importance of the *New Republic* consists precisely in not standing for anything.[27]

Amos Pinchot, the pacifist, complained that they were far too coy about which action(s) they endorsed, remaining safely in the realm of "clever academic controversy."[28] To Bourne, who had been sidelined as a sometime-contributor to the magazine because of his antiwar views, it seemed that the editors cared more about commitment and action for its own sake than for any particular policy or set of programmatic objectives (a view that Dewey came to share a decade later).[29] Thus the editors, from a position of "pragmatic realism," excoriated the pacifists' neutrality as being ineffectual[30] while at the same time they condemned Wilson for advocating neutrality in word as well as deed.[31] The problem seemed to be that neither position allowed the United States a decisive role in shaping international events, and the "new republicans" were chafing under the prospects of being ineffective, or worse, irrelevant, in world affairs.[32] Dewey, however, the nation's preeminent philosopher, defended his *New Republic* colleagues' ambivalence until May 1917, arguing that "our national hesitation" was justified so long as it could not be shown decisively and assuredly that American involvement in the war would advance American notions of democracy and civilization.[33]

Two months later, he changed his mind and began explicitly to defend U.S. entry into hostilities on the novel grounds that war provided an opportunity for socialization and the art of social engineering that would facilitate democratic restructuring. Dewey was not alone in this argument, as even W. E. B. DuBois, among others, was eventually persuaded of its merits. The war, Dewey wrote, provided the opportunity for a "more conscious and extensive use of science of communal purposes" and for "the creation of instrumentalities for enforcing the public interest in all the agencies of modern production and exchange."[34] In other words, the new experts, trained in the art of modern administration and scientific management, could use the opportunity of war to shape public institutions and their policies toward one common objective: the communal, democratic republic that lay at the heart of Dewey's political pragmatism.

Clearly, Dewey was attempting to rescue from war what was valuable in it, namely, the economic well-being of the nation. Private capital would enjoy the increased support and control from a state run by managerial elites, to save it from its own excesses, and the sense of fellowship and solidarity that it could engender, a collectivism that was missing from the public experience. He became so convinced of the orderly and cooperative results that would come from an efficiently run national community mobilized around war and a wartime economy, however, that it took only a small step for him to come out for full-scale intellectual support of the war as an instrument of international progressivism. Intellectuals, he argued, could shape the war to their own ends, turning it into the national enterprise of integration that they craved.[35]

Writing against pacifists rather than antiwar liberals, Dewey condemned them for their "failure to recognize the immense impetus to reorganization afforded by this war; failure to recognize the closeness and extent of true international combination which it necessitates."[36] Their opposition, he seemed to say, had greater stakes than they realized. Their pacifism undermined their antimilitarism, in his logic, for the war could be an agent of prosperity and peace.

To antiwar dissidents in general, he argued that war could become an efficient means of placing private production under public control. "We shall have a better organized world internally as well as externally, a more integrated, less anarchic system" if the war were permitted to facilitate the design of a "federation of self-governing industries with the government acting as an adjustor and arbiter rather than direct owner and manager." Science could be put to work in wartime, in the production and distribution of war materiel, supplies, and information, and in the administration of personnel in a centralized state. Finally, urging intellectuals to take hold of the "social possibilities of war" and shape them in accordance with social-democratic values, he insisted,

> The pacifists [have] wasted rather than invested their potentialities when they turned so vigorously to opposing entrance into a war which was already all but universal, instead of using their energies to form, at a plastic juncture, the conditions and objects of our entrance.[37]

A more effective strategy would have been to join the movement of the possible and thus gain effective power.

These arguments reveal two tensions in Dewey's thought. First, although Dewey believed that the war would bring an expansion of democracy, that is, an expansion of democratic ends, there was no clear sense in his writings of what democratic control of war meant. Moreover, the scientific control of war, or economic production, or even public education involved little or no democratic participation but the control of technocratic elites. A war to save the world for democracy was relying on the professionals, consultants, public-opinion specialists. Means and ends, therefore, were not equilibrated. Second, Dewey believed in the "plasticity" of the course of the war, permitting intervention by intellectuals to steer its course. At the same time, there was a conviction in his thought that the direction of the war was virtually determined, with or without the support of liberals. These contradictions may reflect his fundamental ambivalence over the issue of war and intervention, but they also reveal a surprising lack of flexibility, or lack of conviction in traditional pragmatic thought, such that the disinterested testing of ideas in the real world was foreclosed.

In his ambivalence, Dewey became ironically more accommodationist. In "Conscience and Compulsion," concerning domestic nativist violence and the suppression of civil liberties, he hardened his position. He urged other uncertain intellectuals to "connect conscience with the forces that were moving in another direction," that is, temporarily to support a national security state, including its control of the mails, the prosecution of sedition, and injunctions of dissent, despite their distaste for suppressing civil liberties and the undemocratic nature of that policy. The rationale behind his recommendation was that by joining "conscience" to the "forces" that were violating it, one gained familiarity with what one was fighting for (or against). This option, however, was a little like suggesting that intellectuals get "inside the whale," in George Orwell's phrase, for without leverage to combat those forces and without an understanding of cause or effect, the liberal pragmatist, the problem-solver, did not have the capacity to get beyond. Dewey seemed to recognize this, and by summer 1917 acceded to what was predetermined. "The appeal is no longer to reason; it is to the event." Reason, or what Dewey often called "critical intelligence," had become useless in war. In war, force was all.[38]

Dewey's defense of military involvement was thus multivalent and contradictory. He seemed to argue that democratic ends (social reform) could come out of undemocratic means (war and the suppression of civil liberties) if critical intelligence were used and democratic concessions were temporary. Yet, the more events progressed, the less pragmatic his arguments became and the more he accepted the path of least resistance. By November 1917, Dewey seemed not only to accept the inevitability of war (an unpragmatic concession) but also to conclude that the best way to comprehend it was to identify with it.

Dewey's adjustment came gradually, but the affinity between the war and the young liberal pragmatists was more immediate. In Bourne's analysis, their "congeniality" was the result of several factors, including the uncritical adoption of an instrumentalist philosophy, a certain social psychology specific to this class, and the nature of total war itself. These arguments are interwoven in a wide-ranging critique that, in the last months of his life, included an examination of the nature of the modern state, but in the interests of clarity, I will treat each strand of his critique separately.

Lippmann initially proffered the social reconstructionist argument in April 1917, the same month that Wilson requested and received from Congress a declaration of war, contending that military mobilization promised more than purely political benefits and ought to be viewed in terms of its broader social consequences. The war could usher in the "national integration" that could keep America from drift. It promised even more a means for advancing individual careers, offering possibilities

> to the inventive civilians, to those very reformers and pioneers who all along have preached the very gospel which is now transformed from an amiable hobby into a world necessity. It is a war of engineers, inventors, organisers, social experts, a war of co-operation, technique, productivity and sacrifice.[39]

Here was the great opportunity Croly's "exceptional individuals" and Lippmann's generation of "restless" idealists had been waiting for, a chance to redefine national priorities and affirmatively set the course for social and moral regeneration at home and abroad. The war could be a laboratory in which to experiment with ideas about social order, its great, bold adventure giving direction to their drift and a rationale for putting into practical use their talents and expertise of mastery they had acquired under the tutelage of progressive social scientists. Service to the war became the higher ideal a philosophy of instrumentalism had been looking for, a chance to see its ideas implemented directly in the aid of a common national purpose.

In an unsigned editorial (written probably by Lippmann) in the same month, the editors of the *New Republic* claimed authorship of the war. "Credit" for the war, and presumably for its benefits, should be given to the class that had taken America into it, that is, not the "bankers or capitalists" but the intellectuals themselves.

> The effective and decisive work on behalf of war has been accomplished by an entirely different class—a class which may be comprehensively described as "intellectuals." . . . The American nation is entering the war under the influence of a moral verdict reached after the utmost deliberation of the more thoughtful members of the community.[40]

Even at a time when intellectuals were beginning to assert a sense of class identity and social importance, the claim was audacious. Bourne replied in "The War and the Intellectuals":

> A war made deliberately by intellectuals! A calm moral verdict, arrived at after penetrating study of the inexorable facts! . . . An intellectual class, gently guiding ideas into what other nations had entered only through predatory craft or popular hysteria or military madness.

It was a polemical response, but the essay voiced an American intellectual's skepticism over the myth of the (political) independence of intellectuals. "The American intellectuals, in their preoccupation with reality have forgotten that the real enemy is War rather than imperial Germany. There is work to be done to prevent this war of ours from passing into popular mythology as a holy crusade." Had they wanted to mold public opinion, they might have "spent the time in endeavoring to clear the public mind of the cant of war, to get rid of old mystical notions that clog our thinking. We might have used the time for a great wave of education, for setting our house in spiritual order." If they wanted to "lead the administration, they might conceivably have tried to find some way of securing peace by making neutrality effective. . . . They might have failed. The point is that they scarcely tried."[41] Throwing off the difficult task of pragmatically preparing the nation for peace, they formed an alliance with "the least democratic forces" in society, those "primitive" interests that advanced the notions of a national state and the doctrines of economic privilege. Rather than take credit for the war, he recommended that they ask how "intelligent service" had replaced critical intelligence.

He blamed their education, the new progressivist education, for their inattention to political ends or values worthy of pursuit.

> Their education has not given them a system of large ideas, or a feeling for democratic goals. . . . They are vague as to what kind of society they want, or what kind of society America needs. But they are equipped with all the administrative attitudes and talents necessary to attain them.

They were "liberal, enlightened, aware," but their thought had become "little more than a description and a justification of what is going on." They threw their energies into implementation, and the "admirable adaption of means to ends" replaced experimentation. Turning the boast back on itself, he argued that the war had, in effect, created them.

> The war has revealed a younger intelligentsia trained up in the pragmatic dispensation, immensely ready for the executive ordering of events, pitifully unprepared for the intellectual interpretation or the idealistic focussing of ends. . . . Practically all of this element is lined up in service of the war-technique. There seems to be a peculiar congeniality between the war and these men. It is as if the war and they have been waiting for each other.[42]

The idea that the intellectuals had been, in effect, created by the war recalls Foucault's genealogy of the discourses of modern power/knowledge, where the discourse (practices) of the disciplines (the social sciences, administration, advertisement, intelligence, and surveillance expertise) not only manage, medicalize, and discipline subjects as objects—patients, criminals, soldiers, and so on—but also the experts themselves.[43] For Foucault, however, the idea of human agency as a force moving history was an illusion; for Bourne, it became an illusion in modern times.

Part of Bourne's effort, of course, was to return the young intellectuals to their pragmatic roots by urging them to be more pragmatic or more true to pragmatism's standard of testing ideas in terms of their consequences in the material world. As a student and an ardent believer in pragmatism, he had maintained that it emphasized the importance of social experimentation rather than rational proof as the ground for the truth of an idea and the importance of recognizing the intersubjective (not objective) nature of truth.

> Truth to [James] is thoroughly comprehended *experience,* it is created as we go along, it is what proves its verity by being verified. We thus speak of *more truth* or *less truth,* not of Truth and Error. Relativity is thoroughly scientific; it is the absolutest way of thinking that is theological, and my quarrel with the rationalist is that . . . he is fundamentally unscientific.[44]

Pragmatism's appeal was in the emphasis on the role of subjectivity in the construction of truth and on social experience as the testing ground of ideas in which continent, workable truths could be articulated. Pragmatism did not lead to a set of fixed truths but to a flexible set of contingent truths, to be tried out in one's shifting alliances and encounters with other people. Its promise was in its ability to neutralize the orthodoxy of any philosophy to which it was affixed.

By September and October 1917, Bourne had explicitly named Dewey as leading the intellectual class to embrace "militaristic values and new tastes for power." His "Twilight of Idols," triggered by Dewey's tolerance for the suspension of civil liberties' protections, reflected the "war and laughter" of Nietzsche's original, exposing the cultural damage caused by the war at home as well as the consequences to pragmatism itself.

To separate the issue of pragmatism from its role in the war, Bourne raised two objections. First, he noted that the subordination of vision to technique in Dewey's pragmatism was an abandonment of the philosophy that had inspired young radicals during the prewar years to become actively involved in social change. It is worth quoting the essay at length:

> To those of us who have taken Dewey's philosophy almost as our American religion, it never occurred that values could be subordinated to technique. We were instrumentalists, but we

> had our private utopias so clearly before our minds that the means fell always into its place as contributory. And Dewey, of course, always meant his philosophy, when taken as a philosophy of life, to start with values. But there was always that unhappy ambiguity in his doctrine as to just how values were created, and it became easier and easier to assume that just any growth was justified and almost any activity valuable so long as it achieved ends. . . . It is now becoming plain that unless you start with the vividest kind of poetic vision, your instrumentalism is likely to land you just where it has landed this younger intelligentsia which is so happily and busily engaged in the national enterprise of war. You must have your vision and your technique. The practical effect of Dewey's philosophy has evidently been to develop the sense of the latter at the expense of the former.[45]

If pragmatism "worked," it did so as long as one had one's "private utopia" in hand. Without it, it was a philosophy of mere strategy. In a modern wartime instrumentalism, Bourne found

> no provision for thought or experience getting beyond itself. If your ideal is to be adjusted to your situation, in radiant cooperation with reality, then your success is likely to be just that and no more. You never transcend anything. You grow, but your spirit never jumps out of your skin to go on wild adventures.[46]

Moreover, bureaucratic pragmatism made no provision for the personal point of view that James wrote about because it required conformity and routinized responses to hierarchical command.[47] "There is nothing in the outlook that touches in any way the happiness of the individual, the vivifying of the personality, the comprehension of social forces, the flair of art—in other words, the quality of life."

But, of course, pragmatism's emphasis on the ability to judge consequences told one nothing about how to select among them or order them. Pragmatism had nothing to offer with regard to the criteria needed to judge political values. There were only private values.[48] Moreover, in a liberal society, where private values are valorized, pragmatism accommodates them. For Bourne pragmatism had "worked" because it was a philosophy guided by (radical) social principles, which preceded and informed one's pragmatic adjustments. It was a philosophy with fundamental precepts and ethical principles to substantiate one's pragmatic orientation toward experience. But the pragmatism of Dewey and James required nothing of the kind of centered, principled orientation that Bourne now insisted was a part of it. Pragmatism, as Dewey and James had formulated it, was expressly designed to do away with a priori principles. It looked to experience as a guide. It employed the criterion of consequences to bypass the recurrent questions of philosophical or moral principle. It was designed to demonstrate the practical value of certain social truths, to democratize authority through collective inquiry and education, and to resolve personal anxiety and philosophical doubt by emphasizing the authority of the subjective experience.

Yet the reminder was that pragmatism in theory promised a choice of ends as well as means, a choice guided by one's political values. "Dissatisfied with the given means or ends, one chooses another to effect." To many philosophers and political theorists today, it is precisely this tolerance toward ends that constitutes its appeal. It is agnostic with respect to values, and even to ranking them. Ethical judgments or evaluations of merit are left to others. As a pragmatist, one can be foundationalist or antifoundationalist, humanist or deconstructionist. One can select among a variety of private utopias—democratic, liberal, or feminist. This tolerance has attracted some philosophers and theorists to pragmatism and driven others away from it.[49]

Bourne's second objection to the arguments of the social reconstructionists was that pragmatism ultimately did not work in times of war. It was a philosophy suitable for times of peace and prosperity, when there was a "fund of progressive good will" and a "strong desire for progress," when it could promote experimentation and social reform because institutions were flexible and human resources were plentiful. Schools could be turned into laboratories for educational reform because technicians could control the conditions under which they worked. The means and the practical working out of ideas as an experiment were part and parcel of the ends achieved. But because war "determines its own ends and means," even the old pragmatism was ineffective. In a war administration, where the military environment was not controllable, pragmatism was useless. "War is just that absolute situation which is its own end and its own means, and which speedily outstrips the power of intelligent and creative control. . . . Once entered upon, neither means nor ends can really be revised nor altered."[50] The "inevitables" of total war swept along all other ends in its wake. Hence, the boast of the "realists" that they could direct the war and Dewey's optimism that the war could be turned to democratic ends Bourne viewed with deep skepticism. "If the war is too strong for you to prevent, how is it going to be weak enough for you to control and mould to your liberal purposes?"

His second criticism was different from his earlier, more principled objection to the bureaucratic pragmatism of the younger intelligentsia. Initially Bourne had argued that the pragmatism of "intelligent service" and "adjustment" had become instrumentalism: it had failed to test ideas or to establish its own (independent) ends. In short, pragmatism failed because it was not *principled enough.* Now he argued that pragmatism would not work even if it were tried because it was ineffective, that is, unable to stop the war or change its course; and it was unable to mount a program of social reform because institutions were no longer subject to popular control. This objection was more pragmatic, perhaps, if by that one means that it was an inquiry into pragmatism's "workability." Bourne's argument was a claim that the testing of an idea's truth, and therefore merit, through its practical consequences—the principal pragmatic method—was useless, particularly during wartime.

These objections to an instrumental pragmatism have been criticized as *unpragmatic* distortions of the pragmatic philosophy. Daniel Levine, for instance, defended Dewey against the first charge of an empty, visionless politics by claiming that Dewey's ends were individual freedom; the means he advocated were also individual freedom. Rick Tilman, by contrast, argued that Dewey's ends were progress and that his means vacillated between "welfare state capitalism and genuine socialism."[51] If Dewey's ends are difficult to pin down, the lack of clarity may be due, as C. Wright Mills has argued, to the lack of values in liberalism itself, or in the corporate liberalism of the early century. Because Bourne ultimately linked pragmatism to the politics of the liberal state, which conducted war on the premise of progress and spreading the cause of freedom, it seems clear that he, too, concluded that liberalism had derailed his preferred philosophy.[52]

This conclusion led to a break with the old pragmatism. "I come to . . . a sense of being left in the lurch, of suddenly finding that a philosophy upon which I had relied to carry us through no longer works." He called for a reconceived pragmatism, one that dealt with the realities of power—corporate power, the power of war's imperatives—and recognized that everyone was implicated in them. The pragmatism he proposed understood that knowledge was interested and that the knower was embedded in a complex of social relations that shaped an idea's knowledge and what was known. It was a pragmatism that required a "more skeptical, malicious, desperate, mood" to replace Dewey's optimism. It made the powerlessness to affect events a place for the "vigorous assertion of the values in which the war has no part." Avoiding orthodoxy and propaganda, it began the reconstruction of social values. "It is creative desire more than creative intelligence that we shall need if we are ever to fly."[53]

If Bourne's dispute with Dewey had concerned only the failures of pragmatism in practical affairs or the limitations of progressivist social reform policies, it might be of interest primarily to Dewey scholars or contemporary pragmatists. But their debate was also about the political responsibility of intellectuals in times of peace and war and the nature of war in the liberal state. It raised another question: to what extent can intellectuals be expected to remain independent of the imperatives of war when their participation is so essential to its conduct? Bourne seemed to think that the idea of intellectual independence was an illusion. He did not ask the young intellectuals to be independent; indeed, he asked that they not hide behind the veil of independence. Put differently, his dispute with Dewey and Lippmann was not on the grounds that they were interested or had political objectives but that they had been false to their own standards of independently testing ideas in the real world.

The veil of independence was the disguise of Nietzsche's ascetic priest. Every culture was engulfed in a cloud of ideology about itself and its own spiritual principles, Nietzsche wrote, and the ascetic ideal, the scientific philosophy, was the dominant ideal of the modern age. Its priestly disguise was that of the disinterested intellectual. Nietzsche viewed the ideal as a mere dodge by which philosophers expressed their own inverted wills to power. The myth enabled them to engage in strenuous intellectual activity, but it carried a corresponding sacrifice of animal energy. Modern philosophers, assuming the ascetic countenance and a belief in ascetic values, tried to escape the wrath of priests in ascetically oriented religious cultures, who had the prestige the intellectual lacked. As the natural enemy of the priest, the intellectual assumed the priestly disguise. The disguise itself became a new ideology, however, replacing the desire to be free of religion with its own religion, as cruel in Nietzsche's view as the one against which it had originally risen. The triumph of the disinterested ideal signaled the death of life-serving philosophy.[54]

The "realists" at the *New Republic* were Nietzsche's ascetic priests, enchanted by science and technocracy and interested in power in the form of expertise. Their new science of pragmatism assumed a priestly aura, enchanting them with the allure of technique and of process. In the desire to apply progressive ideas about social control to military ends, the realists represented the moment of unmediated apollonianism, the will to form, in the guise of service to the state.

The idea of intellectual independence was also embedded in the first use of the term "intellectual" in 1898. The intellectuals were the novelists, philosophers, and publicists who took up Alfred Dreyfus's cause, branded by their enemies as critics of society. They defined themselves, however, as the conscience of France. Their moral authority derived from the intellectual vocation itself, as Romaine Rolland argued, from the life of the mind as necessarily distanced from the larger society and immune to its moral degeneration. William James, privately identifying with the defenders of Dreyfus, began to appropriate the term and its political implications of independence to the American context:

> We "intellectuals" in America must all work to keep our precious birthright of individualism and freedom from these institutions [of church, army, aristocracy, royalty]. *Every* great institution is perforce a means of corruption—whatever good it may do. Only in free personal relations is full ideality to be found.

He also suggested in a lecture to college professors that the intellectual center of activity was shifting from the universities to the cafes and literary clubs where the young intellectuals gathered, a move he welcomed as an expansion of intellectual freedom.[55]

Dewey also helped credential the term for American radicals, suggesting in 1908 that he saw glimmerings of an organized intelligentsia forming, which, drawn from all classes and lifting itself above its origins, was capable of solving the riddle of the common good. Seeing intellectuals primarily as catalysts of democratic change, his definition nevertheless carried the implication that the intellectual's freedom from traditional class affiliations produced a superior form of critical consciousness, a disinterested or objective ability that other, class-bound minds could not achieve. Dewey's sense of the intellectual, it can be said, was similar to Mannheim's category of a detached, "free-floating" intelligentsia that formed a substratum in society, as both Dewey and Mannheim located the basis of intellectual authority in the *absence* of bias or interest in the search for knowledge.[56]

Bourne's theory of the role of intellectuals was different from several contemporary theories of the intellectual's political role and responsibility: from Dewey's emphasis on rational or disinterested activity, from Rolland's idealization of the intellectual vocation, and even from Julien Benda's approach and its requirement of fidelity to universal or disinterested values. Where Benda chastised the European intelligentsia for its engagement with politics, especially nationalist politics, because it was detrimental to an appropriately disinterested role, Bourne argued that the intellectual was most himself when he was a meddler, much like the Sartrean intellectual who was most profoundly intellectual when he was politically involved.[57] And where Benda argued provocatively that an intellectual's thought should have no practical utility, singling out James, among others, with favor, for the new "religion" of utility, for Bourne, just the opposite was required of the intellectual, who addressed the day-to-day, practical questions of modern life.[58]

The meddling of the intellectual was a negative role, or perhaps more accurately, a counterhegemonic role, aiming to demystify official values.[59] Recommending that the "malcontented" intellectual take a position "below the battle," that is, outside the dominant frame of public discourse, Bourne argued that the intellectual could entertain political options that were not posed in terms of either/or alternatives: pacifist/interventionist, Anglo-American sympathizer/Germanophile, active/passive. To position oneself "below the battle" was not a means of lying low, contrary to some interpretations, but a disruptive act, a way to redefine the terms of the debate and deliberately to avoid the orthodoxies of current social thought.[60] It was not a stance of political independence; quite the contrary, it was a position of social and political embeddedness, *from which the self emerged.* The modern self was a product of its practices, its discourse, perhaps, who was, as with Nietzsche's pathos, always in the process of becoming.

Ross Posnock has read convincingly Bourne's conception of the self emerging from society's inexorables as social text written by one's environment. This conception is consistent with Bourne's early view of the self as a contingently constructed, decentered self, the product of family upbringing, friendships, membership in "beloved communities," corporate environments, and neighborhood politics. "The self is a network of representations of the various codes and institutions of society," as Bourne wrote.[61] It was indeterminate at the same time that the self was multiply embedded.

Indeed, the notion of the autonomous individual was a fiction that served as a social myth supporting a culture (of liberalism) that prized individualism. It was "group-will" and "group-desire" that existed first, as the new anthropology of Columbia University had taught him, and it was from group affiliation that a self was gradually individuated. But even the individuated self, common to the ideology of liberal societies, was an indeterminate self, following from Nietzsche as well as from James's idea of a multiple self, which was revealed discursively and was constituted by its actions and relations in the material world. Thus, the "glowing" and "vibrant" personality Bourne often embraced was a regulative ideal, a denaturalized, socially constructed identity able to deal with the complexities of the modern world. The idea of personality was a performative self unfolding its inner divisions in its external or social practices.

It was precisely this kind of contingently constructed, fragmented self that the pragmatic liberals of the early twentieth century seemed to have feared. They conceived of the liberal self as an autonomous, preexisting subject, exerting its will on the world as a rational agent. The young intellectuals had entered the war, both as individuals and as a class, with a particular point of view, on the premise that they as political subjects could shape events. In a remarkable profile of their psychology, often overlooked, Bourne argued that this new class, in their aspirations to power and adulthood, which the war gratified, became the product of its larger forces. Uncertain of their status and vaguely committed to the idea of social reform, they escaped into war as an arena for personal ambition and class power. Their "itch to be in the great experience that the rest of the world was having" propelled them into seizing "in a great healing wave of release some doctrine that can immediately be translated into action," and they "regressed" to the "primitive" idea that became a craving for action. And it was action quite literally that they embraced.

> War was seen as the crowning relief of their indecision. At last, action, irresponsibility, the end of anxious and torturing attempts to reconcile peace-ideals with the drag of war towards Hell. An end to the pain of trying to adjust the facts to what they ought to be! . . . The thankfulness with which so many intellectuals lay down and floated with the current betrays the hesitation and suspense through which they have been. The American university is a brisk and happy place these days. Simple, unquestioning action has superseded the knots of thought. The thinker dances with reality.[62]

The language of "regression" and "irresponsibility" suggested the childlike nature of the intellectual class. In joining the rush to war, in Bourne's analysis, they became children again, fulfilling fantasies of being swallowed up by the larger processes, avoiding responsibility, avoiding adulthood. They signed on with a war administration as a way of avoiding responsibility but enjoying a (reflected) power. "A people at war have become in the most literal sense obedient, respectful, trustful children. . . . In this recrudescence of the child, there is great comfort, and certain influx of power." The psychic rewards of avoiding responsibility made the intellectual class among the most enthusiastic supporters of the war.

The significance of the psychological language should not obscure its political content. Bourne's argument was that the state created children by denying them a role to play as citizen-rulers, and they, in turn, fetishized the state, "full of the most naive faith in the all-wisdom and all-power of the adult who takes care of them." Nations required adults, "with a measure of autonomy and power, and with an achieved maturity," but war demanded uniformity of action and opinion, so that even adults, convinced of the necessity of unity, overthrew their "indifference" toward the state and identified with it.

> You feel powerful by conforming, and you feel forlorn and helpless if you are out of the crowd. While even if you do not get any access of power by thinking and feeling just like everybody else in your group does, you get at least the warm feeling of obedience, the soothing irresponsibility of protection.[63]

As Marx wrote, "The political state is as spiritual in relation to civil society as heaven is in relation to earth." During war, Bourne argued, the state's idealism was magnified. It took on dangerous mystical powers, able to compel consent without force, making democratic accountability irrelevant. "War is the health of the state," a refrain he invoked to reinforce the idea of totality and absolution. War became a permanent and ongoing activity of the state, and the "individual as a social being" reached his/her "apotheosis" in total surrender of being to it. Identification with the state "blotted out" the distinction between the individual and society:

> At war, the individual becomes almost identical with society. He achieves a superb self-assurance, an intuition of the right-

> ness of all his ideas and emotions, so that in the suppression of opponents and heretics he is invincibly strong; he feels behind him all the power of the collective community.[64]

The myth of the autonomy of the individual becomes complete in total war; eclipsed by the political agenda, it becomes a means to its end.

The inexorables of total war even blotted out the idea of democratic consent. Testing popular support for the war in February and March 1917, Bourne endorsed a referendum on the question of military involvement, standing by the idea that a war fought for democratic ends must take account of democratic authority. With Max and Crystal Eastman, Winthrop Jordan, Amos Pinchot, and other members of the Committee for Democratic Control, he took out two advertisements in the *New Republic:* "1917—American Rights—1789" and "Do the People Want War?" urging a referendum. The referendum was dismissed in court. But he had begun to suspect that referenda were inadequate means to test democratic sentiment and were irrelevant, in any case, in a modern, technological, total war. "The kind of war which we are conducting is an enterprise which the American government does not have to carry on with the hearty co-operation of the American people but only with their acquiescence."[65] With their "acquiescence," the state could render a philosophy of "creative intelligence" useless and dissent dangerous. Where freedom of choice was impossible, intelligence ceased to have a function, and the prospect of individual responsibility became an illusion.[66] Posnock's reading glosses Bourne's "embrace of the inexorables," ignoring the psychic damage Bourne diagnosed that resulted from the state's infantilization of its citizens. But Posnock's conclusion, that from the radical contingency of the self a "politics of nonidentity" was formed, fully comprehends the engaged political nature of the intellectual position Bourne proposed in being "below the battle."[67]

In "The State," an unfinished manuscript published after his death, Bourne treated the crisis as one of institutions and not of individuals, focusing less on the pragmatists and the liberal intellectuals and more on the state. In the essay he analyzed the institutional, social, and psychological support for the state and its principal activity of international military conflict. He focused on the inner workings of the relationship between the state and war, and their support under capitalism, concluding that "war is the health of the state," that is, that war is the state's profit and prestige and the activity in which it finds its purpose and raison d'être. He theorized that war was a function of the state system, an international network of "military-industrial" dynasties (a phrase first used by Bourne) competing with one another for economic and military supremacy.[68]

In the fragment he also put forward an understanding of the state as a builder of social cohesion or a unifier of the ruling classes. Anticipating the state theories of Gramsci and Nicos Poulantzas, Bourne's analysis, less systematically, examined the means by which the state forged class alliances and built social cohesion, a strategy that at times exacerbated class antagonisms and at other times frustrated them, depending largely on the democratic nature of the state coalitions. Although the state often acted as an instrument of class rule, relying on the traditional methods of force or coercion, it sometimes acted as a builder of hegemony, relying on traditional intellectuals, extracting democratic concessions through a combination of force, fraud, and consent that Gramsci described. In this role, it was a builder of social coalitions and of ideological consensus. The combination of those strategies enhanced not only its own prestige but also the social and intellectual prestige of the groups that supported it.[69]

Although the Bourne legend holds that he discarded the unfinished manuscript in his final days and that it was discovered by friends after his death, there is nothing in the essay that was inconsistent with the direction of his thought in his final essays on war and the mystification of the state. Underlying its widely ranging, discursive exploration was the thread that connected all his writings, namely, the question of democratic change: was it possible in an age of bureaucratic institutions and impersonal, "herd-like" social forces and, if so, what form would it take? What were the preconditions and possibilities for social revolution in America and in the international arena?

In an essay he wrote as a student at Columbia, he first addressed the question of social democratic change and concluded that the prospects of a new "Socialist Industrial Democracy" were encouraging, as the successes of the syndicalists in France and the growing militancy of the IWW in the United States demonstrated. In a move similar to Gramsci's recommendation that revolution need not attack the institutions of government directly—in a "war of maneuver"—it could target the industrial sector, the shop floor, the corporate bureaucracies, and the centers of cultural production—in a "war of position"—because control over social and economic productivity was in the hands of the industrial sector. Further, in Gramsci's view, power resided in culture, articulated most clearly in hegemonic common sense. In Bourne's analysis, modern revolution should be industrial rather than political, and an "industrial democracy" would be the goal because "the industrial is . . . more powerful" than the political state.[70]

But by 1917, something had happened in American society to threaten substantially the prospects of revolution. That something was the war, enhancing the state's prestige and making any potential alignment of the "possessing classes" and the "working classes" impossible.

> We cannot expect, or take measures to ensure, that this war is a war to end war, unless at the same time we take measures to end the State in its traditional form. . . . With the passing of the State, the genuine life-enhancing forces of the nation will be liberated.[71]

Bourne drew a then-common distinction, probably influenced by Rousseau, between the nation, state, and government to make his case about the compatibility of war and the state. The country or nation, Bourne explained, was a peaceful if not homogeneous community of people; it pertained to the "non-political aspects of a people, its ways of living, its personal traits, its literature and art, its characteristic attitudes toward life." The state, on the other hand, was "the country acting as a political unit," acting "as a repository of force, determiner of law, arbiter of justice." The government was simply the political apparatus, or the current administration of the country's political institutions, for carrying into effect the state's functions. "Government . . . is the machinery by which the nation, organized as a State, carried out its state functions." Rather than a locus for democratic participation, government was simply "the idea of the State put into practical operation." As the concrete "framework" for the state's powers, "it is the visible sign of the invisible grace."[72]

The distinction between states and governments was based on their real and ideal aspects. "Government is the only form in which we can envisage the State," Bourne wrote, suggesting that government is a sign but that the state itself was a "mystical conception" whose reality (materiality) was hidden, operating covertly to "direct . . . [the] activities of Government." States are then mystical or ideal but real in the manifestations of their power. They became real, moreover (although remaining mystical), in time of war because, ironically, their ideal or mystical power reached its highest "power and glory." Their reality is a function of their capacity to enchant and deceive. The nation was the counterpoint; it was real, concrete, geographical, organic. It was material because it was part of the people, and the people instantiated it. Nations could be seen as materially and ideally distinct as well. Nations had no motive for war. As Rousseau noted, only states fought wars; nations never did (because, as Rousseau put it, "it is the link between things rather than men that constitutes war").[73]

Bourne concluded similarly that war was the inevitable by-product of a state system. "War is a function of this system of States, and could not occur except in such a system."[74] The state promised universality, as did Hegel's liberal state, the full integration of the citizen into the service of a collective ideal, uniting his particularity (as consciousness) and his universality (as a social being).[75] But only during war could states deliver on the promise and then only to particular classes. Warfare constituted the necessary condition and mediation for the unity of the state's real and ideal capacities. "The more terrifying the occasion for defense, the closer will become the [state's] organization and the more coercive the influence upon each member. . . . War sends the current of purpose and activity flowing down to the lowest level."

Yet the state's promise of universality was partial and strictly class-bound. Like Hegel's bureaucrat, only the middle classes in America could attain universality because they were able to turn "from their selfish and predatory ways" and "become loyal servants of society or something greater than they." The "possessing classes" were permitted to "direct industry and government and all the institutions of society pretty much as before," gaining the "pragmatic satisfaction of governing" even while being stripped of "the psychic burden of adulthood." Thus the propertied classes that had been attempting to forestall the challenges from labor and radical political movements gratefully joined forces with the state, moving from "the direction of a large business in New York to a post in the war management industrial service in Washington," their economic stability ensured by the war's military demands and glorified by the political campaign of state propaganda (or a simulacra, i.e., by symbols of a symbol).[76]

But the economic security of the propertied classes was never threatened seriously, showing the influence of Beard's political history. Having gained for themselves the political, legal, and representational mechanisms necessary to ensure their continual economic and political health, their security, Bourne argued, was fortified by a party system that they controlled, enabling them to make democratic concessions to universal suffrage when it would no longer make a difference to the orderly transfer of power. Although political and social coalitions constituting the American state changed several times, a democratic state was never an actuality in his analysis. Even in the last decade, he wrote, the state coalition "was not likely to crumble before the anger of a few muck-rakers, the disillusionment of a few radical sociologists, or the assaults of proletarian minorities."[77] As the state system succeeded, so did the public schools, the universities, and professional institutions; journals and industries prospered. The information, commodities, and expert specialists that the system produced were designed to fit the system as it operated so that even the psychic gains were illusory. A herd-instinct, always latent, extinguished the "gregarious-instincts," and the state began to hum like a well-oiled machine.

But the unity of state and society was tenuous, Bourne argued, even as the war tried to rationalize and consolidate their activities. "War, which should be the health of the State, unifies all the bourgeois elements and the common people, and outlaws the rest."

With each instance of the state's policy of "white terrorism . . . against pacifists, Socialists, enemy aliens, and a milder unofficial persecution against all persons or movements that can be imagined as connected with the enemy," the "disaffection of labor increased," the "tension intensified."[78]

Ethnic loyalties that ordinarily in peacetime are maintained as a "luxury," "tend to be strengthened" as the state's "invidious policy of Americanism" challenged their identities and intensified the "herd-feeling" within the "sect." And unlike "highly skilled workers who habitually identify with the owning and the significant classes," the "revolutionary proletariat showed more resistance to this unification" than any other social group, even when its "vanguard, as the I.W.W. is," was "remorselessly pursued."[79] The majority of workers remained "notoriously" unpatriotic because their condition was altered only slightly by military production. "From [industrial] serfdom, military conscription is not so great a change," so they entered "the military enterprise . . . with the same apathy with which they enter and continue in the industrial enterprise." Because the "opportunity to regress" to "these primitive childlike attitudes" was never offered to them, they gained none of the psychic rewards of irresponsibility that the "significant classes" enjoyed by surrendering to the state voluntarily. "Having never acquired social adulthood, they cannot lose it."[80] The workers viewed the war as "an upper-class sport" played out in the international arena and a "sport between the hunters and the hunted" in the domestic. The type of manufactured patriotism compelled by a wartime state—manifested in sedition laws, military conscription, and War Issues courses—did not extinguish dissent; it merely drove it underground.

It was in the unstable equilibrium of the social coalitions that traditionally supported the state apparatus, which even in war were not united, that Bourne found hope for a democratic resistance. "The country must be dotted with dissatisfied people who must . . . be appealed to to desire certain things mightily." In "this class of malcontents," Bourne saw as late as 1918 a prospect for a postwar revival of social life.[81] It was a dim hope. Indeed at the same time he anticipated the red scare of the 1920s, a campaign of intimidation and violence waged by "sensational editors, archaic radicals,

. . . sedition-hunting Vigilantes, and by the saving remnant of older liberals."[82] Referring to the novel crime of seditious conspiracy, he warned:

> the punishment for opinion has been far more ferocious and unintermittent than the punishment of pragmatic crime. . . . Even to attempt such a paralysis [of military conscription] is a crime equal to a successful stroke. The will is deemed sufficient. . . . The guardians of the State do not ask whether any pragmatic effect flowed out of this evil will or desire.[83]

The confusion and resignation of subordinates would give way to a more virulent form of social control and would lead, he believed, to a permanent "semi-military State-socialism."

If the war revealed an affinity with pragmatism, it was made possible by a pragmatism that was not self-correcting. It chose one point of view and one political goal, and the liberal state enforced it. Thus the rejection for instrumentalism was more fundamentally a rejection of liberalism, or the absence of guiding values in a political philosophy and culture whose goal became the victory of the liberal state at war.

In Bourne's call for a new kind of pragmatism, the idea of testing several irreconcilable points of view was proposed. This pragmatism (a "post-scientific ideology") would keep these viewpoints alive as contradictory but equally valid truths, rather than resolving them, as the old pragmatism would have done. These contradictory values can be seen in his own alternating appeals, on the one hand, to pursue the "values in which the war has no part" and, on the other, to support the idea of a "moral equivalent" to war offered by William James, in which the virtues of military service (camaraderie, engagement, and commitment) were preserved in the idea of a mass-based mobilization of civilian reformers.[84] For some readers, the contradiction may be grounds for dismissing Bourne's politics as those of an "impossibilist," or alternatively, as the views of a politically quiescent critic removed from the fray, or "above the battle." In my view, his unwillingness to affiliate politically was a strength rather than a weakness, a means of providing the necessary antidote to a feverish political climate. In the escalation of the political during the war, he held back from committing to the "official" point of view.

> The war has brought an immense and terrifying inflation to the political sphere, so that for most people non-governmentalized activity has ceased almost to have significance. But this cult of politics has been inherent in the liberal intellectual's point of view long before the war. Instead of politics taking its place in the many-sided interests of the modern mind, it had the dominant position.[85]

Wartime politics eclipsed the private realm, intimidated cultural production, and suppressed the individual and the idea of human agency.

An analysis of the "politics of nonidentity"—or, more appropriately, the politics of multiple identities—reveals Bourne's concern to theorize a "trans-national" American culture, a patchwork of ethnic and political communities in which individuals expressed multiple loyalties and affiliations. The idea of a transnational America was a counternarrative to the dominant themes of assimilation and Americanization. It constituted a new kind of democratic politics, in which the political and cultural affiliations of America's new immigrants in particular were acknowledged and validated. It was an expression of Bourne's participation in a "vigorous assertion of the values in which war has no part."

7
"TRANS-NATIONAL AMERICA"

In light of our changing ideal of Americanism, we must perpetuate the paradox that our American cultural tradition lies in the future.
—*Randolph S. Bourne, "Trans-National America"*

I believe that we shall find in the current Jewish ideal of Zionism the purest pattern and the most inspiring conceptions of trans-nationalism.
—*Randolph S. Bourne,*
"The Jew and Trans-National America"

When the *Seven Arts* closed in October 1917 after only twelve months of publication, it seemed to many in New York's intellectual community that political dissent had died along with it. Privately Robert Frost complained that Bourne's uncompromising essays of dissent had precipitated the journal's demise:

The Seven Arts

In the Dawn of Creation that morning
I remember I gave you fair warning
The Arts are but Six!
You add Politics
And the Seven will all die a-Bourneing.[1]

The *Seven Arts* was only one of the many casualties of the war. In the political climate of preparedness and war, American culture as a whole was affected. Funding for journals was canceled; editors were cautious. Innocuous or rebellious publications, such as the *Masses,* were taken from circulation by Postmaster General Albert Sidney Burleson, its editors tried for sedition. Radio programs were banned, German music was removed from the airwaves, meetings were broken up by police or vigilantes. The preparedness campaign aimed especially to rout political radicals, pacifists, and the foreign-born. Although President Wilson and George Creel, former muckraker and then-director of the Committee on Public Information, repeatedly condemned vigilantism, the creation of Loyalty Leagues was organized under their direction. In the schools and universities, patriotic curricula were introduced, in one form as the War Issues Course taught by regular professors in the social sciences and history. By 1918 preinduction centers were established for male students in the universities, who took several hours a week of military instruction in addition to their regular classes, wore uniforms, and lived under military discipline. Programs for elementary schoolchildren included the reading of "war biographies" of heroic figures from the Allied countries, and course materials were developed to stress the ideals of "patriotism, heroism, and sacrifice."[2]

The cultural effect of the war at home was a politicization of private and public life:

> We find a liberal war undertaken which could not fail to do far more damage to American democracy at home than it could ever do to the enemy abroad. . . . The war has brought an immense and terrifying inflation to the political sphere, so that for most people non-governmentalized activity has ceased almost to have significance.[3]

Moreover, as the war politicized private activities, it aestheticized politics. The commonly accepted boundaries of modernity between the political, the economic, and the cultural-aesthetic were blurred. The state became a heroic actor whose mission was to create an illusory harmony, a place of escape for the middle class and for the people dislocated by the contradictions of modern society.[4]

Bourne's own experience of U.S. government surveillance in Connecticut redoubled his anxiety:

> I feel very much secluded from the world, very much out of touch with my times, except perhaps with the Bolsheviki. The magazines I write for die violent deaths, and all my thoughts are unprintable. If I start out to write on public matters I discover that my ideas are seditious, and if I start to write a novel I discover that my outlook is immoral if not obscene. What then is a literary man to do if he has to make his living by a pen?[5]

The "terrifying" logic of military preparedness affected the politics of immigration with particular repressiveness. Within a discourse of Americanization, immigration policies were linked to a militant nationalism, aiming to eliminate "enemies within," through deportations, the criminalization of dissent, and vigilantism, and enemies without through international war. In the white imaginary, the demonization of the foreign Other—in the form of ethnicity and national origin—was a means of strengthening solidarity among themselves at a time when their cohesiveness was being challenged internally.[6] As such, this moment of America's internal control over its immigrant self belongs to a longer tradition of American anxiety over primitivism and disorder.[7]

Against the discourse of Americanization, Bourne put forward a counternarrative of transnationalism to challenge both the ideas of "100% Americanism" and cultural pluralism[8] and to propose a new conception of American national identity that was both ethnic and modern, American and cosmopolitan. His theory of transnationalism challenged both theories of American national identity by amplifying the "small narratives" of oppositional, subaltern, and countercultural groups in America's cities. Further, he proposed a practical, collective, pacifist enterprise for intercultural cooperation and social reorganization that was meant to be a counterweight to the military machine and a strategy for survival for America's newest immigrants.

His idea of transnationalism also confronted what was at stake in the debates over immigration and assimilation, that is, the centrality of ethnicity to American identity.[9] For Bourne, the idea of an American national identity that did not take into account its diverse origins and multiple experiences failed to fulfill the "American promise." An American nationalism that ignored the experiences of immigration, common to Anglo-Americans as well as to the newest immigrants, conflated what it meant to be an American, a product of not one, but of several cultures. An American identity that was based only in a neutral, that is, deracinated, cosmopolitanism failed to address the democratic side of civic membership or the possibilities of a common culture. Consequently, the challenge he raised to early twentieth-century cultural-pluralist theories and Americanization programs was also a challenge to the limits of American liberalism, asking how it was possible to create a public interest or a shared moral consensus from a cluster of private interests and cultural differences, and whether, in the *absence* of such shared commitments, a genuinely pluralistic democratic culture was possible?

To understand the idea of transnationalism and its implications, it is necessary to historicize it within the converging contexts of its development: Bourne's personal autobiography as a young intellectual and an outspoken critic of the war; a social history of immigration amid a rising tide of nativism; a political history of military preparedness, in concert with the shift from a liberal to a bureaucratic, corporatized state; and a cultural history of modern cosmopolitanism, emerging in New York, Milwaukee, Madison, and Boston but coming to include the whole of America. In what follows, these four interrelated histories are untangled and briefly examined, followed by an examination of the idea of transnationalism as a counternarrative to the dominant narrative of Americanization. In a concluding section, I will consider transnationalism today as a challenge for America to recover its ethnic identities through aesthetic-expressive forms of cultural production, organization, and discourse.

Bourne's counternarrative grew out of his personal experience of profound and radical marginalization. The self-described Ishmael found that identification with the immigrant, the New Woman, the urban poor, and other outsiders came easily, as they were seen, as he was, as unchosen by Puritan elites and as "alien" by Protestant Yankees. He chose to be a "spiritual vagabond" and "malcontent," "irreconciled" to both official policy and to social-reform programs. Instead of service to the state, his generation of pragmatic-progressives should expend their considerable energies not in war but in building America into the "first international nation." "The war—or American promise. One must choose. One cannot be interested in both."[10]

The roots of his transnationalism began before the war, when he was a student at Columbia University and first began to reject what Henry May has called the "certainties of the Victorian world" and the Arnoldian conception of culture on which they were based. The genteel critics of the school of belles lettres, influenced by Matthew Arnold, regarded culture as the property of the chosen people, set against the shallowness of the philistines. Culture was something to be acquired and consumed passively by people who had no taste or who presumably did not know better. The average person's tastes could be "cultivated" by exposure to the classics, according to Arnold, and through an immersion in culture in this sense, civilization could be saved from the "anarchy" that threatened to dissolve it. In America, Bourne argued, just the opposite had occurred. Instead of culture saving Americans from anarchy, Arnold's "cult of the best" had produced a nation of cultural parasites, convinced of their own cultural inferiority, directing their attention outward toward European standards rather than inward to the cultivation of "inner taste." In "Our Cultural Humility," written in 1914, he suggested in a telling illustration that the Armory Show of 1913, organized in New York City, had the "frankly avowed purpose of showing American artists how bad they were in comparison with the modern French."[11] He rejected the conception of culture as high art, challenging it as Anglophilic and class-bound, and called for a resurgent "cultural chauvinism" that championed contemporary American writers and artists who helped to instill an "intense self-consciousness" of the "soul of this hot chaos of America."

While traveling in Europe in 1913–1914, he began to assemble the ingredients of a dynamic definition of culture that was more anthropological, emphasizing that culture was the interaction among peoples, places, and artifacts rather than merely the cultivation of taste. Culture, in this sense, was a "living effort" of a people's self-expression and solidarity. It referred to the whole range of personal, aesthetic, moral, and religious habits and values that structured a people's unofficial and personal lives, uniting them in a "common consciousness" and collective sense of identity. At its best, culture sustained a sense of belonging and personal identification with a group, or what Bourne called "the good life of personality lived in the environment of Beloved Community."[12] At its worst, it could breed a narrow like-mindedness, provincialism, and a rigid intolerance of the Other.[13]

Indeed, when the eastern Brahmin elite in the United States witnessed the massive influx of immigrants between 1880 and 1920, they became preoccupied with what they perceived to be the forces of "anarchy," of which Arnold had warned, invading their "civilization." As Michael Rogin argues, urban immigrants, the poor, public women, and political dissidents symbolized civilized breakdown, alien control, and the return of the repressed.[14] "Aliens" were feared for the threats they posed to the "American way of life," or the breakdown of boundaries between "us" and "them." At the same time, according to Jacques Lacan, fears of the Other are actually displacements of one's own desire, particularly to enjoy the enjoyment of the Other—that is, to enjoy his festivals and celebrations, his cuisine and language. Desire becomes destructive through fantasies and fascinations about the Other and his "organized enjoyments," in particular, that they are inaccessible to us, that they will threaten "ours," or even that the Other will steal our enjoyments.[15] This explanation suggests that the feared threat to the "American way of life" at the height of immigration was based on "destructive desire," not merely aversion to foreigners.[16]

Indeed, the face of American culture had changed. Between 1870 and 1920, 20 million immigrants came to America. By the end of the first decade of the twentieth century, one in every three Americans was an immigrant or had at least one foreign-born parent. In New York, by 1910, 40 percent were foreign-born. Moreover, the new immigrants, principally from eastern and southern Europe and from Russia, not only outnumbered their English, German, and Irish cohorts by as many as six times,[17] but they also spoke little or no English, brought few or no personal possessions with them, and were often religiously orthodox (primarily Catholic or Jewish). Establishing their own political clubs and civic associations, founding over 3,400 newspapers that served over thirty different nationalities, the newest Americans created a vital, cosmopolitan network of national cultures and neighborhood communities.[18]

Yet increasingly Anglo-Americans saw the new arrivals as dirty, unkempt, abject, unskilled, and decidedly "foreign." Nativist sentiments were voiced by settlement workers, school administrators and teachers, university presidents and professors, town mayors, and journalists of the yellow and liberal presses, and the objections intensified during the 1910s. Anarchists, socialists, and the foreign-born in general were the principal targets of suppression and intimidation, but even within immigrant communities, religious and class factionalism gave way to divisions over American identity and Americanization programs. Prosperous German Reform Jews supported assimilation and Americanization programs, for instance, but poor and working-class, Orthodox eastern European Jews and Zionists opposed them.[19]

By 1915 debates over nationalism and American identity became linked inextricably to the military preparedness campaign and to questions of loyalty and subversion. Under circumstances that Bourne termed "the thinly disguised panic which calls itself 'patriotism,'" German Americans were added to the list of reviled foreigners. "One hundred percent Americanism" became militant and militarist. In 1915 Theodore Roosevelt, a leader of the "citizenship training" movement, told the Knights of Columbus that the duties of patriotism required giving up all other loyalties—those of class, ethnic group, or national origin—for loyalty to America itself. "The only man who is a good American is the man who is an American and nothing else."[20] In a similar vein, Woodrow Wilson, in his first preparedness speech before the Congress, announced: "There are citizens of the United States, . . . born under other flags but welcomed under our generous naturalization laws . . . who have poured the poison of disloyalty into the very arteries of our national life." They must be "crushed out." Two months later, he went further: "Any man who carries a hyphen about him carries a dagger that he is ready to plunge into the vitals of this Republic."[21]

As Wilson acceded to demands for the deportation of immigrants who had failed to learn English after living in the United States for five years, twenty states imposed Americanization programs on the public schools to promote "the language of America" and the inculcation of "American values." Groups per se became suspect, seen as threats to American liberalism and the idea of the solitary, unattached contractarian and bearer of natural rights. In 1915 Wilson made plain his antipathy to (unofficial) groups: "America does not consist of groups. A man who thinks of himself as belonging to a particular national group in America has not yet become an American."[22] In contradiction to the group theory underlying twentieth-century corporate liberalism, first outlined and legitimated in Arthur Bentley's *Process of Government* (1905), anxiety over the spread of groups and the democratization of civil society became pathological.

Within the rising tide of a militant nationalism, three competing theories of American national identity and its ethnic origins appeared: the theory of Anglo-conformity, the melting pot (or assimilation) thesis, and cultural pluralism.[23] Each theory constructed American identity, to use Werner Sollors's terms characterizing the ways in which ethnicity has been symbolized in America, either as "descent" relations, that is, as based in ancestral tradition, family, blood ties, or sacred election; or in "consent" determinations, that is, those grounded in contract, reason, law, or marriage; or in a combination of the two.[24] Although these terms of consent and descent were not meant to be natural, according to Sollors, they do suggest the preoccupation of American writers with foreignness and ethnicity (*ethnikos:* heathen; *ethnos:* other)[25] as an aspect of American identity and a concern with the Other in delimiting American membership.[26]

In its simplest form, the theory of Anglo-conformity posited the notion that America was originally and remained irreducibly one, single, pure strain of Anglo-Saxon stock, originating with the Puritan commonwealth and extending into the nineteenth-century genteel tradition. It insisted on the homogeneity or like-mindedness of the American people (by which its proponents meant themselves), imagining an unbroken line of continuity between the culture of the first English settlers and that of the nineteenth-century "guardians of culture." Accordingly, Anglo-conformists considered cultural identity to be based in descent rather than consent; for them, national identity was something essentially given and fixed, and it admitted of only a limited flexibility for certain classes.[27]

With the preparedness debates, Anglo-conformity turned into a preoccupation with the idea of racial purity and a general fear of "enemies within." The case was made most forcefully by Edward A. Ross in 1900 in praising the Teutonic America, a favored concept within Brahmin circles, and warning that "unchecked Asiatic immigration might lead to the extinction of the American people." These notions were subsequently picked up by Theodore Roosevelt in his invoking the threat of "race suicide" and by Madison Grant in his notorious *The Passing of the Great Race* (1916).[28]

Melting pot–assimilationist images, on the other hand, can be traced back as far as Hector St. John de Crevecoeur's conjectures regarding the new American. "What then is the American, this new man? . . . Here individuals of all nations are melted into a race of men."[29] The melting pot conception of American identity was based on descent relations as well. Its proponents argued that America was a hybrid nation and that Americans were a heterogeneous mixture of many national traditions, mingling and ultimately merging into a unified and harmonious whole. The determinant of cultural identity, it seemed, was less racial than geographic in this conception, as if the special nature of America as a place was the source of the common customs and values that made one an American. American identity was rooted in descent determinations because it involved something outside the individual's agency or will, an identity that was organic or natural rather than self-made.[30]

Under the logic of a militant nationalism, proponents of the assimilationist ideal became paranoid. Voiced by a wide range of spokespersons, from Mary Antin to Frances Kellor to Woodrow Wilson, many assimilationists sought to quell extremist preparedness sentiments and ethnocentrism by appealing to common values among Anglo-Americans and the new Americans, often in terms reminiscent of the nativists' approach. Antin, for example, defended the new immigrants by arguing, "We're hard working, clean, upstanding, but humble recruits for democracy." Other proponents insisted on forced assimilation and Americanization. One preparedness expert, for instance, argued that military service was the only way to "yank the hyphen out of the Italian Americans" and other "imperfectly assimilated immigrants."[31]

The modern variant of cultural pluralism, the third theory of American identity, was formulated by Horace Kallen, a philosopher and Jamesian specialist who taught at the University of Wisconsin, Madison, in a 1915 article, "Democracy *versus* the Melting Pot," an explicit attack on Ross's nativist tract, *The Old World in the New* (1914). As Kallen's title suggests, his antiassimilationist program proposed the thesis that America was composed of many pure strains and ethnic stocks that interacted with and related to one another, forming into a heterogeneous and fundamentally unmeltable whole. Kallen and early twentieth-century cultural pluralists (among them, Robert Park and Robert McIver) valued the variety of groups for the intrinsic worth of difference and diversity. In contrast, James Madison, the early founder of pluralist theory, understood the political value of groups ("factions") for representing diverse interests but was wary of them as impediments to individual liberty and orderly government. In contrast to Madison, as well, modern pluralists saw differences as based in race, class, ethnicity, religion, or national origin (*natio:* origin, birth), whereas for Madison, the "most common and durable" source of factional difference was in property or the private interest in economic security.[32]

Kallen's theory of cultural pluralism therefore was formulated in terms of descent identity. He argued that the inner cultural identity of the immigrant, carried with him into his new land, remained an "inward" experience, regardless of how his external relations changed: "Men change their clothes, their politics, their wives, their religions, their philosophies, to a greater or lesser extent; they cannot change their grandfathers." As if to underscore the distinction between a given, descent identity and a flexible, consent identity, he continued: "An Irishman is always an Irishman, a Jew always a Jew. Irishman or Jew is born, citizen or lawyer, or church-member is made. Irishman and Jew are facts of nature; citizen and church-member are artifacts of civilization." Because the melting pot idea threatened an individual's internal, ethnic particularity, Kallen argued that democracy must be made to apply to groups as well as to individuals, guaranteeing groups the right to exist, so that the immigrant could retain and enjoy his essential, irreducible cultural identity even while participating fully in the civic affairs of the new land.[33]

Kallen used the metaphor of society as an orchestra to illustrate the sort of democracy he advocated that preserved various traditional cultures. "Culture thus constitutes a harmony, which people and nations are the producing instruments, to which each contributes its unique tone, in which the whole human past is present as . . . a background from which the present comes to light." The problem with the metaphor of the orchestra of course, is that each instrument has a particular function, as violins cannot become flutes, and each instrument follows only one part of the orchestral score. A democratic harmony at best can achieve the protection and perfection of given, distinctive cultural differences, but no one can expect to transcend those roles.[34] Kallen's pluralism did not alter or subvert Anglo-Saxon hegemony or question the rules of democratic participation. It sought to preserve ethnic and cultural differences, nothing more. As Irving Howe has pointed out, the argument allowed American Jews a position in American society, but "they would be in it, at least as much as they were allowed to, but not entirely of it."[35]

As an alternative to Kallen's pluralism and as a direct challenge to the theses of assimilation and Anglo-conformity, Bourne fashioned a notion of cultural identity, based partly on descent and partly on consent, and a theory of American nationalism that was explicitly pacifist and internationalist. Like his friend Kallen, he believed that identity was a product of the given "place," that is, the regional, traditional, and familial determinants of a people (descent); but he also recognized that identity was manifested in willed attachments to others (consent) or through affiliations in "communities of sentiment." This socially embedded, constructed self of multiple affiliations was the result of the mix of one's private and public associations, a self that, as Nietzsche determined, was constantly in the process of formation. In Hegel's terms, the process of individuation involved separation from one's primary associations (family, ethnic group) and affiliation with secondary (national and civic) memberships. In this sense, one always existed within a group; the self was irreducibly a social self.[36]

Although Bourne did not adopt Kallen's notion of society as an orchestra or the idea that each group retained an irreducible, static ethnic identity, he took Kallen himself—a German-born immigrant, organic intellectual, a scholar of James, and an active and ardent Zionist—as an exemplar of the "Zionist idea" and an individual with a "spiritual world citizenship," whose multiple levels of identity and consciousness formed a whole American self and a distinctive personality. The Zionist represented the ideal of modern cosmopolitanism to Bourne, "the purest pattern and the most inspiring conception of transnationalism." Bourne spelled out the idea of dual citizenship that underlay his conception of a modern transnationalism: "The Zionist does not believe that there is a necessary conflict between the cultural allegiance to the Jewish centre and political allegiance to a State." Rather, he enjoyed a "dual citizenship," at once a "complete Jew and at the same time . . . a complete citizen of any modern political State where he happened to live and where his work and interests lay."

The idea of dual citizenship lent equal standing to immigrants and natives in any country. Echoing Kallen, Bourne denaturalized (and subverted) his thesis: "Once a citizen, always a citizen, no matter how many citizenships he may embrace."[37] By way of illustration, Bourne singled out Associate Justice Louis Brandeis of the Supreme Court, "at once an ardent Zionist and at the same time an incomparable American leader in economic and social reconstruction." Brandeis, an example of the sort of modern cosmopolitan Bourne had in mind, used as his Zionist credo: "To be good Americans, we must be better Jews, and to be better Jews, we must become Zionists."[38] The idea that Jews in America could be Jewish and American, and more fully so than if their cultural and political terrains were identical, suggested the pattern for the kind of dual citizenship that was possible for every "hyphenated" American. "This dilemma of dual allegiance must be solved in America, it must be solved in the world, and it is in the fertile implications of Zionism that I veritably believe the solution will be found."[39]

Moreover, early Zionism also pointed the way to the sort of nationalism Bourne endorsed, one that was pacifistic and internationalist. The Zionist state was nonmilitary and delimited the role political loyalty should play in the modern world:

> As I understand it, the Jewish State which Zionists are building is a non-military, a non-chauvinistic State. Palestine is to be built as a Jewish centre on purely religious and cultural foundations. It is not to be the home of all the Jewish people. Zionism does not propose to prevent Jews from living in full citizenship in other countries.

Whether Jews living outside Palestine were perceived to be "aliens," "marginal men," or, as Chaim Potok put it, "an inbetween person, at home and not at home at the same time," Judaism had always been perceived as an obstacle to full membership in the lands of exile.[40]

Yet Bourne, reversing the conventional conclusion of exclusion and enclosure, insisted, "the Jew in America is proving every day the possibilities of this dual life."[41] Zionism represented more than marginality or otherness to Bourne. For him and for second-generation American Jews, Zionism represented freedom from both ethnocentrism and 100 percent Americanism. Moreover, there was something distinctively modern, even avant-garde in the Zionist idea that had implications for modern intellectuals in general. Indeed in 1919 Veblen would suggest that the "pre-eminence" of modern Jewish intellectuals was due to their detachment from traditional nationalisms, which freed them from orthodoxy and class bias.[42] But Veblen saw the Jew as shedding alliances, and Bourne saw him as acquiring new ones.

Both men agreed, however, that the mark of an exceptional intellectual was to have overcome the confines of orthodoxy and provincialism, enabling him or her to be truly critical. The cosmopolitan individual, who enjoyed a dual citizenship with divided loyalties and multiple perspectives, represented not so much alienation as a healthy self of fluid identity, "at home" in several worlds. It was as if the split between bourgeois and citizen in the secular state, of which Marx had written in "On the Jewish Question," entailed no necessary contradiction in Bourne's modernist conception but led to a more resilient self. Alienation of this sort, or what Bourne referred to as the unintegrated self, was the most advantageous position for the marginalized, the outsider, or the hyphenate-American. It kept the new immigrant either from drifting along or succumbing to the influences of Anglo-conformity or commercialism.[43]

Modifying Kallen in reference to the mediation of national identity, Bourne wrote:

> Although the Frenchman may accept the formal institutional framework of his new country and indeed become intensely loyal to it, yet his Frenchness he will never lose. What makes up the fabric of his soul will always be of this Frenchness.

What Bourne seemed to be saying in Kallenesque language is that one would never conceive of saying, "I used to be French," or "I used to be Jewish." That is, one cannot unlearn what one knows about one's self. In some sense, one always retains an element of one's parentage or, quoting Bourne, "dwells still in his native environment." Thus a "Frenchman" is always a French man, but in a particular context he is also more than French, and not French—that is, not the French man he once was. We carry "nations within us," Bourne suggested, those of origin and of choice. Like the Zionist, the transnational lived in both worlds at once. As such, one learns to reinvent oneself as the Other, the first step toward bridging the gap between parochial identities.[44] In this modern conception of the cosmopolitan individual, consent- and descent-identities were thoroughly mediated through active participation in the building of a democratic culture.[45]

In reversing the conventional depiction of Jews and other immigrants as marginalized, Bourne transvalued the meaning of marginality itself. Marginality, in another light, was a form of embeddedness, an anchor that kept one either from being sucked into the "centripetal" forces of the city or scattered into atomized isolation by the centrifugal forces of liberal society. Without this "spiritual internationalism," Bourne maintained, "America ran the real danger of becoming a queer conglomeration of the prejudices of past generations, miraculously preserved here, after they have mercifully perished at home."

Consequently, he could not condone the maintenance of political loyalty to a homeland or of unchanging cultural practices.

> [Those who] fondly imagine that they are keeping the faith . . . have not really kept the faith. *The faith is a certain way of facing the world, of accepting experience. It is a spirit and not any particular form.*[46]

The point is significant. An unmediated descent identity was premodern; it did not affect a negotiation between old and new cultures or between former and present selves. A successful cosmopolitanism involved a mediation of consent- and descent-identities in one's experiences in the new land. More important, Bourne was suggesting that a modern cosmopolitan identity was not reducible to a particular pedigree or set of experiences. Rather, it entailed a certain "spirit" or stance—toward oneself and the world—that de/formed and re/formed the individual. As a certain practice and discourse, one's ethnic and cultural identity was continually made and remade, in contact with other individuals and groups.

Traditional nationalism, therefore, was at best a temporary source of identification for the hyphenate-American. It would not do because it was mired in the past, in a "weary old nationalism—belligerent, exclusive, inbreeding," and was rapidly becoming obsolete by the breakup of geopolitical units, the international "mobility of labor," and the rise of the multinational corporations. The idea of transnationalism did not do away with nationalism or national identity; it treated it as a point of departure for a new conception of American national identity.[47]

On a practical and theoretical level, Bourne wanted to expose the melting pot ideal as a failure and a hoax.[48] It was a failure because, though cultural communities were broken up and dispersed, individuals retained strong memories of their former lands. "Assimilation, in other words, instead of washing out the memories of Europe, made them more and more intensely real."[49] But it was also a hoax because it formulated a corrupt ideal that was foisted upon the new immigrants. Assimilation was designed to take place in terms of the dominant culture and produce results "congenial to the ruling class." Americanization meant "Anglo-Saxonizing," when it succeeded. When assimilation failed, on the other hand, it sentenced immigrants to "the most rudimentary planes of America life, the American culture of the cheap newspaper, the 'movies,' the popular song, the ubiquitous automobile." They become "the flotsam and jetsam of American life." Dispersion became the lot of every immigrant; "America has become a vast reservoir of dispersions." Yet he was careful to note that the "cultural wreckage of our time" comes "from the fringes of the Anglo-Saxon as well as the other stocks."[50]

Linking the Anglo-Saxon with the European immigrants as "detached fragments of peoples" clearly suggested that Anglo-Americans were also immigrants. "We are all foreign-born or the descendants of foreign-born, and if distinctions are to be made between us they should rightly be on some other ground than indigenousness." Only American natives were able to claim an organic link to a national identity; every group arriving since had been a "hyphenate." "The Anglo-Saxon was merely the first immigrant, the first to found a colony. He has never really ceased to be the descendant of immigrants."[51]

The idea that "all Americans are immigrants" ignored the very real historical differences between immigrants and "colonized minorities," to borrow from Alan Wald, in terms of their absorption into the American economy, the forms of discrimination they experienced, and their cultural acceptance (language, religion) in the larger society.[52] Moreover, it is a claim that comes close to the "we are all ethnics" position that gained some degree of popularity in the 1950s and that has reemerged in the debates over cultural diversity and multiculturalism since the 1980s. Cultural and ethnic studies scholars are rightly concerned with the false universalism implicit in this position and the tendency to "reduce" race, as Sollors does, to "one aspect of ethnicity."[53] In my view, the emphasis on ethnicity also has the effect of reinforcing the hegemony of liberalism ("individualism, mobility, self-reliance, free enterprise"), because liberal values are conceptualized as neutral, and in some sense "natural," rather than as a "particular set of interests" conceived within a middle-class society, which have emerged from contestation and challenge during the last three centuries.[54] As Slavoj Zizek cautioned, the "massive presence" of the "world system" of global capitalism is rendered "invisible" by debates over cultural differences and ethnic particularity, which do not challenge it but take it for granted.[55]

But if Bourne's transnationalism too readily universalized the experience of immigration and the condition of rootlessness and dispersion, it was too restrictive by its inclusion of (only) European immigrant groups. He wrote to address a specific historical crisis, the politics of immigration and the ideology that justified deportations, vigilantism, and Americanization programs, and to defend, in particular, American Jews from the "terrible like-mindedness" of the Anglo-Saxon culture. The politics of race, he noted in private correspondence, suggested a different problematic. Nevertheless, at the heart of his effort was a concern to define just what it meant to be an American and to decouple that meaning from its Anglophilic associations. In this pursuit of "what an Americanism might rightly mean," his silence over the racialism of American identity is a striking omission.[56]

The idea of transnationalism rewrote America's story of origin. Although Bourne did not repudiate the idea of an organic founding, he argued that the founding must be extended into the new century. "In light of our changing ideal of Americanism, we must perpetuate the paradox that our American cultural tradition lies in the future." Every arriving group of immigrants had an equal claim to reshaping American culture. Each group that arrives in America becomes a co-founder, an equal participant in shaping America's identity. America was being constantly refounded and regenerated with each arriving group. Thus new immigrants could become part of an organic continuum, an ongoing and continuous founding, and help to define a modern America. "America shall be what the immigrant will have a hand in making it."

A new way of conceptualizing American national identity was needed, a way through which ethnic minorities and Anglo-Americans might find common cause in democratic opposition to corporate commercialism.

> What I mean by co-operative Americanism . . . is, an ideal of a freely mingling society of peoples of very different racial and

> cultural antecedents, with a common political allegiance and common social ends but with free and distinctive cultural allegiances which may be placed anywhere in the world that they like.[57]

Stated differently, American transnationalism would begin where classical pluralism had left off: with the idea of democracy as a confederation—decentralized, pluralistic, self-critical, and self-correcting, in a Deweyan formulation of democracy that *creates* a public in the process and practice of democratic participation.

Borrowing from William James, Josiah Royce, and Horace Kallen, Bourne reconstructed the contours of an American pluralism that reflected its oppositional *and* democratic nature. From James, he took the image of a "plura-verse"—the idea that the universe is "more like a federal republic than an empire or a kingdom"[58]—and applied it to American society. America was in miniature what Europe was in general, a "federation of cultures," a "unique sociological fabric . . . a weaving back and forth, with the other lands, of many threads of all sizes and colors." The idea of a federated America suggested that it had no cultural core. It was like an onion: all layers, with no center.[59]

From Royce, Bourne derived his communitarianism, the idea that a beloved community could act as a brake against the modern maladies of rootlessness and, alternatively, conformism. In such places—such as Columbia University or the editorial offices of the *Seven Arts*—Bourne discovered the "international intellectual world of the future," where he "breathe[d] a larger air" and felt himself a "citizen of a larger world." In particular, Bourne looked to the cities for this democratic and oppositional form of cultural politics. In the cities' multiethnic, polycentric culture, Bourne found the makings of a viable, countercultural alternative to the ward politics of the urban machine. In its neighborhoods, "communities of sentiment" were supported, where "little pools of workers, appreciators of similar temperaments and tastes" emerged in its working and living communities. In the cities *(metro-poleis)*, artisanal or bohemian activities were producing alternatives to the corporate commercialism of the movies, dance halls, and amusement parks. In the cities, the beginnings of a new kind of expressivism could be found, a dionysian energy and a certain *dis*order that presumed competition between groups and the *absence* of certain shared values and norms without a common integrating force.[60]

His conception of the possibilities of the modern metropolitan experience, therefore, challenged the progressives' concerns over the dangers of the city. Like the progressives, Bourne saw the city as disruptive. It signified not simply freedom from provincialism but liberation from patriarchy, the bourgeois family, and traditional gender roles. Unlike the progressives, who sought to contain its disruptive potential in organized leisure, planned amusements, settlement work, and reformist politics, he encouraged the expression of that energy in new forms of art. Cities reshaped the possibilities of art, in group pageants, community festivals, and neighborhood theater productions. Group pageants, like the Paterson Pageant, were modern incarnations of dionysian feasts and rites; they exploded the division between artist and audience and brought art to all classes. Their appreciation of the dionysian undercurrent in urban culture had a regenerative appeal:

> The outburst of Pagan expressiveness is far more revolutionary than any other social change we have been making. It is a New Freedom that really liberates and relaxes the spirit from the intolerable tensions of an over-repressed and mechanicalized world.[61]

In contrast to the urban realists, dadaists, and impressionists of the early twentieth century, who represented the city architectonically by identifying New York with its skyscrapers, elevated railways, electric lights, and human congestion,[62] Bourne saw the city as a center of human vitalism, containing a primal, almost sexual, primitive energy of mass man:

> Who can walk the lighted streets at night and watch the flowing crowd, the shining youthful faces, the eager exhilaration of the sauntering life, or who can see the surge of humanity on holiday or Sunday, without feeling the strange power of this mass-life? . . . In this garish, vulgar, primitive flow of Broadway, are not new gods being born? This exaltation of the flowing

> crowd, is it not one with the mystic thrill of the dancing savage, a new affirmation of life?

For millions of Americans, city life was "the real religion, the daily toil the real sacrifice, the evening saunter and amusement the real worship." Finally, cities generated their own kind of group life, the "merging of one's petty individuality and cares into this throbbing dynamic life" such that "the individual is transcended." In the city, one recognized that "the highest reality of the world is not Nature or the Ego, but the Beloved Community."[63]

The connection between metropolitanism and cosmopolitanism suggests the distinct modern subtext of Bourne's transnationalism. In the city, one reached another state of consciousness, expressing oneself in ways not directly reducible to the past, in particularistic blends of current and past cultures and traditions. Modern urban transnationalism contained elements of diversity and a little disorder. The frenzied release of crowds on Broadway had their pacific and intimate counterparts in the city's beloved communities, acting as loci of group life. Both situations were faces of the "hot chaos" of modern urban life: the anonymity of the crowd and the intimacy of strangers commuting on the same bus; the willed mutual commitments of different minds and spirits bound together by friendship, common ideals, or both. Each was an alternative means of offsetting the misguided apollonianism of the rational and the iron cages of the technological.[64]

Bourne's modern, urban transnationalism ultimately failed to supplant the narratives of Americanization and cultural pluralism and the politics of corporate liberalism. The four intersecting histories—personal, social, political, and cultural—reinforced one another to close off the opportunity for "spiritual internationalism" and a "cooperative Americanism." Bourne's death in 1918 was followed by the 1919–1920 alien raids, supervised by J. Edgar Hoover and Attorney General A. Mitchell Palmer. The 1920s saw a further increase in anti-immigration fever and the criminalization of dissent, when for the first time surveillance and crime control were combined under one agency, the Federal Bureau of Investigation. The race riots of 1919, which Hoover blamed on subversive forces, also helped bring to a close the unrestricted immigration of the previous decade. The commercialism and consumerism of the 1920s displaced and dispersed much of the artistic experimentation of the prewar years. For these and other reasons—including an end to the cooperative internationalism among European nations that Bourne noted before the war—the countercultural, pacifistic counternarrative of transnationalism remained what it had been at the outset: a call to create a "progressive democratic reconstruction of America" hospitable to difference.

As with most of Bourne's political prescriptions, the politics of transnationalism were a form of cultural politics. As Casey Blake has aptly remarked, historians have traced the ways in which cultural activities—the amusement park, baseball, the motion picture—brought together ethnic working classes, "but Bourne understood that power relations did not disappear when Americans went to the same movies or cheered the same baseball teams, and his critique of consumer culture—like his protest against more coercive forms of Americanism—was ultimately made on political grounds.[65]

In my view, his transnationalism was also, to borrow a phrase from Winni Breines, a form of "prefigurative politics," oppositional and alternative forms of politics and education less concerned with challenging directly the policies of the liberal state and more concerned with creating alternative public spaces in which to work out collective solutions to political problems. Prefigurative politics attend to personal and political discontents by redefining problems experienced by the unorganized, marginalized members of society, enabling them to gain a sense of personal authority and collective integrity that is missing in traditional interest-based associations. For instance, the halfway houses of the civil rights movement served as crucial political and social resources for cultivating alternative political strategies.[66] In freeing individuals to develop nonstatist communities as substitutes for the patriarchal family, the provincial town, the public school, and the organized pressure group, prefigurative politics anticipate possibilities for society at large. They are, at the same time, practical experiments in social reorganization, working in concrete ways to restructure relations among work, family, and community.[67]

Consequently, transnational politics begin where democratic politics already exist: in the prefigurative politics taking place in America's subcultures, schools, churches, and neighborhoods. In the aesthetic-expressive realm of contemporary culture, one need only think of the origins of rap music or the multicultural music coming out of Los Angeles to appreciate the explosion of traditions being suggested: a mix of Asian, Mexican, Latino, and Anglo music and instrumentation that is wholly new, an exuberant yet respectful merging of the old and new.[68] As the contestation over otherness increasingly takes place in the aesthetic-expressive realm, these local, decentralized centers of identity can be transformed into loci and strategies of power. These alternative forms of group identity and organization are important, even when operating semiautonomously in terms of goals and strategies, because they redefine normal politics, taking it out of the state and returning it to the city *(polis)*, bringing it closer to the lived experiences of the many.[69] The impulse toward nonstatist, oppositional cultural politics is important to nourish, not because minorities are able to join the mainstream but because they help redefine it. The prefigurative politics of a democratic transnationalism suggest a cultural politics that is beyond militarism, and importantly, beyond liberalism. As such, it offers a significant narrative of dissent.

8
"CREATIVE DESIRE"

> One keeps healthy in wartime not by a series of religious and political consolations that something good is coming out of it all, but by a vigorous assertion of values in which the war has no part.
>
> —*Randolph S. Bourne, "A War Diary"*

> It is the creative desire more than the creative intelligence that we shall need if we are ever to fly.
>
> —*Randolph S. Bourne, "Twilight of Idols"*

Perhaps it was Lewis Mumford who gave currency to the idea of Bourne as a war casualty retreating from politics in his final year. Writing in the 1930s, he saddled Bourne with the responsibility of "shaping the dangerously a-political sensibilities of intellectuals in the twenties,"[1] a remarkable claim, given the more likely causes of the withdrawal of intellectuals from politics after the war, including the red scare, a postwar disillusionment, and the relative lack of support in America for its artists and writers. Nevertheless, it is an interpretation shared by others, even the people who knew Bourne, often substantiated by pointing to the fact that he never wrote about the war after the closing of the *Seven Arts* and that the single piece of political theory he did write, the fragment on the state, was discarded in the trash in his room, its writing broken off in mid-sentence. His friends and literary executors, moreover, tried to recast him as a cultural critic rather than as a political radical. Van Wyck Brooks, for instance, his friend and the author of *The Wine of the Puritans,* who repeatedly urged Bourne to remain silent on the war, recounted how he had anticipated Bourne's full flowering into one of the nation's foremost literary critics who would help to heal the split between the "highbrow" and "lowbrow" that he, Brooks, found to be severing America's cultural identity.[2]

Historians have similarly discounted Bourne's politics or concluded that he abandoned all interest in politics after the *Seven Arts* closed. They have argued along one of two lines. One group has maintained that Bourne became disenchanted with politics because it was inseparable from war, and having renounced the war, he renounced all political involvement and turned to art as the only salvation for the regeneration of American society. The other has suggested that because Bourne was ultimately ineffective either in stopping the war or in shaping liberal politics in general, his contribution to American politics was, in the final analysis, negligible.

Charles Forcey, in his influential study of the wartime debates among *New Republic* liberals, belongs in the first group in concluding that Bourne "rejected politics in favor of the delights of artistic anarchism" and offered no "practical alternatives" to the support of American participation in World War I.[3] Paul Bourke's thesis, as well, found Brooks's political passivity to have influenced Bourne so substantially that "the effect was to produce in him an almost total repudiation of politics altogether." In Bourke's reading, the antiwar essays published in the *Seven Arts* constitute "a sustained polemic against political involvement of any kind," and the unfinished manuscript, "The State," made "it clear that the enemy had become, simply politics."[4]

The important study by Christopher Lasch, in contrast, belongs with the second group of historians in arguing that the "new radicals" of Bourne's generation had consistently confused politics and culture, proposing "political solutions for cultural problems and cultural solutions for political problems." This confusion made them ineffective politically, and ultimately, insignificant as political radicals, unable to shape state policies to radical ends. Casey Blake's assessment of Bourne's political thought followed from this Laschean perspective, concluding that Bourne's search for "beloved community" was, in the end, insufficiently civic-minded and inclined toward the romantic. With Blake's study, the historical judgment has come full circle in recapitulating Mumford's disappointment with Bourne's politics as "romantic defeatism."[5]

These are significant criticisms, and any assessment of the importance of his political thought in the history of American dissent depends on a serious consideration of them. I analyze Bourne's literary and cultural criticism, and his theory of the roles of the artist and the cultural critic in modern society, in light of these criticisms. Specifically, I address the claim that Bourne's turn to cultural issues signaled a retreat from political engagement and argue for an alternative reading, that his cultural criticism was an intrinsic part of his political theory. My argument requires looking at Bourne as a particular kind of political theorist, one whose subject was frequently political but whose analyses often were not. (More often, in fact, his subject was culture.) An interest in culture does not in itself signify a diminution of political commitment if, as Bourne believed, cultural solutions could stimulate political responses. His attention to culture, therefore, makes sense immanently as a political critique.

I also address the related and perhaps more important claim that the kind of cultural politics he did advance—namely the production of art, literature, and theater by small cooperatives, literary clubs, and theater collectives—ran the risk of exclusivity and insularity, compromising the democratic ideals to which he was committed. I suggest that his cultural materialism and his theory of the function of art underlay his support of these groups and that he turned to them as a form of prefigurative politics, as exercises in social democracy, reorganizing already existing social relations. Moreover, he believed the art and literature produced in the new cooperatives were more democratic than either the works created by the individual artist, supported by bourgeois patronage, or the products of mass culture because the former were produced collaboratively and were available to all classes, and they rejected the division between the highbrow and lowbrow. Further, he repudiated the antidemocratic implications of the idea of cultural leadership, suggested by Brooks, political leadership as a notion that was too close to vanguardism.[6] Ultimately, I argue that the art he most admired—group art, pageantry, imagist poetry, the novels of Dreiser and Dostoyevsky—can be seen to illustrate his democratic commitments, expressing the "paganism" of the modern experience, tracing the thread of desire underlying human ambitions, or doing both.

The arguments of Brooks and Mumford, as well as many historians, are based on an implicit assumption that cultural concerns are somehow outside the domain of normal politics, as if culture were a place to which one withdrew when real politics gets too rough. This assumption reflects a bias toward liberal politics as normal politics, insofar as liberalism presumes a sharp division between public and private and leaves the private as distinctly reserved for cultural pursuits and personal (read: unorganized) solutions. The possibility that culture itself may be a locus of politics itself or that cultural criticism may have political significance is not considered because, by definition, they were outside the realm of politics.

Moreover, because liberal politics are largely consensus politics, interested in building coalitions among elites (assuming there is no fundamental cleavage among them over principles or core values), they aim to forge compromises over the minutiae of policy formulation and implementation rather than the formation of the values of a common life. As liberal politics in America has been elite politics, in some fundamental sense, ascribing to itself the tasks of administration, regulation, and social control, they have not been concerned with the construction of communitarian values or attention to personal fulfillment through democratic participation, which it has assumed already exists. Because Bourne rejected liberal politics and its institutional forms, he is considered to have abandoned all politics.

But it was the liberal politics of the *New Republic* and the Wilson administration that Bourne repudiated, not politics itself. His rejection of politics was based on the view that the "war liberals" had distorted politics, overestimating its importance and using the government to intervene in private activities. With the escalation of the political, the boundary between the public and the private, on which liberalism depended, collapsed; and politics consumed personal lives, trampled academic freedom, and disfigured cultural meanings. Despite the democratic objectives of many progressives, politics had become an occupation for elites, an increasingly insular form of politics that no longer needed to rely on the consent of the majority but only on its acquiescence. In short, the enemy was not politics but an elite politics that knew no limits.

Bourne explained his position to Brooks, as if anticipating the criticism that he was retreating from politics.

> Do we [malcontents] deny that politics has no influence on the everyday personal and social life of a nation? Of course not. What we object to is the calm uncritical attitude toward this relation. Nothing arouses the curiosity of these malcontents more than this question of how political systems, political changes, political manipulations, do affect the civilized life as it goes on around us.[7]

"The real antithesis" between the liberals and himself, as he put it, was the difference "between interest in expensively exploiting American material life, and interest in creatively enhancing American personal and artistic life."[8] Liberal politics had aspirations to "mastery" that aimed to remake society directly. But political reform had to take account of and preserve the culture it believed itself to be saving.

> The conservation of American promise is the present task for this generation of malcontents and aloof men and women. If America has lost its political isolation, it is all the more obligated to retain its spiritual integrity.

Accordingly, he advised against any attitude or activity that minimized the importance of art or literature or culture in general. "This nobly-sounding sense of the futility of art in a world of war may easily infect conscientious minds. And it is against this infection that we must fight."[9]

In 1917 he signaled the move he was about to make. "One keeps healthy in wartime not by a series of religious and political consolations that something good is coming out of it all, but by a vigorous assertion of values in which the war has no part."[10] His concern with American culture was an effort to discover and articulate those "values" and "ends" that were unexamined in, or absent from, the political agenda. Therefore he came out for "politics taking its place in the many-sided interests of a modern mind."[11]

As Carl Resek has suggested, Bourne thought art and politics could be separated "only at each other's peril,"[12] agreeing with the editors of the *Seven Arts* that the health of the arts was a public concern. James Oppenheim, in the journal's opening editorial, announced their philosophy:

> It is our faith and the faith of many, that we are living in the first days of a renascent period, a time which means for America the coming of that national self-consciousness which is the beginning of greatness. In all such epochs the arts cease to be private matters; they become not only the expression of the national life but a means to its enhancement.[13]

As public matters, the arts—including the art of politics—were the appropriate subject for the radical critic. The modern critic had to become aware of and able to discuss the relation of literature and art to the larger social environment. Although the precise relation of art and politics, or for that matter culture and politics, ultimately eluded Bourne, his efforts to examine the products and practices of cultural life, in terms of their aesthetic, social, and political aspects and influences, should be seen as part of a wholesale effort to weld radical politics and radical culture into a coherent theory and practice, or form of life.

Waldo Frank argued that Bourne had achieved that integration, joining through his work "the political and cultural currents of advance." In his cultural criticism, he aimed to link revolutionary politics with an appreciation of experimental art and thus tried to create a new mode of discourse and cultural ideal. His cultural criticism focused on the aspects of social life that nurtured and shaped the writer and broadened the reader's awareness of the writer's milieu. Cultural criticism in this sense was an extension of his rebellion against the older generation and its Arnoldian "cult of the best" and a repudiation of his own generation's preoccupation with administrative politics. Bourne set for himself as a radical critic the goal of welding a radical politics and cultural criticism into a coherent theory and practice, believing in its democratic potential.[14]

If Bourne was a formalist on arriving at Columbia University, identifying art with the expression of the spiritual and the ethical, by the time he returned from his European tour five years later, he was a socialist realist, looking to the political impact of art and literature. Whether either philosophy of the role of art in society and the standards for judging it had democratic implications requires an understanding of his reasons for supporting them.

His early aestheticism can be seen in a college essay, "The Suicide of Criticism," in which he challenged the anti-intellectualism and antirationalism of the "new criticism." Joel Spingarn, his professor and a noted expert in Renaissance art, maintained that art had nothing to do with morality, only with expression, and must not be interpreted in terms of any other criteria. The new critic must renounce "standards" and ask only "what has the author tried to express, and how has he expressed it?" Bourne's 1911 critique made a case for the validity of criticism guided by art, and vice versa. To blur the distinctions between art and criticism meant the suicide of each. "Art is purposive; it means control and concentration. For the artist does not strive merely to express himself, but to *make a point.* And this making a point is what we mean by *form.*" Bourne insisted in his essay on the importance of artistic form and on the value of its ethical content. "The attempt to root out the ethical is a deadly blow at the very existence of Art." Although Spingarn's expressionism did not strike Bourne as immoral, as it did Paul Elmer More and Irving Babbitt, the "new humanists," it did seem to be an endorsement of intellectual anarchy and aesthetic romanticism.[15]

By the time he returned from Europe in 1914, Bourne had abandoned the ethical interpretation of art. There was no single or absolute standard of what was "good" or "best," as the variety of literary and performing arts in Europe showed that each country defined for itself its own standards and its own canon. He blamed the new humanism of the genteel critics rather than the expressionism of the new critics for turning art education into "almost a branch of moral education." Under the influence of Babbitt, More, Paul Shorey, and Stuart Sherman, Americans had learned that "to be cultured has meant to like masterpieces" and to worship the classics.

> I am not denying the superlative beauty of what has come to be officially labeled "the best that has been thought and done in the world." But I do object to its being made the universal norm. For if you educate people in this way, you only really educate those whose tastes run to the classics. You leave the rest of the world floundering in a fog of cant.[16]

When culture was "reserved for the few," the majority was left to the culture of commercialism and advertising and the popular novel, and America's writers and artists went unknown and unsupported. Yet the purpose of an education in art was not only to recover America's artists or to cultivate popular taste but also to enhance social sensitivity.

> The mere callousness with which we confront our ragbag city streets is evidence enough of the futility of the Arnold ideal. To have learned to appreciate a Mantegna and a Japanese print, and Dante and Debussy, and not to have learned nausea at Main Street, means an art education which is not merely worthless but destructive.[17]

The roots were less Platonic than Rousseauian. Bourne's primary concern was not with the idea that the arts created a false or an illusory reality, which individuals confused with the real world, but with the consequences of the Arnoldian standard. The cultivated person, like Rousseau's patron of the theater, learned to ignore the misery of the poor as he became civilized, losing his natural empathy *(amour de soi)* and becoming egoistic and self-regarding *(amour propre)*.[18] Rousseau's genealogy of the corruption of men anticipated Bourne's assumptions about the original sociability of humans and the process of separation or individuation, justified by the bourgeois ethos of individualism. Yet Bourne's modernism deviated from Rousseau's return to a premedieval communitarianism in his conviction that the arts could attend to the problems of modern alienation and social misery—not only in the ways in which they were produced but in their effect on consciousness. Therefore, the development of aesthetic taste and the standards to judge it became a political imperative.

> Life [is] enriched by a certain . . . sensitiveness to art . . . and the complete lack of it . . . brutalizes the people. So if you can do anything towards spreading that sensitiveness . . . you have a work before you as important as that of the best social reformer. Any general improvement in taste means a demand for a rise in the standard of living, and this rise is *the* great fulcrum, I am convinced, in social progress. Until people begin really to *hate* ugliness and poverty and disease, instead of merely pitying the poor and the sick, we shall not have, I fear, any great social advance.[19]

The change in Bourne's thinking about the role of art and the standards for judging it came in part from his encounters with the "social art" of the Continent. In a letter from Europe, he wrote of his enthusiasm for its public arts and city planning. "I am immensely interested in civic art, town planning and kindred movements over here." Europeans took city planning seriously, considering "cities as communal homes," unlike the architects who planned American towns, which were dingy and sprawled chaotically, and American cities, where they were "obsessed with the individual building." European city planners worked with the community and its space holistically to create designs in accordance with people's needs.[20] Such a possibility was ignored by American architects, who considered architecture as high art and were therefore contemptuous of city planning or the "common humdrum building" of apartment houses and office buildings, preferring to leave them to commercial builders.[21]

In "American Use for German Ideals," an article that provoked a storm of controversy and demands that its author be deported for treason,[22] he praised the bold and exciting architectural styles of the

University of Jena and the Stuttgart Theater, the estimable town planning of the city of Ulm, the municipally built and owned apartment buildings in Munich, the model garbage-disposal plant in Furth, and the garden-city workingmen's suburb in Lichtenhof, where

> everywhere, as in the great ages of creative art, the styles are those in which form grows out of function, so that the work of factories and water-towers and railroad bridges suggests the motives of design. Steel and cement set the lines for wholly novel forms.[23]

Architecture was potentially the most democratic of arts, "because of its completely social nature." It had the ability to shape people's conceptions of space, productivity, feelings of belonging and intimacy, and freedom.[24] In the culture of the cafe, for instance, private buildings often served as public spaces with multiple purposes, alternative arenas for the life of citizenship, for shared speech, action, and recognition. Here the private sphere could be relied on to draw out the impulse toward a life lived in common. Bourne even believed that architecture could become part of the solution to the problems of homelessness, poverty, and slum life.

It was a romantic conception perhaps that individuals could find the life of "beloved community" in the heart of the city, but it also revealed a modernist, and Nietzschean, romance about the function of art. It suggested that art had a utilitarian or social function as well as an ideological or spiritual one. His cultural modernism combined both theories of the relation of art and society. It acknowledged that art had a direct material application and could be a tool of social reform, and it suggested that the arts could be a source of cultural regeneration by their potential to transform consciousness and reinspire common ideals, such that their ideological value was a prerequisite to the transformation of social arrangements.[25]

Bourne's views were based on the premise that the production of art was a social practice. How the artist produced was as important as what was produced and how it was understood. He took as his subject the artist as creative agent, the choices the artist made in the creative process, and what the text revealed and refracted about the social environment in which the artist produced.

Although he seemed to hold the view that art was created autonomously, the conditions of that autonomy varied, and the texts could give readers clues as to the state of art in the larger social process. In this way, the modern critic could judge art and literature immanently but also in social terms. He saw his own task as a culture critic as that of laying bare the relation between art and society and of making that relation more apprehensible to artists and their audiences.[26]

This view of art as a collective process, influenced by the conditions of family, community, and work and later developed by E. P. Thompson and Raymond Williams, also attended to the ideological consequences of art. The process of creation influenced not only what was produced but also the consciousness of the producers and their audiences. As an ideational force, it had the potential to politicize them or, at least, to increase their "social sensitivity." This materialist perspective—in which culture is a practical form of social organization that shapes its ideological effect—explains his support for the artists' cooperatives, neighborhood theaters, and literary collectives of the early twentieth century. Each of them was involved in a new form of cultural/social production as participants of artistic and critical communities unconnected with, and sometimes opposed to, the state and its cultural/national-patriotic norms. Artists and critics living and working together as members of "self-conscious cultural nuclei," in contrast to the ways in which art was traditionally produced by individual artists and supported by cultural elites, created new forms of art: group art, pageantry, avant-garde dance, and performance art, shaped by their collective organization. They also produced a

> new social consciousness [that] demand[ed] its poetry . . . new gods of a collective humanity . . . [a] new social religion [that] has on the one hand its elevated sentiments of democracy and a restored Christianity, [and] also down in the heart of the people its Pagan side, vague, formless, terrible, the stirrings of an incalculable force.[27]

The pageantmakers were the "Prosperos of today, conjuring up by their magic all the latent charm and beauty that is among us."

The democratic implications of this new kind of art were evident in the effect on its audiences. Group pageants and community festivals were modern incarnations of dionysian feasts and rites responding to the "elemental cravings" of moderns and, according to Bourne, satisfying the "social hunger" for community. Although group art did not guarantee great art—the Washington Square Players disappointed him because they lacked discipline and a sense of the dramatic[28]—the artists invoked a new "social purpose," which meant "work[ing] towards a creative, imaginative and inter-stimulating community life, in which personality and expressiveness shall flourish as they cannot under present institutions."[29] Because of their liberating potential, Bourne encouraged every cultural worker to "search out its own group, its own temperamental community of sentiment," writing for one another and criticizing freely. "We are now to form little pools of workers and appreciators of similar temperaments and tastes."[30]

The potential insularity of these groups, as has been noted by literary critics and historians, did not go unnoticed in Bourne's cultural criticism. Some groups would be homogeneous ethnically, or in terms of class or nationality. "Each national colony in this country seems to retain its foreign press, its vernacular literatures, its schools, its intellectual and patriotic leaders, a central cultural nucleus." Other groups would be internationalist and, like the *Seven Arts,* multiethnic, where, as he wrote of himself, he "breathe[d] a larger air." He supported them because he thought they would give new Americans an anchor in the tide of commercialism and a defense against the "most rudimentary . . . American culture of the cheap newspaper, the 'movies,' the popular song, the ubiquitous automobile."[31] He also endorsed the groups as alternative forms of social organization and brakes on the ethos of individualism. And he championed them as democratic alternatives to the practice of private patronage, which privileged the individual artist and effectively kept the public from participating in an artistic education.

The standards of the social patron had become the standards for society, and ironically, he found them to have a leveling influence.

> "Society," we say, whether it be in the form of the mob or the cultivated dinner-circle, is the deadly enemy of the literary

> artist. Literary promises can be seen visibly fading out in the warm beams of association with the refined and the important. And social glamour was never so dangerous as it is today when it is anxious to be enlightened and liberal. Timidity is still the reigning vice of the American intellect, and the terrorism of "good taste" is yet more deadly to the creation of literary art than is sheer barbarism. The literary artist needs protection from the liberal audience that will accept him though he shock them, but that subtly tame him even while they appreciate.[32]

The dangers of social patronage seemed to underscore the need for artists and critics to band together, writing for one another, criticizing each other.

The new form of mass culture, the motion pictures, contributed to the split between the highbrow and the lowbrow. With the current diet of melodrama in the "movies," he argued, "we seem to be witnessing a lowbrow snobbery. In a thousand ways it is as tyrannical and arrogant as the other culture of universities and millionaires and museums." Yet he did not "put the thing down to the low intelligence of a dear deluded public." Melodrama was officialism's "movie interpretation of life," seen in the panicked support for a sanatorium to deal with the tuberculosis crisis or the contest between corrupt city officials and more corrupt supporters. Thus, whether it was the standards of the social patron or of officialdom, the leveling of taste offended his democratic sensibilities. "I don't know which ought to be more offensive to a true democrat—this [stale culture of the aristocrat] or the cheapness of the current life that so sadly lacks any raciness or characteristic savor."[33]

Yet, for a social democrat, he advanced a seemingly undemocratic position for judging cultural texts. "All good writing is produced in serene unconsciousness of what Demos desires or demands. It cannot be created at all if the artist worries about what Demos will think of him or do to him." A truly democratic art was constructed by ignoring the standards imposed by the current social order. "The artist writes for that imagined audience of perfect comprehenders. The critic must judge for that audience too."[34] It was a position that recapitulated Walt Whitman's credo, used as the motto of *Poetry,* the

Chicago-based journal of avant-garde verse: "To have great poets, there must be great audiences too."

Bourne was ambivalent, however, over the elitist implications of this theory of culture. In "The Artist in Wartime," he fashioned an imaginary debate over the relation of the artist to the war among three aspects of his own conflicted mind. The protagonists were "Clement," an aspiring novelist whose worry that literature was an indulgence in a world gone mad with war produced in him an artistic paralysis; "Sebert," a "flaneur" and sybarite who was able to write because he serenely disregarded the war with the justification that "society [was] a hysterical mob" and could not be saved; and an unnamed narrator, who worried that Clement's depression made art useless in war and futile to pursue and that Sebert's dismissal of the war was socially irresponsible, insular, and self-absorbed. Bourne did not resolve the question of the futility of art during war, because, in addition to being conflicted himself, he realized that both positions destroyed art: the first by suicide, the second by becoming an accomplice to the war's effort. "Suppose all the world agreed with [Sebert]? Would it be safe for anything, even for Sebert himself?" The debate, a modern *Rameau's Nephew,* is significant for the insight it lends into Bourne's divided mind over the autonomy of art and the artistic process. To produce in blissful ignorance of social corruption or malaise was unacceptable; but at the same time, an artistic sensibility must protect itself from a forgiving (uncritical) culture.[35]

He concluded that "cultural 'Modernists'" must learn to write for one another and ignore, for the short term, not only the standards of the social patron but also the sterile debates between the new humanists, who measured all art in terms of the classics, and the new critics, who advocated a subjectivist art-for-art's-sake appreciation of the "expressiveness" of art.

> Far better for the mind that aspired towards "culture" to be told not to conform or worship, but to search out its own group, its temperamental community of sentiment, and there deepen appreciations through sympathetic contact.

He encouraged the formation of these "cultural nuclei," despite the risks of insularity, because he expected that they would disagree with one another and thereby police their potential elitism. Disharmony could be expected, even a certain disorder, as was evident in the ongoing debates among the social realists, the modernists, and members of the avant-garde. But such struggles were essential to the vitality of the artistic spirit. "Far better a quarrel among these intensely self-conscious groups than the issues that had filled the *Atlantic* and the *Nation* with their dreary obsolescence."[36]

As an example, he undertook a friendly dispute with Harriet Monroe, *Poetry*'s editor, in 1918, for her position that art should be judged immanently, or strictly in aesthetic terms.

> You can discuss poetry and a poetry movement solely as poetry—as a fine art, shut up in its own world, subject to its own rules and values; or you can examine it in relation to the larger movement of ideas and social movements and the peculiar intellectual and spiritual color of the time. To treat poetry in terms of itself is the surest way to drive it into futility and empty verbalism.[37]

What he meant by "more careful and better oriented criticism," was a "discussion of a larger scope," which understood art "as an expression of life . . . separating the false in [the critics'] work from the true, and placing them in relation to a larger intellectual and artistic whole." It was important for critics to "broaden their imaginative and intellectual horizons." The call for a new criticism was, in short, a call for self-criticism.

> The problem of the literary artist is how to obtain more of this intelligent, pertinent, absolutely contemporaneous criticism, which shall be both severe and encouraging. It will be obtained when the artist himself has turned critic.[38]

Therefore, while maintaining the distinction between the function of art and the function of criticism, he showed a growing appreciation of the need for each cultural worker, the artist and the critic, to learn from the other. The involvement of the audience, not only the literary critics, was important to the realization of the artist's vision.

He explicitly rejected Brooks's call for a "new literary leadership." Because culture was a collective process, the possession and practice of everyone, all must be involved in its creation and preservation. If critics were to take any part in this social enterprise, they would first need to overcome their own class and cultural backgrounds, which the young intellectuals in their political leadership failed to do. Even if they could, he cautioned that any sort of critical literary leadership should be constructed only as "a pious hope, a youthful insolence," not as a fact that could be "weighed tangibly." At most, it could be a "vital myth," an inspiration, but it "could not point to things done. It could only be a ferment or a goad. You would not expect it to be anything else." His alternative was the leadership of the class of "malcontents" and "desperate spiritual outlaws," individuals from all social classes, who were too entangled in America and its "promise" to go into exile and too dissatisfied with things as they were to be apathetic. "The country must be dotted with dissatisfied people who cannot accept any of the guides offered to them." Their leadership would be more democratic but also more political than the cultural leadership of the critic, who, like Brooks, stayed resolutely out of politics.[39]

In his own literary criticism, Bourne addressed not only what texts revealed but also what they distorted or concealed. Contradictions between form and content, or contradictory meanings, often disclosed the unconscious tensions in the writer's sense of himself, the world, or both. The new critic and would-be literary radical had to make those contradictions known to the artist and to his audience and interpret their meaning in social terms. Anticipating Bakhtin's theory of critical dialogics, Bourne determined that the task of the cultural critic was not to repair the text or to complete the literature but to unveil its contradictions and identify the principle that underlay its conflicted meanings and contradictory elements. As he put it, "The new critic must intervene between public and writer with an insistence on clearer and sharper outlines of appreciation by the one, and the attainment of a richer artistry by the other."[40]

In much the same way that the ironist was to heighten contradictions but not resolve them, so the new critic would interpose himself between the artist and his audience and attempt to render an interpretation that had meaning to the audience in their personal lives. The radical critic, in taking a middle position between the author and the public, interpreted for artists and their audiences the social significance of the creative vision and the multiple meanings in the text itself. It was a role decidedly unlike that of the postmodern critic "against interpretation," in that it involved an active intervention in the interpretation of meaning, according to aesthetic and social standards. His role, decidedly secondary to that of the artist in stimulating the imagination and transforming consciousness, nevertheless was an essential part of the artistic process. As long as the critic was aware of its limitations, criticism could be a vital arbitrator of cultural taste.

Perhaps because Bourne was concerned primarily with literature, he did not question the limitations of art to express the depths of human suffering or its inability to capture the common experience. Later pop artists and painters, perhaps because of the limitations of the media, became self-referential, incorporating common objects into paintings in an effort to depict the culture of materialism. Bourne's sense of the artistic sensibility seemed to admit of the need to be ironically self-referential as one means of capturing what he called the "personal point of view." As he saw it, the work of artists, and poets in particular, brought one closer than any other form of expression to the subjective and primal forces in the human experience, the dionysiac given form through the artist's touch.

Nevertheless, he remained concerned with the importance of form, more so than were the cultural nationalists on the *Seven Arts* (save Brooks), yet not as much as the later *Dial* critics in the 1920s were, though never to the exclusion of the work's social significance. At a minimum, Bourne argued, artists must not sacrifice form for exuberance. The contemporary fashions of art for art's sake (for example, Walter Pater's aestheticism) and art for society's sake (for instance, H. G. Wells's socialism) sacrificed form for effect and did not give art the freedom to grow or experiment.[41] On the other hand, much of Vachel Lindsay's writings, especially the *Congo* and *General Booth,* struck him as "imitative" and "banal."[42] Amy Lowell's "imagist" poetry achieved the right balance. She chose the form to accord with her "revolutionary tone. . . . Her sound intuition gets the better of her class-feeling even in her attitude towards the war." In her literary criticism as well, she treated poetry as a significant element of daily life, "neither as a refined dessert to be consumed when the day's work is done, nor as a private hobby which the business man will deride if he hears about it."[43]

In an overlooked essay, "A Sociological Poet," he offered an appreciation of the imagism of Jules Romain and the Belgian poets of the European renaissance of the 1910s. He also indicated of his search for the sources of democratic culture, admiring it for reflecting the "social conscience" of the age and a new sociability that revived the instinctual social consciousness and the sense of being a "collective person" of man's primitive ancestors. Romain's poetry "shows the way of that return," singing the song of "the life of the common soul." He was "a Whitman industrialized," a "poet of the crowd" and of "mass-life."[44]

He admired the work of Dreiser most of all, in *Sister Carrie* and *The Genius,* for its unsentimental rejection of Puritan optimism and its "habit of redemption" and for Dreiser's frank treatment of the themes of power and sex.[45] His raw naturalism, also seen in *A Hoosier Holiday,* revived Bourne's faith in American literature. It seemed that only Dreiser understood the "sense of determinism that pervaded all life." He tried to reach below the "conventional superstructure" to the life force of desire. "One feels that this chaos is not only in the Genius's soul, but also in the author's soul, and in America's soul."[46] The attention to the relation between the artist's spiritual health and the material culture in which the artist lived—suggesting that both were texts to be interpreted—was a frequent theme in Bourne's literary criticism. The author's characters could be understood as particular representations of both the modern condition and the author. Yet this tracing of desire cannot be construed as a psychoanalytic interpretation of authorial subjectivity but as a recognition that desire was intertwined with material reality. "A good novelist catches hold of the thread of human desires. Dreiser does this, and that is why his admirers forgive him so many faults."[47]

Bourne did not dismiss Dreiser's lack of form, however. He had "the artist's vision" but none of the "sureness of the artist's techniques." His "clumsy" technique, his indistinct style, his resort to a conventional form, the long, episodic structure of the nineteenth-century novel, and his tedious details, "which are too minute to be even good photography," compromised his artistic skill. Still, Bourne wanted to forgive him because Dreiser tried to "make something artistic out of the chaotic materials that lie around us in American life." His sincerity and straightforwardness counted for a great deal in a culture of melodrama and Victorian sentimentalism.

Earlier American novelists were better at sociology and autobiography because their manner was straightforward, and they made no pretense at fiction. In 1916 he decided that Upton Sinclair's *King Coal,* an attempt to integrate fiction and fact, was the best compromise that had been achieved by an American novelist. Yet he likened sociologic fiction to "a movie transcription of life" or "sociological observation 'filmed.'" Like the popular movie, its characterization was shallow, its plot made one "smile," and it was motivated by a melodramatic urge to get its "message" across. Given its different purposes, he suggested, the standards for judging sociological fiction ought to be different from those for art and literature. "All we say is, Does the novel make visible conditions as they are and as they ought to be speedily altered?" After a fashion, Sinclair had succeeded, but largely because his attempts at drama were so feeble and poorly integrated into the reportage that the reader could easily extract the story without losing any of the drama of the grim conditions of coal-mining camps or the brutal repression of the Colorado coal strike by unorganized miners in 1913–1914.[48]

On the other hand, Ernest Poole had "erred in attempting art," and H. G. Wells's sociologic novels sacrificed art for effect, the characters exploited in an effort to convey a political point. Zola was the only "master of the sociological novel" Bourne could recommend, because he managed to transmit dispassionately the passions of human relations.

> Zola lives because . . . he laboriously painted in every segment of his canvas, documenting sensual impression and confused aspiration, as well as institutional circumstance, so as to produce, through sheer massiveness and breadth, a feeling of personal life.

Similarly, although with a different technique, Dostoyevsky captured "the inner life we know. . . . After reading *Crime and Punishment,* you are yourself the murderer. For days the odor of guilt follows you around." Because the twentieth century was attempting to splinter traditional dualisms between "spirit" and "matter," "intellect" and "instinct," Dostoyevsky appealed to the modern sensibility, making no distinctions between "the normal and the abnormal, or the sane and the insane." In shattering conventional dualisms, he brought his readers into the "full warm unity of emotional life." The reader felt a part of the unfolding drama. "In Dostoevsky's novels it is not only the author that is immanent. The reader is also absorbed." Older writers often exploited their subjects, but he did not impugn their motives. "There was no falsification" in the presentation of a neatly dualistic life in the writings of Scott, Balzac, Dickens, Thackeray, and Trollope, because

> they were writing for an epoch that really had stable "character," standards, morals, that consistently saw the world in a duality of body and spirit. They were a reflection of a class that really had reticenses, altruisms, and religious codes.

Bourne's literary criticism accommodated the historical context of the artist's work.[49]

The newer artists that compelled his imagination and inspired his idealism were those writers who, like himself, had shed conventional certainties. Willa Cather, one of the new American artists, understood the new ethical and social landscape and was conscious that her readers were of different classes. In *My Antonia,* Bourne wrote, Cather did not purport to set down "eternal truths" but gave her readers an "understanding of what these people have to contend with and grope for that goes to the very heart of their lives." She was "convincing" because her "novel has that serenity of the story that is telling itself, of people who are living through their own spontaneous charm," in contrast to the "cluttered" prose and "self-conscious" moralisms of William Allen White.[50]

In the work of the novelists Bourne admired—Cather, Dreiser, and Twain, among the Americans, and Zola, Dostoyevsky, Tolstoy, Lagerlöf, Nexö, Gorky, and Rolland, among the Europeans—he saw reflected the dionysian undercurrent of human personalities, affecting the readers and drawing them into the work. In terms of technique and stance, the novelists did not condescend, but neither did they insert themselves into the story as a conscious presence. The artists either let the story "tell itself" or kept a serene distance from the material. In either case readers were not aware of the writers' art or their presence or message. The story breathed in the readers themselves; they became a part of it. In contrast to Brecht's later theory of critical detachment, Bourne seemed to be suggesting that audiences must become involved in the work itself to have the work live in them in order to recognize themselves in it, or to imagine living the life depicted and understand more fully their place in the social order. It was the critic's task to bring the audience out of the work again, interpreting its meanings in terms of social conditions.

Bourne worried at times that American writers were unable to present convincingly the struggle of life as experienced by the lower classes, not because they were ignorant of it but because they adopted a patronizing attitude rather than "the delicate art of sympathetic detachment." In 1916 he had decided that Sinclair's socialist realism would have to do for Americans until a form could be found "in which the writer not only keeps the faith towards his sociological material, but creates also a drama of personal life."[51] By 1918 he had changed his mind. "It is not enough that a book should be radical." For a novel to be great, it had to tell its story artfully, and critics whose judgment did not distinguish between a writer's ideology and his art, or who judged the latter in terms of the critic's own political persuasions, were "propagandists," substituting one "orthodoxy" for another.[52]

Nevertheless, the contradictions in Sinclair's journalism-cum-literature suggested to Bourne that there was still room for new forms of art in America that responded to the cosmopolitan sensibilities of the best-educated, most culturally heterogeneous public to that time. The difficulty of finding those new forms to capture the "new spirit" he understood to be the result of peculiarly modern problems of man, rootless, drifting, but also threatened by militarist or socially repressive orthodoxies of public and private comportment.[53] The new art would have to address and confront the competing loyalties of America's artists and their publics; and with the efforts of a social criticism, those angles and contradictions could be made conscious and socially meaningful.

Writing of himself as "Miro" in "History of a Literary Radical," one of his last essays, Bourne suggested he had reached a turning point in his cultural education. "Miro had a very real sense of standing at the end of an era." He had learned to "put literature into its proper place, making all 'culture' serve its apprenticeship for him as interpretation of things larger than itself, of the course of individual lives and the great tides of society." Having undergone a "transvaluation of values," he no longer believed that art revealed truth or virtue but social life itself and its undercurrents of desire and power. The new art must express what it knew best, namely the social nexus in which it was embedded. "The American has to work to interpret and portray the life he knows."[54]

In a remarkable anticipation of the debates of the 1980s over opening the canon of Western literature in the universities to literature of Western colonials and other nations, Bourne argued that literature had no national limitations and that in a practical sense it was no longer a question of importing "alien culture in the form of 'comparative literature' " but of understanding that an internationalist world order had brought into being its own form of art. The call for a new inclusiveness in university studies and in the literary marketplace was meant to challenge the militarization of culture, first put into effect by the War Issues course in 1918 on university campuses (later transmogrified in fall 1919 at Columbia University to a required course, "Contemporary Civilization").[55] The literature that spoke to him and his generation evoked the common experiences of many people in various countries and had the effect of transfiguring their consciousness, creating in them a sense of solidarity with people of divergent traditions.

> Miro found the whole world open to him, in these days, through the enterprise of publishers. He and his friends felt more sympathetic with certain groups in France and Russia than they did with the variegated "prominent authors" of their own land. Winston Churchill as a novelist came to seem more of an alien than Artzybachev.[56]

The new literary radicals were "cultural 'Modernists'" of "classical background"—not "cultural vandals"—who mined the cultural past for writers belonging to a "certain eternal human tradition of abounding vitality and moral freedom"; through them the new radicals "buil[t] out the future."[57]

As a culture critic and literary radical, Bourne had turned to Nietzsche for inspiration. He believed that art, a combination of the apollonian will to form and the dionysian will to chaos, could mend a culture and reinspire its ideals. Yet he also tried to turn Nietzsche into a democrat, suggesting that the "American tribe of talent" would come from no single class or national culture but from those individuals with a "taste for spiritual adventure, and for sinister imaginative excursions." The prospects of a democratic cultural revival came appropriately from the margins, in rebellion against social patronage and the mass culture of Main Street.[58]

9
EPILOGUE

> The country must be dotted with dissatisfied people who cannot accept any of the guides offered to them.
>
> —*Randolph S. Bourne to Van Wyck Brooks, 1918*

> We can be skeptical constructively, if, thrown back on our inner resources from the world of war which is taken as the overmastering reality, we search much more actively to clarify our attitudes and express a richer significance in the American scene.
>
> —*Randolph S. Bourne, "A War Diary"*

Bourne contributed to the construction of his own myth, as I suggested at the outset of this book. Through the artful creation of personality and the crafting of auto–American-biographies designed to unite his destiny with that of his generation, he wanted, he wrote, following Nietzsche, to turn his life into a work of art. In his autobiographical writings, he constructed himself as a witness to, and prophet of, his generation's ideals, formed by their experiences in the modern world of corporate liberalism. Living as an "unintegrated self," he participated in "both worlds"—the puritan world of restraint, rationality, and guilt and the pagan world of personal expressivity, alternative families, and social activism—a contradictory situation that he regarded as a common one for young moderns. With an ironic stance of "creative skepticism," he traveled between "both worlds," in his words, comparing "the is and the ought," much as Nietzsche's aesthetic impulse moved dialectically between the dream and the reality, to compare, to "build out a new world."[1]

But of course he could not control his story, and by the 1920s, he had become a mythic figure, a martyr to the war, and a voice of conscience. Part of the myth relied on the idea that his radicalism was a function of his personal dislocation, or more plainly, that his "irreconcilability" was a result of his physical differences—his hunched back, his twisted face, his dark cape worn to hide his misshapen body—and of his marginality, which made it easier to dismiss his politics, as did Amy Lowell ("deformed body, deformed mind"). For his critics, his radicalism was the result of his being an alienated and embittered outsider, longing to belong. For others who knew him, he was marked—indeed, chosen—as the prophetic voice of the age. As they told it, the afflictions of the body were overcome, disembodied by the miracle of speech, in Dreiser's account, or by acts of moral courage, in the memoirs of Oppenheim and Frank. One of Oppenheim's poems is typical:

> For in himself
> He rose above his body and came among us
> Prophetic of his race,
> The great hater
> Of dark human deformity
> Which is our dying world.

For Dos Passos, his ability to transcend reached biblical proportions.[2]

Perhaps it was his iconic status that delayed serious studies of his work.[3] For decades, his name appeared as a footnote in histories of the twentieth century, principally as an opponent of World War I, protesting that "war is the health of the state." There were a few exceptions, a full-length biography, Max Lerner's valuable assessment of his theory of the state, and the recovery of his antimilitarist writings and personal letters by the editors of *Twice-a-Year* in the 1940s. With Christopher Lasch's influential study of the "new radicals" in the 1960s, Bourne scholarship took a dramatic turn. He became the subject of several biographies, a central figure in intellectual histories of the early twentieth century, and a political critic considered by political theorists to be a significant influence on the tradition of American dissent. His communitarianism was recovered by Wilson Carey McWilliams as a critique of liberalism, its emphasis on friendship and fraternity as a counterweight to its individualism. Thomas Bender established Bourne as a public intellectual, the last of the independent intellectuals, committed to a cosmopolitan American culture and a democratic society. In Robert Westbrook's definitive intellectual biography of Dewey, Bourne emerged as its hero, his criticism of Dewey's wartime instrumentalism vindicated by Dewey's later embrace of it in a stance of "cultivated naivete."[4]

The critical reception was different from the myth in that it was not uniformly celebratory. Lerner dismissed Bourne's critique of the liberal state as reductionist and insensitive to the distinctions between imperialism and totalitarianism, depending too closely on the working class to defend against the "anti-democratic and anti-humanist" state. Harold Laski, by contrast, rebuked Bourne for ignoring the corporatist nature of liberalism. Charles Forcey sought to restore Bourne's politics to the plane of liberal respectability, concluding that the differences between his political criticism and that of the progressives were a matter of style, not of content. Sidney Kaplan reached the same conclusion but saw Bourne as a "half-way figure" between liberalism and socialism/syndicalism. More recently, Sheldon Wolin characterized Bourne as sympathetic to conservatism because of his interest in restoring community values and rescuing America's "usable past," although Casey Blake's study of the Young Americans of the early twentieth century carefully distinguished his communitarianism as a combination of the romantic anticapitalist and republican traditions in American thought, leaning, perhaps, too far toward romanticism.[5]

The revolution in Bourne scholarship prompted by Lasch's work also altered the analytic framework, introducing a psychosocial analysis of political ideas. Historicizing the "new radicalism" of Bourne's generation as a response to the growing crisis of liberalism in the twentieth century, Lasch interpreted Bourne's critical dissent as a product of both personal and generational alienation. As a member of the first class of self-described intellectuals, Bourne (and his generation of new radicals) was alienated from his middle-class background because of the breakdown of family values, the absence of discipline, and the reliance of weak and ineffectual parents as well as the schools on experts to administer private relations. The progressives, according to Lasch, sought reintegration in society by supporting programs that aimed to impose a (repressive) social order through practical or intellectual forms of control, but Bourne pursued a form of personal politics based on friendship rather than on citizenship, an immature assessment of political agency that was inadequate as a political solution to the crisis of authority in the family and in other social institutions. Blake's study of the Young Americans reflected the Laschean psychological analysis, arguing that the breakdown of the late Victorian family (read: the absence of the father and the failure of material nurturance) turned these culture critics inward, in an infantile craving for "oceanic" wholeness or unity, searching for a "beloved community" that consequently weakened their civic commitments.[6]

The new radicals' lack of attention to institutional politics and their turn to personal politics formed the basis of the Laschean critique. Lasch seemed to be troubled by the influence of the new radicalism on the culture of contemporary America. His argument, subsequently debated for almost three decades, suggested that the politics of the new radicalism led indirectly to the further breakdown of the family and patriarchal authority in the later part of the twentieth century; the decline in marital love; the rise of a culture of narcissism, with its turn to experts, therapy, personal expression, and the general escape from adult responsibility; and, as a particular example of its excesses, its influence on the personal politics of the New Left.[7]

Lasch's critique of the crises of capitalism, and his disdain for the culture of narcissism that ironically supported it, is less important to my analysis than the psychological premises on which it is based. Lasch seems to fear the loss of the idea of a stable, unified self, able to establish internal boundaries and discipline and to enforce the reality principle, to determine the limits of the possible. I have suggested that Bourne's rejection of the terms of a liberal discourse can be seen to extend to his rejection of the liberal conception of the self, on which it is based. Lasch, and to a lesser extent, Blake, is wary of the breakdown of boundaries—between self and society, love and friendship, history and truth—yet Bourne recognized and welcomed the collapse. This is not to say that he embraced a sense of the performative self, playing out a "drama" of fantasies on a refracted mirror stage (Lacan), but he did regard the self as a "network of representations of the various codes and institutions of society," a socially embedded and fragmented or multiply affiliated self, that prefigured the postmodern self, constructed by self-alienation (separation).

The "unintegrated self" of Bourne's social psychology confronted the possibilities of boundary breakdown—between the masculine and the feminine, the young and old—and, in particular, did not fear the feminine, or in Bourne's terms, the dionysian. It is important to be clear. The construction of a "vital" and resilient self in Bourne's understanding did not collapse the boundaries between self and other or between the natural and the social, contrary to Ross Posnock's reading, but it did, as Posnock suggested, permit a fluidity of affiliations and an instability of perspective that Bourne cultivated to keep his radicalism from collapsing into orthodoxy. Therefore, if one considers the Freudian self as the norm, with its well-integrated super ego, then the "unintegrated self" of Bourne's psychology, with its embrace of the feminine, will seem to be immature or stuck in adolescence.[8]

Bourne's "unintegrated self" had its political and intellectual corollary in his stance of "creative skepticism" in that he was both connected to the particularities of day-to-day politics and at the same time grounded in theory. This position, which Posnock termed the politics of nonidentity, meant that Bourne's political commitments were constantly in flux, contingent on specific circumstances but relying on "intellectual suspense" to test them critically. In a letter written to Paul Strand in 1917, Bourne described the difficulty of translation and transcendence:

> Being of marked physical deficiency and therefore draftless, I often fear that I write about the war without that poignant sense of it that must come to the men who have the direct

> issue made for them. I feel it all, but I may be too much "in the air," as they say. One is happy, however, in these times, to find one's self saying anything that brings help to anybody.[9]

In this rare reference to his physical disability, Bourne underscored the dangers of abstraction. "Intellectualism is the 'liberal' curse, the habit of moving in concepts rather than in the warm area of pragmatic life," he wrote to Brooks. The restlessness of a "creative skepticism" reformulated the experimentalism of pragmatism and recovered the Jamesian "personal point of view."

Despite the many troubling implications of Lasch's critique of the culture of self-love, his thesis cannot be dismissed out of hand. The implication that Bourne was stuck in suspended adolescence or, more generally, was unable to offer a mature or constructive politics to deal with the political crises of corporate capitalism is a recurrent theme in Bourne scholarship. It has found its expression in Mumford's disappointment in Bourne's "romantic defeatism," and, more recently, in Michael Walzer's reading of Bourne's final writings as a retreat into "despair" and "distance."[10]

Against the psychosocial imagery, I would like to address the same issue by repositioning Bourne's politics within the Nietzschean terms of this book and particularly in the metamorphoses of the three spirits. In Zarathustra's first speech, he relates the voyage of the spirit: "Of the three metamorphoses of the spirit I tell you: how the spirit becomes a camel; and the camel, a lion, and the lion, finally, a child."[11] In Nietzsche's allegory, the camel was the stage of the "yea-sayer," the long-suffering, willing bearer of pain, who would carry any burden and submit to any pain. It was the soul's moment of reaction, enduring life's contradictions and accepting them as natural. The lion represented the "nay-sayer," the rebel whose form of rebellion was in absolute negativity against all that went before. The lion was not creative in his revolt but sought only to be free. The final stage, the moment of the child, was the stage of willful innocence and potential rebirth. Through the act of forgetting, that is, in the willful remembering of one's past and of taking it in, a return to the stage of childlike joy was possible. Only those individuals who were stuck in their pasts, who had grievances they could not forget, were unable to move to the last stage, unable to act to liberate themselves. They were at war with their own time and at war with themselves.[12]

The interpretation of Bourne as stuck in the stage of Nietzsche's lion—in the position of always saying no—is persuasive in light of the breadth of his critique and the persistence of his "irreconcilability." His hostility to bureaucratic institutions, his antistatism, his repudiation of scientific management and professional expertise, and his animus toward the myths of progress aided by technology were consistent and absolute. His fears of conformism under the "herd instinct" of the family, the school, the state, and the communities of feminists and the literati followed him from his first writings on the generational conflict. His critique of the misdirected faith in science—not of science itself—and the experiments in social reform and welfare administration placed him outside the progressive community in the view of many people within it. His critique of a one-dimensional mass culture and its commercialism left him in a compromising position for a cultural democrat. Many of these positions are unsupportable today, even for people on the left—because such views underestimate the possibility of democratic resistance and dismiss the constructive role of statist politics—but they raise the question of whether the nature of his dissent was so thoroughgoing that it precluded any constructive or creative politics of affirmation.

My point is that Bourne's politics, although largely anti-institutional, were neither defeatist nor irredeemably negative. His support for the prefigurative politics of a transnational American culture was not in itself anti-institutional. Indeed it redefined the nature of politics and opened up the political space to outside voices and alternative sites of engagement. His politics of cultural experimentation were grounded in a democratic impulse that communities of artists and writers could reorganize social relations in their own practices as well as produce art for all classes. His belief that cultural solutions could stimulate political responses grounded his enthusiasm for the transforming influences of architecture and city planning.

Moreover, Bourne did indeed endorse some forms of institutional politics, what I have called prefigurative politics, or the neighborhood-based politics of halfway houses, settlements, experimental schools, and cooperatives that involved feminine labor, self-help, and nonstatist alternatives to centralization and bureaucratic management. Prefigurative politics were not substitutes for centralized institutional politics, but they were practical, experimental, and alternate spaces for education and engagement, where the relations between family, work, and the community were reorganized. His redefinition of the political was a breakdown of the boundaries between institutions and culture, public and private, on which liberalism depended.

Put in Nietzschean terms, Bourne saw power (or the will to power) in both nature and in convention, constituting individuals and structuring their activity and discourse. While Nietzsche dissolved the concepts of community and culture (and past and future) in the interest of creating the autonomous individual, Bourne aimed to free men from both nature and convention for participation in "beloved community." In his fragment, "Old Tyrannies," his resignation to the forces of social determinism, the fact that "we live a completely social life" in which we "have never overtaken the given," seems complete. Perhaps it was less a cry of despair, as most have read it, and more a recognition of the need to create alternative communities without the "sect-pressures" of both natural and conventional groups.

> Let us compel the war to break in on us, if it must, not go hospitably to meet it. Let us force it perceptibly to batter in our spiritual health. This attitude need not be a fatuous hiding in the sand, denying realities. When we are broken in on, we can yield to the inexorable. Those who are conscripted will have been broken in on. . . . [Others] can resist the poison which makes art and all the desires for more impassioned living seem idle and even shameful. For many of us, resentment against the war has meant a vivider consciousness of what we are seeking in American life.[13]

These communities, in my view, were not insular enclaves or an opportunity for escape into romantism but an anchor against the centripetal forces of society, dispersing individuals and atomizing them, and the centrifugal forces of the state, imposing a national/patriotic identity.

Perhaps the issue of Bourne's negativism might be differently phrased, in order to inquire into the implications of his dissent. If one chooses to analyze power from outside the state and outside mass society, is one in a difficult position to look for a source of resistance? Is one forced into a position of a solitary critic, or can one find a basis for a democratic criticism that speaks to the common experience in the common language? The answer seemingly depends on a reading of Bourne's critical position, "below the battle," the space where he worked out both his critique and his proposals for America's "promise." Taking a position "below the battle," he argued, was a stance for impossible situations: when one is forced to choose between two fixed or false choices or when choices are foreclosed by the "inexorables" of social and political forces, making individual resistance ineffective and mass protest untenable. It was not a position of political quiescence, contrary to Blake, or of aloofness. "This does not mean any smug retreat from the world, with the belief that the truth is in us and can only be contaminated by contact."[14] It was a position that was necessary for the "malcontents" of all classes, who "cannot accept any of the guides offered to them."[15]

Ironically, at the same time that Bourne's stance was a concession of the limits of dissent—for the critic who is below the battle cannot influence official policy, but neither need the critic support it—it created the precondition, indeed the necessity, for a creative politics worked out in the unmapped space of the impossible. Its "creative skepticism" resembled Nietzsche's aesthetic impulse, moving between dream and reality, or in Bourne's terms, between the is and the ought. The tension was creative; the comparison of alternatives, the shifting of the light, in his photographic metaphor of the ironic vision, altered the nature of reality, until the normal became the deviant and the sane became insane. By altering perception, heightening imagination, and shattering illusions, irony was both constructive and destructive. "If the ironist is destructive, it is his own world he is destroying; if he is critical, it is his own world that he is criticizing . . . his irony is his critique of life." His effort, like Nietzsche's artist, was to show other moderns how to see the world differently and thereby to change it.

Perhaps it does not misconstrue the nature of his dissent therefore to conclude that he was not caught in Nietzsche's "laughing lion" but was drifting to the stage of the child, trying to recover a youthful innocence that came, for Nietzsche, in remembering the slaughter that founded nations so that if one took it in, it burned in one's memory in order not to repeat it. "We have art in order to not die from the truth," according to Nietzsche. Bourne's call for "creative desire," in a similar fashion, may be a means to recover from the truth:

> A more skeptical, malicious, desperate, ironical mood may actually be a sign of more vivid and more stirring fermenting in America today. It may be a sign of hope. That thirst for more of the intellectual "war and laughter" that we find Nietzsche calling us to may bring us satisfactions that optimism-haunted philosophies could never bring. Malcontentedness may be the beginning of promise. That is why I evoked the spirit of Williams James, with its gay passion for ideas, and its freedom of speculation. . . . It is the creative desire more than the creative intelligence that we shall need if ever we are to fly.[16]

In this way, the politics of affirmation would come of necessity from a position "below the battle."

NOTES

CHAPTER 1. INTRODUCTION

1. John Dos Passos, *U.S.A.* (Boston: Houghton Mifflin Company, 1937), pp. 119–21.

2. The literature of remembrance is extensive. It includes Waldo Frank, *Our America* (New York: Boni and Liveright, 1919), p. 310; Van Wyck Brooks, "Introduction," in *History of a Literary Radical and Other Essays by Randolph Bourne* (New York: B. W. Huebsch, 1920), pp. ix–xxxv, *The Confident Years: 1885–1915* (New York: E. P. Dutton and Company, 1952), pp. 491–512, and *Fenollosa and His Circle: With Other Essays in Biography* (New York: E. P. Dutton and Company, 1962), pp. 259–321; James Oppenheim, "Randolph Bourne: Died December 22 [*sic*], 1918," *Dial* 66 (January 11, 1919): 7; "Randolph Bourne," *Liberator* 1 (February 1919): 14–15; "The Story of the *Seven Arts,*" *American Mercury* 20 (June 1930): 156–64; Elsie Clews Parsons, "A Pacifist Patriot," *Dial* 68 (March 1920): 368–70; Lewis Mumford, "The Image of Randolph Bourne," *New Republic* 64 (September 24, 1930): 151–52; John Chamberlain, *A Farewell to Reform* (Chicago: Quadrangle, 1965); Dorothy Teall, "Bourne into Myth," *Bookman* 75 (October 1932): 590–99; Floyd Dell, *Homecoming* (New York: Farrar and Rinehart, 1933); Theodore Dreiser, "Appearance and Reality," in *American Spectator Year Book* (New York: Frederick A. Stokes Company, 1934), pp. 204–6; Joseph Freeman, *An American Testament: A Narrative of Rebels and Romantics* (New York: Farrar and Rinehart, 1936); Alyse Gregory, *The Day Is Gone* (New York: E. P. Dutton, 1948); Horace Gregory, "Salvos for Randolph Bourne," in *Selected Poems of Horace Gregory* (New York: Viking Press, 1951); and Sherman Paul, "Randolph Bourne and the

Party of Hope," *Southern Review* 2(3) (July 1966): 524–41—reprinted in *Makers of American Thought: An Introduction to Seven American Writers,* ed. Ralph Ross (Minneapolis: 1963; rpt., University of Minnesota Press, 1974), pp. 120–56; Edward Abrahams, *The Lyrical Left: Randolph Bourne, Alfred Stieglitz, and the Origins of Cultural Radicalism in America* (Charlottesville: University Press of Virginia, 1986); and Casey Blake, *Beloved Community: The Cultural Criticism of Randolph Bourne, Van Wyck Brooks, Waldo Frank, and Lewis Mumford* (Chapel Hill: University of North Carolina Press, 1990). For a summary of the literature of legend, see A. F. Beringhause, "The Double Martyrdom of Randolph Bourne," *Journal of the History of Ideas* 18 (October 1957): 594–603, and Bruce Clayton, *Forgotten Prophet: The Life of Randolph Bourne* (Baton Rouge: Louisiana State University Press, 1984), pp. 3–5, 263–66. See also unpublished memoirs by Waldo Frank, Floyd Dell, and Arthur Macmahon in the Randolph S. Bourne Papers, Butler Library, Rare Books and Manuscript Collections, Columbia University, New York.

3. Michael Gold, "America Needs a Critic," *New Masses* 1(6) (October 1926): 7–9.

4. Dwight MacDonald, "War and the Intellectuals: Act II," *Partisan Review* 6 (Spring 1939): 10–20; "Editors' Statement," *Twice-a-Year,* 5–6 (Fall–Winter 1940, Spring–Summer 1941): 11–16; cf. Max Lerner, "Randolph Bourne and Two Generations," in *Ideas for the Ice Age* (New York: Viking, 1941), 54–78.

5. See Christopher Lasch, *The New Radicalism in America, 1889–1963: The Intellectual as a Social Type* (New York: Random House, 1964), and James Vitelli, *Randolph Bourne* (Boston: Twayne Publishers, 1981).

6. The last reprint of Bourne's writings was published in 1977 in *The Radical Will: Randolph Bourne, Selected Writings, 1911–1918,* ed. Olaf Hansen (New York: Urizen Books, 1977, 1978). The University of California Press reprinted the Hansen text in 1992.

7. See Clayton, *Forgotten Prophet.*

8. For instance, a common theme in Bourne scholarship is the causal link between personal alienation and political dissent. See Mark Harris, "Randolph Bourne: A Study in Immiscibility" (Ph.D. diss., University of Minnesota, 1956); Melvyn Rosenthal, "The American Writer and His Society: The Response to Estrangement in the Works of Nathaniel Hawthorne, Randolph Bourne, Edmund Wilson, Norman Mailer, and Saul Bellow" (Ph.D. diss., University of Connecticut, 1968); John Adam Moreau, *Randolph Bourne: Legend and Reality* (Washington, D.C.: Public Affairs Press, 1966); and Clayton, *Forgotten Prophet.* Cf. Kenneth S. Lynn, "The Rebels of Greenwich Village," *Perspectives in American History,* no. 8 (Cam-

bridge: Harvard University Press, 1974), pp. 335–77, reprinted in *The Air-Line to Seattle: Studies in Literary and Historical Writing About America* (Chicago: University of Chicago Press, 1983), pp. 60–92, and Michael Walzer, "The War and Randolph Bourne," in *The Company of Critics: Social Criticism and Political Commitment in the Twentieth Century* (New York: Basic Books, 1988), pp. 45–63.

9. The shift from the modern to the post-modern sensibility has been characterized, first by Nietzsche, as that from the moral to the aesthetic.

10. For a similar view, see Alan Trachtenberg, "Introduction: The Genteel Tradition and Its Critics," in *Critics of Culture: Literature and Society in the Early Twentieth Century*, ed. Alan Trachtenberg (New York: John Wiley, 1976).

11. By liberalism I mean a political culture that is based on the principles of government by consent, the protection of individual liberties, and the preservation of private interests. As J. David Greenstone has argued, the liberal tradition in America was a divided one: while centering on these core values, it debated the proper balance between the protection of negative liberties and the attainment of positive freedoms. At stake was the nature of democratic liberties and the degree to which the government should play a role in securing them as well as the prospects for creating a common culture while preserving individuality. At the beginning of the twentieth century, as R. Jeffrey Lustig argues, the locus shifted from recognizing individual rights and preferences to recognizing those of organizations and groups. In a corporate liberal society, the market was still regarded as the space in which individual "development" could be realized but in an economy that was now organized. Individual reason was replaced by bureaucratic rationality and political equality by the procedural guarantee of equality of opportunity. Individuals who were not organized or who did not conform to corporate organization were atomized or displaced, and those who were organized became anonymous, part of a mass. The observation that liberalism in the twentieth century depoliticized America's public is also a statement that politics had escalated, in Bourne's words, to manage and organize social relations. Cf. Louis Hartz, *The Liberal Tradition in America* (New York: Harcourt, Brace and Company, 1955); R. Jeffrey Lustig, *Corporate Liberalism: The Origins of Modern American Political Theory, 1890–1920* (Berkeley: University of California Press, 1982); J. David Greenstone, *The Lincoln Persuasion: Remaking American Liberalism* (Princeton: Princeton University Press, 1993); and Rogers M. Smith, "Beyond Tocqueville, Myrdal, and Hartz: The Multiple Traditions in America," *American Political Science Review* 87(3) (September 1993): 549–66.

12. Blake, *Beloved Community,* especially chapter 5.

13. Cf. Eldon J. Eisenach, *The Lost Promise of Progressivism* (Lawrence: University Press of Kansas, 1994).

14. Sacvan Bercovitch, *The Puritan Origins of the American Self* (New Haven: Yale University Press, 1975).

15. See Ross Posnock, "The Politics of Nonidentity: A Genealogy," *boundary 2* 19(1) (1992): 34–68, for an elegant and noteworthy contribution to the theory of ironic criticism, linking Bourne's politics of "intellectual suspense" to John Dewey's "cultivated naivete" and to Max Horkheimer's and Theodor Adorno's efforts to uproot traditional Marxism through "immanent critique."

CHAPTER 2. A POLITICAL GENEALOGY

1. Studies of the prewar rebellion are numerous. The first, and in many ways the best, is Henry May's *The End of American Innocence: The First Years of Our Own Time, 1912–1917* (New York: Oxford University Press, 1959). See also Van Wyck Brooks, *America's Coming of Age* (New York: B. W. Huebsch, 1915); Daniel Aaron, *Writers on the Left* (New York: Oxford University Press, 1977), pp. 5–145; James Burkhart Gilbert, *Writers and Partisans: A History of Literary Radicalism in America* (New York: John Wiley, 1968), pp. 8–45 and passim; June Sochen, *The New Woman in Greenwich Village, 1910–1920* (New York: Quadrangle Books, 1972); John P. Diggins, *The American Left in the Twentieth Century* (New York: Harcourt Brace Jovanovich, 1973), pp. 3–106; Richard H. Pells, *Radical Visions and American Dreams: Culture and Social Thought in the Depression Years* (New York: Harper and Row, 1973), pp. 1–42; Kenneth S. Lynn, "The Rebels of Greenwich Village," *Perspectives in American History,* no. 8 (Cambridge: Harvard University Press, 1974), pp. 335–77; Arthur Frank Wertheim, *The New York Little Renaissance: Iconoclasm, Modernism, and Nationalism in American Culture, 1908–1917* (New York: New York University Press, 1976); Judith Schwartz, *Radical Feminists of Heterodoxy, Greenwich Village 1912–1940* (Norwich, Vt.: New Victoria Press, 1986); and Thomas Bender, *New York Intellect: A History of Intellectual Life in New York City, from 1750 to the Beginnings of Our Own Time* (New York: Alfred A. Knopf, 1987), pp. 207–62.

2. Mabel Dodge Luhan, *Intimate Memories: Movers and Shakers* (New York: Harcourt, Brace and Company, 1933), 3: 83.

3. Steve Golin, "The Paterson Strike Pageant," *Socialist Review* 69 (May–June 1983): 45–78. See also Steve Golin, *The Fragile Bridge: Paterson Silk Strike, 1913* (Philadelphia: Temple University Press, 1988), a book that came to my attention after I wrote this chapter.

4. For the impact of the Armory Show, see Meyer Schapiro, "Rebellion in Art," in *America in Crisis,* ed. Daniel Aaron (Hamden, Conn.: 1952; rpt., Archon Books, 1971), pp. 203–42.

5. For a superb interpretive history and historiography of modern American poetry, see Cary Nelson, *Repression and Recovery: Modern American Poetry and the Politics of Cultural Memory, 1910–1945* (Madison: University of Wisconsin Press, 1989).

6. Judith Butler, *Gender Trouble: Feminism and the Subversion of Identity* (New York: Routledge, 1990), pp. viii–ix.

7. Eldon Eisenach, *The Lost Promise of Progressivism* (Lawrence: University Press of Kansas, 1994). It should be noted that Eisenach scrupulously includes many dissenting voices within progressivism itself, such as those of Jane Addams and Charlotte Perkins Gilman. At the same time, however, he counts among the progressives individuals whose political sympathies ranged from socialist to liberal, which raises a question about the elasticity of the term and requires him to include the full range of views in his analysis. Cf. Michael Lind, *The Next American Nation: The New Nationalism and the Fourth American Revolution* (New York: Free Press, 1995), pp. 55–96.

8. Morton White, *Social Thought in America: The Revolt Against Formalism* (1947; rpt., Boston: Beacon Press, 1964).

9. For a sophisticated analysis of Holmes's legalism, see G. Edward White, *Justice Oliver Wendell Holmes: Law and the Inner Self* (New York: Oxford University Press, 1993).

10. John P. Diggins, *The American Left in the Twentieth Century* (New York: Harcourt Brace Jovanovich, 1973), pp. 27–38; cf. John P. Diggins, *The Promise of Pragmatism: Modernism and the Crisis of Knowledge and Authority* (Chicago: University of Chicago Press, 1994), especially chapter 3, a greatly revised history of the left and a lament over its decline into postmodernism.

11. H. Stuart Hughes, *Consciousness and Society: The Reorientation of European Social Thought, 1890–1930* (New York: Vintage, 1961).

12. Randolph S. Bourne, "Denatured Nietzsche," *Dial* 63 (October 25, 1917): 389–91.

13. Alfred Kazin, *On Native Grounds: An Interpretation of Modern American Prose Literature* (1942; rpt. New York: Harcourt Brace Jovanovich, 1982), p. 63. See also John Milton Cooper, Jr., *The Warrior and the Priest: Woodrow Wilson and Theodore Roosevelt* (Cambridge, Mass.: Belknap Press, 1983), for an inventive application of the dionysian and the apollonian to Roosevelt and Wilson, respectively.

14. John Higham, "The Reorientation of American Culture in the 1890s," in *Writing American History: Essays on Modern Scholarship* (Bloomington:

Indiana University Press, 1970), pp. 73–102. For two very different versions of the construction of the New Woman at the turn of the century, see Sochen, *New Woman,* and Carroll Smith-Rosenberg, "The New Woman as Androgyne: Social Disorder and Gender Crisis," in *Disorderly Conduct: Visions of Gender in Victorian America* (New York: Alfred A. Knopf, 1995), pp. 245–96 and passim.

15. See, for example, T. J. Jackson Lears, *No Place of Grace: Antimodernism and the Transformation of American Culture 1880–1920* (New York: Pantheon, 1981). James Livingston offers a prodigiously researched and provocative rereading of the implications of the shift from proprietary capitalism to a consumer capitalism in *Pragmatism and the Political Economy of Cultural Revolution, 1850–1940* (Chapel Hill: University of North Carolina Press, 1994). His thesis, that this much-studied change in political and cultural economies produced—as Foucault would have it—both a repressive and a generative force for individual freedom (although Livingston relies primarily on a dialectic informed by Hegel and Marx, on the one hand, and the American pragmatists, on the other) is important to evaluate and should not be ignored by any serious scholar of the period. Unfortunately, his book came to my attention after I wrote this chapter. See also the profound critique of the development of consumer capitalism by William R. Leach, *Land of Desire: Merchants, Power, and the Rise of a New American Culture* (New York: Vintage Books, 1993).

16. Randolph S. Bourne, "The Two Generations," *Atlantic Monthly* 108 (May 1911): 591–98, reprinted in *Youth and Life* (New York: Houghton Mifflin Company, 1913), p. 48.

17. The characterization of generational shift from a culture of "character" to a culture of "personality" began with Warren Susman, *Culture as History* (New York: Pantheon, 1985), pp. 213–14, 220, and has been recently refined by Richard Wightman Fox, "The Culture of Liberal Protestant Progressivism, 1875–1925," *Journal of Interdisciplinary History* 23(3) (Winter 1993): 630–60. Cf. Livingston, *Pragmatism.*

18. Bourne, "Two Generations."

19. See especially Michael Paul Rogin, *Fathers and Children: Andrew Jackson and the Subjugation of the American Indian* (New York: Vintage Books, 1975), and "Liberal Society and the Indian Question," reprinted in Michael Rogin, *Ronald Reagan, the Movie and Other Episodes in Political Demonology* (Berkeley: University of California Press, 1987), pp. 134–68.

20. Randolph S. Bourne, "Twilight of Idols," *Seven Arts* 2 (October 1917): 688–702.

21. Cf. Eisenach, *Lost Promise,* who sees the war as the failure of progressivism's promise to construct a national unity based on democracy as

a civic religion, nationalism, and a common American identity (pp. 48–73).

22. For theories of representation and signification in discourse analysis, see, for example, Anne Norton, *Republic of Signs: Liberal Theory and American Popular Culture* (Chicago: University of Chicago Press, 1993), pp. 1–8; Linda Zerilli, *Signifying Woman: Culture and Chaos in Rousseau, Burke, and Mill* (Ithaca, N.Y.: Cornell University Press, 1994), chapters 1, 5; and S. Paige Baty, *American Monroe: The Making of a Body Politic* (Berkeley: University of California Press, 1995), pp. 8–19.

23. See Hannah Fenichel Pitkin, *The Concept of Representation* (Berkeley: University of California Press, 1972). I think it is this fiction of representation as relying on an (unspoken) consent of an (absent) subject that is at the heart of Carole Pateman's brilliant study of the elision (and subordination) of women from social-contract theory. See Carole Pateman, *The Sexual Contract* (Stanford, Calif.: Stanford University Press, 1990). Cf. Butler, *Gender Trouble,* pp. 5–9 and passim.

CHAPTER 3. ISHMAEL

1. Randolph S. Bourne, "History of a Literary Radical," *Yale Review* 8 (April 1919): 468–84; reprinted in Randolph S. Bourne, *History of a Literary Radical and Other Essays* (New York: B. W. Huebsch, 1920), pp. 1–30.

2. The essay was also a commentary on the debates in the universities over education in the canon. On Bourne's self-education, see Jinx Roosevelt, "Randolph Bourne: The Education of a Critic, an Interpretation," *History of Education Quarterly* 17(3) (Fall 1977): 257–74. Roosevelt suggests that America's cultural heroes are frequently those individuals who have rejected formal institutions or membership in organizations whose rebellion is made possible by the very strength of these institutions. In this view, Bourne's radicalism is superficial relative to his affirmation of America's liberal order. Cf. Bruce Clayton, *Forgotten Prophet* (Baton Rouge: Louisiana State University Press, 1984), who associates Bourne's self-education with the popular literary convention of depicting oneself as an innocent, whom others know to be actually wiser, e.g., the self-education of Huckleberry Finn and Tom Sawyer (p. 15).

3. Susan Juster, "'In a Different Voice': Male and Female Narratives of Religious Conversion in Post-Revolutionary America," *American Quarterly* 41(1) (March 1989): 34–62.

4. Randolph S. Bourne, "The Handicapped: By One of Them," *Atlantic Monthly* 108 (September 1911): 320–29, reprinted and revised as

"A Philosophy of Handicap," in *Youth and Life* (Boston: Houghton Mifflin Company, 1913), pp. 339–65. Citations are from "A Philosophy of Handicap," in *The Radical Will: Randolph Bourne, Selected Writings, 1911–1918,* ed. Olaf Hansen (New York: Urizen Books, 1977), pp. 73–87. Bourne also began a chapter of what may have been an autobiographical novel, published posthumously as "An Autobiographical Chapter," *Dial* 68 (January 1920): 1–21. Outlines of two autobiographical novels are also available in the Bourne Papers, Box 11 and Reel 4A (unnumbered).

5. Sacvan Bercovitch, *The Puritan Origins of the American Self* (New Haven: Yale University Press, 1975), p. 8.

6. My reading of Nietzsche is informed by Tracy Strong, *Friedrich Nietzsche and the Politics of Transfiguration* (Berkeley: University of California Press, 1975), p. 233, quoting from Nietzsche's *Gay Science.*

7. Randolph S. Bourne, "The Adventure of Life," in Hansen, ed., *Youth and Life,* pp. 182–83.

8. Randolph S. Bourne to Dorothy Teall, April 11, 1915, Bourne Papers, reprinted in *The Letters of Randolph Bourne,* ed. Eric Sandeen (Troy, N.Y.: Whitston, 1981), p. 297.

9. Friedrich Nietzsche, *Birth of a Tragedy,* trans. Francis Golffing (New York: Doubleday, 1956), pp. 51–52, 137.

10. For the concept of context as embedded in text, see Dominick LaCapra, *Rethinking Intellectual History: Texts, Contexts, Language* (Ithaca, N.Y.: Cornell University Press, 1983), pp. 185, 312. On the problem of historical validity as discursive, see also Hayden White, *Tropics of Discourse: Essays in Cultural Criticism* (Baltimore: Johns Hopkins University Press, 1987), p. 3.

11. Carl Resek, "Introduction," in *War and the Intellectuals: Essays by Randolph S. Bourne, 1915–1919* (New York: Harper and Row, 1964), p. viii.

12. John Adam Moreau, *Randolph Bourne: Legend and Reality* (Washington, D.C.: Public Affairs Press, 1966), pp. 3–4.

13. Van Wyck Brooks, *Fenollosa and His Circle: With Other Essays in Biography* (New York: E. P. Dutton, 1962), pp. 259–321.

14. Quoted in ibid.

15. In his collected papers is a rough sketch of a back brace, on a medical prescription form, which he may have been investigating for future use. There is no indication that he had the brace made (Bourne Papers).

16. James Oppenheim, "The Story of the *Seven Arts,*" *American Mercury* 20 (June 1930): 163; Theodore Dreiser, "Appearance and Reality," *American Spectator Yearbook,* no. 11 (New York: Frederick A. Stokes, 1934), pp. 204–9; and Ellery Sedgwick, *The Happy Profession* (Boston: Little, Brown, 1946), p. 223.

17. Randolph S. Bourne, "Randolph Bourne: Diary for 1901," *Twice-a-Year* 5–6 (Spring–Summer 1941): 89–98. "Fragment of a Novel" offers a view of childhood in terms of his relationship with his grandmother, Nanno, the obvious center of the household and head of the family (Bourne Papers).

18. Bourne, "The Handicapped," pp. 75, 76.

19. Philip E. Slater, *The Glory of Hera: Greek Mythology and the Greek Family* (Princeton: Princeton University Press, 1968), p. 388.

20. Bourne, "The Handicapped," p. 76.

21. Randolph S. Bourne to Simon Pelham Barr, January 19, 1914, Bourne Papers, reprinted in Sandeen, ed., *Letters,* p. 209.

22. Randolph S. Bourne to Alyse Gregory, January 13, 1915, Alyse Gregory Papers, Beinecke Library, Yale University, reprinted in Sandeen, ed., *Letters,* p. 286.

23. Bourne, "The Handicapped," p. 75. Warren Susman, *Culture as History* (New York: Pantheon, 1985), suggests that the problem of being "in but not of the world" involved a crucial question of strategy for radicals in Europe and the United States (p. 76).

24. Records of the city register suggest that Charles continued to drift. In the *New York Directory of 1910,* the following listing appeared: "All the Magazines and Books at Lowest Rates. Charles R. Bourne, Magazine Specialist, Subscription Books, Advertising Specialties, Printing and Engraving, Lithography, Typewriter Supplies, Account Books, Stationery, Classical and Popular Music, 10 cents." Waldo Frank offers a somewhat different chronology, suggesting that Charles "made a fortune from his candy stores in Cleveland and lost it in the great depression" (*Memoirs of Waldo Frank,* ed. Alan Trachtenberg [Amherst: University of Massachusetts Press, 1973], p. 241). This report is unlikely, as Charles died in 1926. Cf. Kenneth Lynn, "The Rebels of Greenwich Village," *Perspectives in American History,* no. 8 (Cambridge: Harvard University Press, 1974).

25. Bourne, "Fragment of a Novel," pp. 332–33.

26. Biographical details are scarce, but available material comes from a variety of sources. Bourne's letters, diaries, and autobiographical writings are collected in the Bourne Papers. John Moreau's biography, *Bourne,* is based on interviews with relatives and friends; cf. Clayton, *Forgotten Prophet.*

27. Randolph S. Bourne, "What Is Exploitation?" *New Republic* 9 (November 4, 1916): 261–62; see also Bourne, "Sabotage," *Columbia Monthly* 10 (November 1913): 1–2.

28. Bourne, "The Handicapped," p. 78.

29. Ibid., pp. 74–75, 77–78; Bourne, "The Dodging of Pressures," in *Youth and Life,* p. 124.

30. Bourne, "The Handicapped," pp. 79–81.

31. Ibid., p. 81.

32. Randolph S. Bourne to Mary Messer, February 7, 1914, "Some Pre-War Letters (1912–1914)," *Twice-a-Year* 2 (Spring–Summer 1939): 79–81; Bourne, "The Virtues and Seasons of Life," *Youth and Life,* p. 62.

33. William James, *The Varieties of Religious Experience* (New York: Longmans, Green, 1902), especially pp. 132, 163, 206, 236–53. For a revealing account of James's personal efforts to overcome his past, see Cushing Strout, "William James and the Twice-Born Sick Soul," *Daedalus* 117 (Summer 1968): 1062–82.

34. As Strout argued, the sick soul "grasped more profoundly the personal nature of reality" because it did not hypostatize experience into an abstraction or scientific principle. It relied on the self as the fundamental locus of reality and was concerned with the private destiny of the individual. See also Michael Weinstein, *The Wilderness and the City* (Amherst: University of Massachusetts Press, 1982), chapter 5.

35. Bourne, "The Adventure of Life," p. 158.

36. Bourne, "The Handicapped," p. 79.

37. Randolph S. Bourne to Prudence Winterrowd, March 2, 1913, Bourne Papers, reprinted in Sandeen, ed., *Letters,* p. 76.

38. Ezekiel 18:31.

39. Louis Filler, *Randolph Bourne* (Washington, D.C.: American Council on Public Affairs, 1943), p. 31.

40. Bourne wrote several reviews of faculty publications, including one by Franz Boas, *The Mind of Primitive Man,* in *Columbia Monthly* 9 (November 1911): 31–32, and "Individuality and Education," *Columbia Monthly* 9 (January 1912): 88–90, a review of Edward Thorndike's studies of social influence on personality development. Bourne's master's thesis, "A Study of the Suburbanizing of a Town and the Effects of the Process upon Its Social Life" (Bourne Papers), is revised as "Social Order in an American Town," *Atlantic Monthly* 111 (February 1913): 227–37.

41. Charles A. Beard to Randolph S. Bourne, May 15, 1914, Bourne Papers.

42. The story is told in more detail in Moreau, *Bourne,* pp. 192–93, and Clayton, *Forgotten Prophet,* pp. 255–56.

43. For the details of the *Dial* affair, see Nicholas Joost, *Scofield Thayer and the Dial: An Illustrated History* (Carbondale: Southern Illinois University Press, 1964), pp. 4–13, 37, 78, 188, 201, 230–32, 265, 271–72. See also Randolph Bourne to Alyse Gregory, n.d. [Summer 1918] and August 2, 1918, Gregory Papers, reprinted in Sandeen, ed., *Letters,* pp. 415, 419, and Bourne to Sarah Bourne, October 12, 1918, Bourne Papers, reprinted in Sandeen, ed., *Letters,* p. 423.

44. James Oppenheim, ed., "Foreword," *Untimely Papers* (New York: B. W. Huebsch, 1919), p. iv.

45. Warren I. Susman, "'Personality' and the Making of Twentieth-Century Culture," reprinted in *Culture as History,* pp. 271–85; cf. Richard Fox, "Apostle of Personality," *Times Book Review,* January 13, 1985, and Raymond Williams, *Keywords* (1976; rpt., New York: Oxford University Press, 1977), pp. 194–97.

46. On the shifts in meaning and language usage in the early decades of the twentieth century, see Paul Fussell, *The Great War and Modern Memory* (1975; rpt., Oxford: Oxford University Press, 1977), pp. 1–35 and passim.

47. Randolph S. Bourne to Dorothy Teall, April 11, 1915, Bourne Papers, reprinted in Sandeen, ed., *Letters,* p. 297; Bourne, "For Radicals," in *Youth and Life,* pp. 286, 299, 300.

48. Bourne "The Adventure of Life," p. 180.

49. Bourne "For Radicals," p. 295.

50. Bourne, "The Dodging of Pressures," p. 283.

51. Randolph S. Bourne, "Paul Elmer More," *New Republic* 6 (April 1, 1916): 245–47 (review of *Aristocracy and Justice*).

52. Bourne, "The Adventure of Life," p. 187.

53. The phrase is Paul Gilroy's, in *The Black Atlantic: Modernity and Double Consciousness* (Cambridge: Harvard University Press, 1993).

54. Bourne, "History of a Literary Radical," in Bourne, *History of a Literary Radical and Other Essays,* p. 22.

Chapter 4. Irony and Radicalism

1. Randolph S. Bourne, "The War and the Intellectuals," *Seven Arts* 2 (June 1917): 133–46.

2. Randolph S. Bourne, "The Price of Radicalism," *New Republic* 6 (March 11, 1916): 161.

3. Alan Trachtenberg, "Introduction," in *Critics of Culture: Literature and Society in the Early Twentieth Century,* ed. Alan Trachtenberg (New York: John Wiley, 1976).

4. William James, *The Letters of William James,* ed. Henry James (Boston: Atlantic Monthly, 1920), 2: 100–101; see also William James, "The Social Value of the College-Bred," *McClure's* 3 (1908): 419–22.

5. Even during the war, Bourne supported the idea of intellectual leadership only as a "vital myth," as a "ferment or a goad." See Randolph S. Bourne to Van Wyck Brooks, March 27, 1918, Bourne Papers, reprinted in *The Letters of Randolph Bourne,* ed. Eric Sandeen (Troy, N.Y.: Whitston, 1981), pp. 410–14.

6. Ross Posnock, "The Politics of Nonidentity," *boundary 2* 19(1) (Spring 1992): 34–68. See also Theodor Adorno, *Prisms* (Cambridge: MIT Press, 1967), pp. 31–32, on the dangers of high abstraction.

7. M. M. Bakhtin, *The Dialogic Imagination: Four Essays,* ed. Michael Holquist, trans. Caryl Emerson and Michael Holquist (Austin: University of Texas Press, 1981), pp. 366, 369.

8. Self-masking was a frequent pragmatic discursive strategy for Bourne whereby he could remake himself several times over, or as Bakhtin noted with respect to the integral role of the mask in carnival, to indicate the "incongruity of man with himself," a gap the modern novelist exploited (Bakhtin, *Dialogic Imagination,* pp. 36–37). Bourne's masking took several forms. He signed his early (college) essays with pseudonyms, with names of places or persons (e.g., Aurelius Bloomfield, Juvenis, J. Lowes (for G. Lowes Dickenson, the Greek scholar and pacifist). He included himself as a subject in several essays, the Poet in "The Major Chord" (a prose-poem), the conscientious objector in "Below the Battle," the friend and the narrator in "Making One's Own Contribution," "Fergus," and "The Artist in Wartime." In his autobiographies, he was Miro and Gilbert (for Gilbert Murray, the poet). Each device of self-distancing and mimesis was a signification of his multiple positions, alternatively author and subject, author and text, narrator and narrated. For an example of parody, see "One of Our Conquerors," *New Republic* 4 (September 4, 1915): 121–23, a profile of Nicholas Murray Butler, president of Columbia University.

9. Randolph S. Bourne, "What Plato Means to Me," [n.d.], Bourne Papers, unpublished manuscript.

10. Randolph Bourne, "The Life of Irony," *Atlantic Monthly* 111 (March 1913), reprinted in *Youth and Life* (Boston: Houghton Mifflin, 1913), pp. 106–7. All citations are from the reprinted edition. The collective determination of truth finds its source in James, Dewey, and Peirce. See, for example, William James, "The Sentiment of Rationality," in *Pragmatism and Other Essays* (New York: Washington Square Press, 1963), pp. 87–104. The idea of evaluative and creative "communities of sentiment" was later developed in Bourne's writings on cultural nationalism.

11. Bourne, "The Life of Irony," p. 107.

12. Daniel Aaron, "American Prophet," *New York Review of Books* 25 (November 23, 1978): 37–38.

13. Randolph S. Bourne, "The War and the Intellectuals," *Seven Arts* 2 (June 1917): 146.

14. In Lacanian discourse, the Real functions as this regulative fiction, in the space between the represented (the symbolic) and the representation (reality).

15. Bourne, "The Life of Irony," pp. 109, 116, 124–25.
16. Ibid., pp. 107, 120.
17. Ibid., 109.
18. Olaf Hansen, ed., "Introduction," in *The Radical Will* (New York: Urizen Books, 1977), p. 37.
19. "Bourne, The Life of Irony," p. 110.
20. Ibid., pp. 108–9.
21. Ibid., pp. 109, 105.
22. Georg Lukács, *The Theory of the Novel* (1971; rpt., Cambridge: MIT Press, 1977), pp. 14, 74, 75, 93.
23. Randolph S. Bourne, "The Art of Theodore Dreiser," *Dial* 62 (June 14, 1917): 507–9.
24. Thomas Mann, *Reflections of a Non-Political Man* (1918; New York: Frederick Unger, 1983), p. 419 and chap. 12.
25. Friedrich Nietzsche, *Beyond Good and Evil,* trans. Walter Kaufmann (New York: Vintage Books, 1966), p. 52.
26. Bourne "The Life of Irony," p. 123.
27. Randolph S. Bourne to Carl Zigrosser, March 16, 1912, Bourne Papers, reprinted in Sandeen, ed., *Letters,* p. 50.

CHAPTER 5. YOUTH

1. Randolph S. Bourne to Alyse Gregory, December 1, 1914, Gregory Papers, reprinted in *Letters of Randolph S. Bourne,* ed. Eric Sandeen (Troy, N.Y.: Whitston, 1981), p. 276.
2. Randolph S. Bourne to Prudence Winterrowd, May 18, 1913, Bourne Papers, reprinted in Sandeen, ed., *Letters,* p. 86.
3. Randolph S. Bourne, "Youth," in *Youth and Life* (Boston: Houghton Mifflin, 1913), p. 20.
4. Randolph S. Bourne, "The Adventure of Life," in *Youth and Life,* pp. 167–68.
5. See, for example, [Max Coe], "Karen, A Portrait," *New Republic* 8 (September 23, 1916): 187–88, reprinted in Olaf Hansen, ed., *The Radical Will* (New York: Urizen Books, 1977), pp. 443–52; [Max Coe], "Making One's Own Contribution," *New Republic* 8 (August 26, 1916): 91–92; and Randolph S. Bourne to Alyse Gregory, January 19, 1914, Bourne Papers, reprinted in Sandeen, ed., *Letters,* p. 207.
6. See Randolph S. Bourne to Alyse Gregory, March 13, 1914, Gregory Papers, reprinted in Sandeen, ed., *Letters,* pp. 230–32; and [Unsigned],

"Social Workmanship," *New Republic* 4 (August 28, 1915): 108, a review of *The Field of Social Service,* ed. Philip Davis.

7. See [Unsigned], "The Issue in Vocational Education," *New Republic* 3 (June 26, 1915): 191–92, and [Unsigned], "A Policy in Vocational Education," *New Republic* 10 (February 17, 1917): 63–65.

8. For the scrubwomen controversy, see Randolph S. Bourne, Letter to the Editor, *Columbia Spectator* (February 24, 1913): n.p., and Letter to the Editor, *Columbia Spectator* (March 1, 1913): n.p., in the Bourne Papers. For the canon controversy, see "History of a Literary Radical," *Yale Review* 8 (April 1919): 468–84.

9. On this point, I share Edward Abrahams's view that "along with most cultural radicals, Bourne found the dominant political ideology of the era, progressivism, severely limited. The politics of reform, he thought, were designed mainly to make the system work and to preserve the status quo. Bourne regarded reformers as though they were engineers, and not architects" (see Abrahams, "Randolph Bourne on Feminism and Feminists," *Historian* 43 [May 1981]: 366).

10. Robert Wohl, *The Generation of 1914* (Cambridge: Harvard University Press, 1979), pp. 208–9. See also Annie Kriegel, "Generational Difference: The History of an Idea," *Daedalus* 7(4) (Fall 1978): 29–30.

11. Wohl, *Generation of 1914,* pp. 3, 38, 207.

12. Sherman Paul, "Randolph Bourne," reprinted in *Makers of American Thought,* ed. Ralph Ross (1966, rpt., Minneapolis: University of Minnesota Press 1974), pp. 120–56. On the distinctions between a community of choice and a community of age, see Kriegel, "Generational Difference," pp. 28–29.

13. Wohl, *Generation of 1914,* pp. 204–5.

14. For a thoughtful critique of generational theory as a "packaging of time" and a "commodification" of history, see Paul Lyons, "Teaching the Sixties," *Socialist Review* 15(1) (no. 79): 71–91. Lyons argues that generational consciousness, which he finds pervasive in contemporary American social thought, encourages the assumption that history runs "in discrete parts," obscuring the "continuity of the past into the present and future." The "worst consequence" of generational thought is "the packaging of time," so that "consciousness restricts itself to the decade one consumes," and self-identity is restricted to the time of one's youth or adolescence. Looking backward, in addition, becomes a passive experience rather than a process of critical history, and historical decades and generations become reduced to objects of nostalgia and fashion (pp. 72, 75–77, and passim).

15. Wohl, *Generation of 1914,* pp. 36–41.

16. Laura L. Nash, "Concepts of Existence: Greek Origins of Generational Thought," *Daedalus*, 107(4) (Fall 1978): 2. See as well this entire issue, which is devoted to the theme of generations.

17. Kriegel, "Generational Difference," pp. 28–29. See also the literature on students as a youth class organized around collective grievances to challenge traditional authority relations: Irving L. Horowitz and William Friedland, *The Knowledge Factory: Student Power and Academic Politics in America* (Chicago: Aldene Publishing Company, 1970), especially chap. 5, pp. 118–48; Paula S. Fass, *The Damned and the Beautiful: American Youth in the 1920s* (New York: Oxford University Press, 1977); and Helen Lefkowitz Horowitz, *Campus Life: Undergraduate Cultures from the End of the Eighteenth Century to the Present* (New York: Alfred A. Knopf, 1987), especially chap. 4, pp. 82–97.

18. Wohl, *Generation of 1914*, pp. 203–4. See also Kriegel, "Generational Difference," pp. 26–31.

19. Wohl, *Generation of 1914*, pp. 206–7, 210–12. See also Kriegel, "Generational Difference," pp. 26–28.

20. As Wohl indicates, the Great War ultimately split that generation in two, so that those people who survived perceived their lives to be divided into "before," "during," and "after" experiences, coinciding with the "stages of life known as youth, young manhood, and maturity" (*Generation of 1914*, p. 210).

21. G. Stanley Hall, *Adolescence: Its Psychology and Its Relations to Physiology, Anthropology, Sociology, Sex, Crime, Religion, and Education* (N.p.: Telegraph Books, 1981).

22. Cornelia A. P. Comer, "A Letter to the Rising Generation," *Atlantic Monthly* 108 (February 1911): 145–54 (emphasis added).

23. Randolph S. Bourne, "For Radicals," in *Youth and Life*, pp. 295–96.

24. Bourne, "Youth," pp. 14–15; Bourne, "The Two Generations," *Atlantic Monthly* 108 (May 1911): 591–98, reprinted in *Youth and Life*, pp. 31–52; Bourne, "For Radicals," pp. 294–95. The grammar of "youth" in his writings followed a nineteenth-century tradition of denoting a generational entity in terms of chronological age; so "youth," as a singular noun, denoted generally a postadolescent male in his early- to mid-twenties, and "youths," as a plural noun, signified young adult men. Within that locution, however, gender referents were sometimes applied, especially in the collective form, so that "youths" referred to young adults of both sexes, or, more ambiguously, of either sex. Bourne usually gender-specified his meaning in his writings, juxtaposing youths to "feminines." If he used no qualifier, however, his meaning was ambiguous, but as I suggest in this chapter, it was intentionally so as a way of universalizing the possibilities

of "perpetual youth." "Youth" as a singular noun, generally capitalized, was Bourne's term of art, a floating signifier to invoke either the experimental spirit of scientific modernism or the dionysian revelry of the artistic imagination. It was a term signifying a certain attitude or sensibility, thus a certain spirit of adventure and willingness to change, common potentially to both sexes and all generations, and it could change its signification depending on the encoding of the other, the older (Puritan) mind. For a semiology of "youth" in Europe, see Wohl, *Generation of 1914,* pp. 42ff.

25. Bourne, "Youth," p. 15.

26. The phrase is Hansen's, ed., *Radical Will,* p. 25.

27. James Hoopes, "The Culture of Progressivism: Croly, Lippmann, Brooks, and Bourne and the Idea of American Artistic Decadence," *Clio* 7(1) (1977): 91–111. See also Van Wyck Brooks, "The Younger Generation of 1915," in *The Confident Years: 1885–1915* (New York: E. P. Dutton and Company, 1952), pp. 491–512; Sidney Kaplan, "Social Engineers as Saviors: Effects of World War I on Some American Liberals," *Journal of the History of Ideas* 17 (June 1956): 347–69; Daniel Aaron, "American Prophet," *New York Review of Books* 25 (November 23, 1978): 36–40; Michael True, "The Social and Literary Criticism of Randolph Bourne: A Study of His Development As a Writer" (Ph.D. diss., Duke University, 1964). My view, in line with Hansen's, is that the idea of youth was meant to suggest a stance toward life for any individual of any generation. As a metaphor it functioned as an inspirational myth to encourage creativity, and even greatness, through deeds, consistent with Bourne's Sorelian and Nietzschean inclinations.

28. See, for instance, Randolph S. Bourne, "Maurice Barres and the Youth of France," *Atlantic Monthly* 114 (September 1914): 394–99; "Berlin in Wartime," *Travel* 24 (November 1914): 9–12, 58–59; "Impressions of Europe, 1913–14," *Columbia University Quarterly* 17 (March 1915): 109–26.

29. Randolph S. Bourne to Prudence Winterrowd, May 18, 1913, Bourne Papers, reprinted in Sandeen, ed., *Letters,* pp. 84–85.

30. Randolph S. Bourne, "The Virtues and Seasons of Life," in *Youth and Life,* p. 90.

31. On conservative youths, see Bourne, "Youth"; on the excesses of youthful rebellion, cf. Randolph S. Bourne, "The Dodging of Pressures," in *Youth and Life,* p. 266: "The youth of to-day are willful, selfish, heartless, in their rebellion."

32. Randolph S. Bourne to Carl Zigrosser, November 16, 1913, Bourne Papers, reprinted in Sandeen, ed., *Letters,* pp. 172–73.

33. See Michael Rogin, "Max Weber and Woodrow Wilson: The Iron Cage in Germany and America," *Polity* 3 (Summer 1971): 566–67.

34. Jane Addams, "The Subjective Necessity of Social Settlements,"

reprinted in *The American Intellectual Tradition: Volume 2, 1865 to the Present,* 2d ed., ed. David A. Hollinger and Charles Capper (1892; rpt., New York: Oxford University Press, 1993), pp. 159–64.

35. Cf. Kenneth Lynn, "The Rebels of Greenwich Village," *Perspectives in American History,* no. 8 (Cambridge: Harvard University Press, 1974), pp. 335–77.

36. See Carl Zigrosser, *My Own Shall Come to Me* (Philadelphia: Casa Laura, 1971), for a history of the Ferrer School and Zigrosser's career as an art museum curator.

37. Ronald Steele, *Walter Lippmann and the American Century* (Boston: Little, Brown, 1980), chap. 4, and William E. Leuchtenburg, "Walter Lippmann's *Drift and Mastery,*" in *Drift and Mastery,* ed. William E. Leuchtenburg (Madison: University of Wisconsin Press, 1985), p. 3.

38. Anne Norton, *Republic of Signs* (Chicago: University of Chicago Press, 1993), p. 130.

39. Walter Lippmann, *Drift and Mastery* (1914; rpt., Madison: University of Wisconsin Press, 1985), p. 16.

40. Lippmann, *Drift and Mastery,* pp. 16–19, 101–12. Cf. Christopher Lasch, *The New Radicalism in America, 1889–1963: The Intellectual as a Social Type* (New York: Vintage Books, 1965), p. 185. Lippmann's change of heart came, at least in part, from Graham Wallas's tutelage; see Leuchtenburg, "Introduction," and Steele, *Lippmann,* chap. 7.

41. Lippmann, *Drift and Mastery,* p. 98.

42. On the progressives' emphasis on education and training as a means of shaping social behavior and moral character, see Richard A. Hofstadter, *Anti-Intellectualism in American Life* (New York: Alfred A. Knopf, 1963), pp. 299–390; Robert A. Carlson, "Americanization as an Early Twentieth Century Adult Education Movement," *History of Education Quarterly* 10 (Winter 1970): 440–64; and Lasch, *New Radicalism,* p. 85.

43. Lasch, *New Radicalism,* argued that what Lippmann and the progressives feared most was conflict itself (pp. 162). See also C. Wright Mills, *The Sociological Imagination* (New York: Oxford University Press, 1959), pp. 84–91. Cf. Fass, *The Damned,* pp. 13–52, who distinguishes Lippmann, a "traditionalist," from the "progressives" of the *New Republic* in terms of their differing views on social conflict, the need for order and opportunities for cultural renewal.

44. Lippmann, *Drift and Mastery,* pp. 42–44, 98–99, 146–51, 155–56, 154–57.

45. Randolph S. Bourne to Dorothy Teall, June 14, 1915, Bourne Papers, reprinted in Sandeen, ed., *Letters,* p. 303.

46. Bourne, "The Two Generations," pp. 40–41.

47. Ibid., pp. 33–39; Bourne, "Our Educational Prospect," *New Republic* 3 (June 26, 1915): 202–3.

48. See Joseph Featherstone, "Foreword," in *Randolph Silliman Bourne: Education Through Radical Eyes,* by Thomas N. Walters (Kennebunkport, Maine: Mercer House, 1982), p. i.

49. Bourne, "The Dodging of Pressures," pp. 118, 116.

50. Randolph S. Bourne, "Education as Living," *New Republic* 8 (August 5, 1916): 10–12. Bourne's critique of the progressives' emphasis on centralization, administration, efficiency, and expertise also appears in his articles endorsing the proposed installation of several Gary-type schools in the Bronx and Brooklyn, New York, in 1915 and, in an unrelated development, on the separation of administration from curricular development in the colleges. See [Unsigned], "The Schools from the Outside," *New Republic* 1 (January 30, 1915): [Unsigned], "The Organic School," *New Republic* 4 (August 21, 1915): 10–11; "Democracy and University Administration," *Educational Review* (May 1915): 455–59; "Medievalism in the Colleges," *New Republic* 4 (August 28, 1915): 87–88; "The Portland School Survey," *New Republic* 5 (January 8, 1916): 238–39; "The School Situation in New York," *New Republic* 6 (February 5, 1916): 6–8; and "Experimental Education," *New Republic* 10 (April 21, 1917): 345–47.

51. Diane Ravitch provides a graphic illustration of rote learning techniques and behaviorist training in her study of the history and politics of the New York City school system. She recounts that a visitor to a classroom noted the following exchange: "The teacher drew a line on the blackboard and asked, 'What is this?' The first pupil replied, 'It is a line.' The teacher: 'What kind of a line?' The second pupil: 'It is a straight line.' The teacher then drew a crooked line and asked, 'What is this?' The third pupil: 'It is a crooked line.' The teacher: 'Wrong.' At once the fourth pupil said, 'It is a line.' And the teacher: 'What kind of a line?' Fifth pupil: 'It is a crooked line.' The teacher explained (to the visitor) that the student who made a wrong answer was new to the class and had not yet learned the set routine of two questions and two answers." Diane Ravitch, *The Great School Wars: A History of the Public Schools as a Battlefield of Social Change, New York City, 1908–1973* (New York: Basic Books, 1974), p. 128. For Bourne's critique of a teacher-centered education emphasizing rote learning, see "The College Lecture Course as the Student Sees It," *Educational Review* 46 (June 1913): 66–70; "In a Schoolroom, *New Republic* 1 (November 7, 1914): 23–24; [Unsigned], "Puzzle Education," and [Unsigned], "What Might Be in Education," review of *What Is and What Might Be,* by Edmond Holmes, *New Republic* 1 (January 2, 1915): 10–11 and 28; [Unsigned], "The Schools from the Outside," *New Republic* 1 (Jan-

uary 30, 1915): 10–11; "When We Went to School," *New Republic* 2 (February 27, 1915): 101–3; "The Wasted Years," *New Republic* 3 (June 5, 1915): 120–22; "Medievalism in the Colleges," pp. 87–88; and "Education as Living," pp. 10–12. In this regard, Bourne's educational theory anticipates the critique of the "banking" system of education later formulated by Paulo Freire.

52. Studies of the progressive movement in educational reform have analyzed in greater detail its conflicting biases and contradictory goals. See, in this regard, Hofstadter, *Anti-Intellectualism*, pp. 173–322 and passim; Sol Cohen, *Progressives and Urban School Reform: The Public Education Association of New York City, 1895–1954* (New York: Teachers' College of Columbia University, 1963); Lawrence A. Cremin, *The Transformation of the School: Progressivism in American Education, 1876–1957* (New York: Vintage, 1961); Ravitch, *Great School Wars*, pp. 107–85; and Featherstone, "Foreword," pp. i–ix.

53. See, for instance, Randolph S. Bourne, "John Dewey's Philosophy," *New Republic* 2 (March 13, 1915): 154–56; [Unsigned], "Our Educational Prospect," *New Republic* 3 (June 26, 1915): 210–11, a review of *Schools of Tomorrow*, by John Dewey and Evelyn Dewey; Bourne to John Erskine, April 25, 1916, Bourne Papers, reprinted in Sandeen, ed., *Letters*, p. 367.

54. John Dewey and Evelyn Dewey, *Schools of Tomorrow* (New York: E. P. Dutton, 1915), pp. 287–316 and passim; and *Democracy and Education: An Introduction to the Philosophy of Education* (New York: Macmillan, 1916), pp. 81–100.

55. Only one commentator, a friend of Bourne's, draws the connection between Bourne's socialism and his educational democracy. See Carl Zigrosser, "Randolph Bourne and the Gary Schools," *The Modern School* 6(4) (October 1917): 155–57. See Randolph S. Bourne, [Unsigned} "The Democratic School," *New Republic* 4 (October 23, 1915): 297–99.

56. Bourne, "The Democratic School."

57. Ibid., p. 297.

58. Randolph S. Bourne, *The Gary Schools*, intro. William Wirt (Boston: Houghton Mifflin Company, 1916). See also "Schools in Gary," *New Republic* 2 (March 27, 1915): 198–99; "Communities for Children," *New Republic* 2 (April 3, 1915): 233–34; "Really Public Schools," *New Republic* 2 (April 10, 1915): 259–61; "Apprentices to the School," *New Republic* 2 (April 24, 1915): 302–3; "The Natural School," *New Republic 2* (May 1, 1915): 326–28; "The Democratic School," 297–99; "The Gary Public Schools," *Scribner's Magazine* 60 (September 1916): 371–80; and "New York and the Gary School System, *Educational Administration and Supervision* 2 (1916): 284–89.

59. See, for instance, Randolph S. Bourne, "Continuation Schools,"

New Republic 7 (June 10, 1916): 143–45, and "Extending the University," *New Republic* 9 (January 6, 1917): 259–60.

60. For the political battle over the Gary plan in New York, see Featherstone, "Foreword," pp. vi–vii.

61. See, for instance, Randolph S. Bourne, "New York and The Gary School System," 277–84; [Unsigned], "The School Situation in New York," *New Republic* 6 (February 5, 1916): 6–8; [Unsigned], "Politics Against the Schools," *New Republic* 6 (February 12, 1916): 32–33; [Unsigned], "Education for Work," *New Republic* 6 (March 11, 1916): 145–46; [Unsigned], "Organized Labor on Education," *New Republic* 7 (May 6, 1916): 8–9.

62. Hofstadter, *Anti-Intellectualism,* pp. 375–77.

63. See, for instance, Randolph S. Bourne, "The Professor," *New Republic* 3 (July 10, 1915): 257–58; "Who Owns the Universities?" *New Republic* 3 (July 17, 1915): 269–70; [Juvenis], "One of Our Conquerors," *New Republic* 4 (September 4, 1915): 121–23; and "Thinking at Seventy-Six," *New Republic* 12 (August 15, 1917): 111–13, a review of *The New Reservation of Time* by William Jewett Tucker.

64. Bourne, "The Adventure of Life," p. 267.

65. Bourne, "Youth," pp. 25, 27, and "The Two Generations," p. 51.

66. Bourne, "Youth," pp. 19–20.

67. Bourne, "The Adventure of Life," p. 179; "Some Thoughts on Religion," reprinted in *Youth and Life,* p. 196. See also Mills, *Sociological Imagination,* pp. 76–99.

68. Randolph S. Bourne to Carl Zigrosser, April 19, 1912, Carl Zigrosser Papers, University of Pennsylvania, reprinted in Sandeen, ed., *Letters,* p. 52.

69. Bourne, "Some Thoughts on Religion," p. 196.

70. Randolph S. Bourne to Prudence Winterrowd, March 2, 1913, Bourne Papers, reprinted in Sandeen, ed., *Letters,* p. 67.

71. Bourne, "The Adventure of Life," pp. 166–67.

72. Randolph S. Bourne to Prudence Winterrowd, February 5, 1913, Bourne Papers, reprinted in Sandeen, ed., *Letters,* pp. 71–72.

73. Randolph S. Bourne to Prudence Winterrowd, March 2, 1913, ibid., p. 71.

74. Randolph S. Bourne, "Maeterlinck and the Unknown," *New Republic* 1 (November 14, 1914): 26, a review of *The Unknown Guest,* by M. Maeterlinck, and *The New Philosophy of Henri Bergson,* by E. LeRoy. Cf. Randolph S. Bourne, "The Mystic Turned Radical,"*Atlantic Monthly* 109 (February 1912): 236–38.

75. Randolph S. Bourne to Alyse Gregory, January 19, 1914, Gregory Papers, reprinted in Sandeen, ed., *Letters,* p. 206.

76. Sherman Paul, *Randolph Bourne* (Minneapolis: University of Minnesota Press, 1966), p. 130.

77. A typical *New Republic* editorial endorsing the importance of social control stated, "The underlying notion of modern radicalism is to substitute a conscious social control for accident and confusion" ([Unsigned], *New Republic* 5 [November 6, 1915]: 1). Herbert Croly's *Promise of American Life* (New York: Macmillan, 1909), a foundational text for American progressives, conceived of social reform as a consequence of personal regeneration through an inner transformation to an ethic of self-control. "The individual released, disciplined and purified, will be the soil" for a "Christian Sparta" (p. 99). See also Edward Stettner for an analysis of Croly's political theory in *Promise* as aligned with the liberalism of L. T. Hobhouse (*Shaping Modern Liberalism* [Lawrence: University Press of Kansas, 1993], pp. 50–53).

78. ["Juvenis"], "The 'Scientific Manager,'" Bourne Papers, (n.d.), first published in Hansen, ed., *Radical Will*, pp. 290–303. See also "What Is Exploitation?" *New Republic* 9 (November 4, 1916): 12–14, reprinted in Hansen, ed., *Radical Will*, pp. 285–89; "New Ideals in Business," *Dial* 62 (February 22, 1917): 133–34; Review of *America and the New Epoch*, by Charles P. Steinmetz, and *An Approach to Business Problems*, by A. W. Shaw, and reprinted in Hansen, ed., *Radical Will*, pp. 294–97. Cf. ["Juvenis"], "The Architect," *New Republic* 5 (January 1, 1916): 222–23, and reprinted in Hansen, ed., *Radical Will*, pp. 279–81. Cf. Casey Blake, *Beloved Community* (Chapel Hill: University of North Carolina Press, 1990), who finds Bourne's cultural radicalism to be more sympathetic to the scientific foundations of progressivism, citing Bourne's own instrumentalism in his support of the idea of a civilian corps of young reformers as the "moral equivalent" of military troops and his early support of Dewey, rather than James (pp. 93ff); cf. Abrahams, "Bourne on Feminism and Feminists," p. 366.

79. Bourne, "The Experimental Life," p. 229.

80. Randolph S. Bourne to Simon Pelham Barr, January 19, 1914, Bourne Papers, reprinted in Sandeen, ed., *Letters*, p. 207.

81. See, for instance, Nancy Cott, *The Grounding of Modern Feminism* (New Haven: Yale University Press, 1987), p. 35.

82. Randolph S. Bourne to Prudence Winterrowd, April 28, 1913, Bourne Papers, reprinted in Sandeen, ed., *Letters*, p. 82. Cf. Carroll Smith-Rosenberg, "The New Woman as Androgyne: Social Disorder and Gender Crisis, 1879–1936, in *Disorderly Conduct: Visions of Gender in Victorian America* (New York: Alfred A. Knopf, 1985), pp. 245–96.

83. Randolph S. Bourne to Alyse Gregory, January 19, 1914, Gregory Papers, reprinted in Sandeen, ed., *Letters*, p. 207.

84. Randolph S. Bourne, "Chivalry and Sin," review of *The Cry of Youth,* by Harry Kemp, and *The Americans,* by John Curtis Underwood (n.d.), first published in Hansen, ed., *Radical Will,* pp. 485–88.

85. Randolph S. Bourne to Alyse Gregory, January 19, 1914, Gregory Papers, reprinted in Sandeen, ed., *Letters,* p. 207.

86. Bourne, "Chivalry and Sin," p. 488.

87. Randolph S. Bourne to Prudence Winterrowd, November 3, 1913, Bourne Papers, reprinted in Sandeen, ed., *Letters,* p. 171.

88. Randolph S. Bourne to Carl Zigrosser, April 2, 1912, Zigrosser Papers, reprinted in Sandeen, ed., *Letters,* p. 51.

89. Contemporary feminist theorists of power have also redefined power "as energy, strength, and effectiveness" that "need not be the same as power which requires domination of others." See Nancy Hartsock, "Political Change: Two Perspectives on Power," *Quest* 1(1) (Summer 1974): 10–25, and "Staying Alive," *Quest* 3(3) (Winter 1976–1977): 2–14.

90. Randolph S. Bourne to Prudence Winterrowd, November 3, 1913, Bourne Papers, reprinted in Sandeen, ed., *Letters,* p. 171.

91. Randolph S. Bourne to Alyse Gregory, January 19, 1914, Gregory Papers, reprinted in Sandeen, ed., *Letters,* p. 207.

92. Lippmann, *Drift and Mastery,* p. 126.

93. For a more sympathetic reading of Lippmann's views of the feminist movement and on science, see David A. Hollinger, "Science and Anarchy," *American Quarterly* 29 (1977): 463–75, reprinted in Hollinger, *In the American Province: Studies in the History and Historiography of Ideas* (Bloomington: Indiana University Press, 1985), pp. 44–55.

Chapter 6. Intellectuals at War

1. For a review of the myths surrounding Bourne's opposition to the war, see A. Beringause, "The Double Martyrdom of Randolph Bourne," *Journal of the History of Ideas* 18 (1957): 594–603.

2. Friends and colleagues who viewed Bourne's "irreconcilability" as pacifism include Elsie Clews Parsons, "A Pacifist Patriot," *Dial* 68 (March 1920): 367–70, and Freda Kirchwey, "Randolph Bourne," *Nation* 3 (December 1, 1920): 619, review of Van Wyck Brooks, *History of a Literary Radical and Other Essays.* See also Sherman Paul, *Randolph Bourne* (Minneapolis: University of Minnesota Presss, 1966); Paul F. Bourke, "The Status of Politics 1909–1919: The *New Republic,* Randolph Bourne and Van Wyck Brooks," *Journal of American Studies* 8(2) (August 1974): 198–99; Michael Walzer, "The War and Randolph Bourne," in *The Company of Critics* (New

York: Basic Books, 1988), p. 56; and Gary Bullert, *The Politics of John Dewey* (Buffalo: Prometheus Books, 1983), p. 63. (Bullert also claimed that Bourne was an anarchist.) Cf. John Moreau, *Randolph Bourne* (Washington, D.C.: Public Affairs Press, 1966), pp. 160–61. Bourne's own distinction between his position and that of the religious or political pacifist, conscientious objector, or both is developed in "Below the Battle," *Seven Arts* 2 (July 1917): 270–77, and "Conscience and Intelligence in War," *Dial* 63 (September 13, 1917): 193–95. For a further indication that Bourne did not dismiss out of hand a policy of armed defense, see "The Collapse of American Strategy," *Seven Arts* 2 (August 1917): 409–24, for a discussion of the strategy of a limited naval war aimed at the "destruction of the attacking submarines" of the German forces.

3. Thomas Bender, *New York Intellect* (New York: Alfred A. Knopf, 1987), p. 243.

4. See, however, Charles Beard, "A Statement," *New Republic* 13 (December 29, 1917): 249–51. For Bourne's defense of Cattel and Dana, see "The Inquisition of Columbia," *New York Tribune*, March 16, 1917; "Conspirators," *Seven Arts* 2 (August 1917): 528–30; and "Those Columbia Trustees," *New Republic* 12 (October 20, 1917): 328–29. On academic freedom, see "Who Owns the Universities?" *New Republic* 3 (July 17, 1915): 269–70; "Democracy and University Administration," *Educational Review* (May 1915): 455–59; and "The Idea of a University," *Dial* 63 (November 22, 1917): 509–10. See also Carol S. Gruber, *Mars and Minerva* (Baton Rouge: Louisiana State University Press, 1975), p. 205; and Clyde Barrow, *Universities and the Capitalist State* (Madison: University of Wisconsin Press, 1990), especially chapters 7 and 8.

5. Heinrich von Treitschke, *Politics* (New York: Macmillan, 1916), 1: xxxi, 64–65, and 3–106 passim. Treitschke venerated the power of the state, particularly as revealed in war, and scorned the "dream of eternal peace," in which people's attention would be diverted from the state and "underrate" it.

6. John Diggins, *The American Left in the Twentieth Century* (New York: Harcourt Brace Jovanovich, 1973), pp. 34–39; cf. John Diggins, *The Promise of Pragmatism* (Chicago: University of Chicago Press, 1994), chap. 3, where knowledge for James was linked to desire—the desire to know, the need to resolve doubt—and therefore to pleasure or the satisfaction of desire. See also Howard M. Feinstein, *Becoming William James* (Ithaca, N.Y.: Cornell University Press, 1984), for James's desire to resolve the anxieties of a "sick soul." Cf. Diggins, *Promise,* chap. 5, on Dewey's pragmatism as an attempt to merge religious faith with scientific analysis. For a similar interpretation, see Alan Ryan, *John Dewey and the High Tide of Amer-*

ican Liberalism (New York: Norton, 1995). Cf. Robert B. Westbrook, *John Dewey and American Democracy* (Ithaca, N.Y.: Cornell University Press, 1991), who sees Dewey alternatively as a social or a moral democrat.

7. Randolph S. Bourne, "Twilight of Idols," *Seven Arts* 2 (October 1917): 688–702, reprinted in *War and the Intellectuals,* ed. Carl Resek (New York: Harper and Row, 1964), p. 56. For a sympathetic study of Dewey's shift from issues of education to issues of central planning and political action, see Alan Cywar, "John Dewey: Toward Domestic Reconstruction 1915–20," *Journal of the History of Ideas* 30 (1969): 385–400, and "John Dewey in World War I," *American Quarterly* 21 (1969): 578–95. Paul F. Bourke also recalled that Dewey thought philosophy "recovers itself when it ceases to be a device for dealing with the problems of philosophers and becomes a method, cultivated by philosophers for dealing with the problems of men" (quoted in Bourke, "Philosophy and Social Criticism: John Dewey 1910–1920," *History of Education Quarterly* 15 [Spring 1975]: 6).

8. Cf. Bruce Clayton, *Forgotten Prophet* (Baton Rouge: Louisiana State University Press, 1984), who argued that Bourne committed "intellectual suicide" with his antiwar articles, effectively putting his career as a political critic to an end (p. 202).

9. James Oppenheim offered an affectionate tribute to Bourne in "The Story of the *Seven Arts,*" *American Mercury* 20 (June 1930): 156–64, acknowledging the risks of publishing Bourne's essays, which he, as editor, willingly undertook.

10. Randolph S. Bourne to Everett Benjamin, November 26, 1917, Bourne Papers, reprinted in *Letters of Randolph Bourne,* ed. Eric Sandeen (Troy, N.Y.: Whitston, 1981), p. 404.

11. The details of the *Dial* controversy are told most authoritatively by Nicholas Joost, *Scofield Thayer and the Dial* (Carbondale: Southern Illinois University Press, 1964), 4–13, 37, 78, 188, 201, 230–32, 265, 271–72, and Joost, "Culture vs. Power: Randolph Bourne, John Dewey and the *Dial,*" *Midwest Quarterly* (April 1968): 245–58. See also letters from Bourne, Bourne Papers, reprinted in Sandeen, ed., *Letters,* pp. 415, 419, 423. The story is a complicated one. After the *Dial* came out in support of the war in 1917, Bourne's position there became increasingly precarious. Martin Johnson, the journal's editor, was wary of the confrontational tone of his articles and decided that Bourne was a liability who had to go. Through the intercession of Scofield Thayer, a friend and admirer of Bourne's and a financial backer of the journal, Bourne's demotion or outright firing was prevented for about a year, and he remained unsuspecting of the contest between Thayer and Johnson. Meanwhile, Johnson was courting Dewey, and one of Dewey's demands was that Bourne be let go. Bourne

remained on the editorial board in 1917 at Thayer's insistence but was not invited to editorial conferences and was isolated by the supporters of Johnson and Dewey; in the last year he wrote only reviews. Eventually the staff became so split over the feud between Thayer and Johnson, and Bourne and Dewey, that when the journal moved to New York, Johnson reorganized the staff and placed Dewey in charge. Bourne was out of a job; Thayer resigned in support of Bourne and within a year had severed all ties with the journal, including financial support. Ironically, Dewey left the journal within the next year, traveling first to California and then to China to set up education programs.

12. See Westbrook, *Dewey and American Democracy,* pp. 195–212; Diggins, *Promise,* pp. 250–59; Ryan, *Dewey,* pp. 157, 341; and Posnock, "Politics," 49–54. Westbrook documents carefully the changes in Dewey's thought after the war and argues that Dewey ultimately embraced Bourne's critique of instrumentalism and considerably more radical politics, thus vindicating Bourne's wartime critique (a conclusion to which Diggins takes exception). The nature of Dewey's postwar politics, although outside the purview of this book's focus, nevertheless appears to be quite different, in my view, from Bourne's politics both before or during the war. Though Dewey became a noninterventionist in World War II, Bourne's argument was that modern war exaggerated the bipolarity of liberal politics so that neither militarism (intervention) nor pacifism (nonintervention) was an adequate response to the political and cultural aspects of international conflict and cooperation. Moreover, his politics both before and during the war were distinctly nonstatist, often personal politics; and Dewey's politics—which he sometimes called a "radical liberalism" and which Westbrook has called a democratic socialism—seem nearly always to have included some degree of state intervention or involvement.

13. C. W. Mills, *Sociology and Pragmatism* (New York: Oxford University Press, 1966).

14. Bourne, "Below the Battle," in Resek, ed., *War and the Intellectuals,* pp. 15–21. The title inverts Romaine Rolland's "Above the Battle" and by implication its pacifist stance. See also Bourne, "A War Diary," *Seven Arts* 2 (September 1917): 535–47, reprinted in Resek, ed., *War and the Intellectuals,* pp. 41, 43.

15. Posnock, "Politics," p. 35.

16. Bourne, "A War Diary," p. 45.

17. David Kennedy, *Over Here* (New York: Oxford University Press, 1980), chap. 1.

18. Bourke, "Status of Politics," pp. 186–87.

19. Herbert Croly to Randolph S. Bourne, September 15, 1914, Bourne Papers.

20. Edward Stettner, *Shaping Modern Liberalism* (Lawrence: University Press of Kansas, 1993), chap. 7.

21. Editorial, *New Republic* 1 (November 7, 1914): 1. See also Croly's letter to Dorothy and Willard Straight, which suggested that the role of the critic was to "transmute the experience the American people will obtain . . . into socially formative knowledge" (quoted in Bender, *New York Intellect,* p. 227).

22. William E. Leuchtenburg, "Progressivism and Imperialism: The Progressive Movement and American Foreign Policy, 1898–1916," *Mississippi Valley Historical Review,* 39(3) (December 1952): 483–504. See also William Appleman Williams, *The Tragedy of American Diplomacy* (New York: Dell, 1959) for the view that U.S. diplomacy has been based on objectives of imperialism and economic expansion.

23. Leuchtenburg, "Progressivism," p. 490, quoting Herbert Croly in *Willard Straight* (New York: Macmillan, 1924), pp. 422ff., 503.

24. Croly, *Promise of American Life,* pp. 289–90, 301–33, 169.

25. Ibid., p. 500.

26. There is some debate among historians over the nature and content of the *New Republic*'s foreign policy during the years of preparedness and mobilization. Bourke ("The Status of Politics," pp. 176–87) argues that Croly in particular, and the editors in general, lacked any commitment to specific political reforms or policies but aimed deliberately to transcend the contingency of social and political events or programs and to discuss issues of a more "permanent" nature. In Bourke's reading, their abstract and idealistic rhetoric signified their intent to speculate on hypothetical institutional arrangements and social plans, articulating common principles and broad objectives rather than narrow, partisan preferences. Charles Forcey, by contrast, in *The Crossroads of Liberalism: Croly, Weyl, Lippmann, and the Progressive Era, 1900–1925* (New York: Oxford University Press, 1961), p. 270 and chap. 8, passim, argues that the *New Republic*'s editors "effectively made over Wilson's foreign policy into their own," a policy that did not square with their own liberal principles but that they eventually had to embrace, once the turn of events took away their hopes of controlling them. Finally, Christopher Lasch, *The New Radicalism in America, 1889–1963* (New York: Vintage Books, 1965), pp. 184, 192, and chap. 6, passim, suggests, along with Bourke, although for different reasons, that the editors lacked a specific or concrete foreign policy and agrees with Forcey, again on a somewhat different basis, that they "improvised" a foreign policy, but only when it was forced upon them by political, military,

and diplomatic events, and they became dissatisfied with neutrality because it contributed to their passive observation from the sidelines. The consensus, if there is one, seems to be that, for whatever combination of reasons, a specific foreign policy did emerge among the *New Republic*'s editors, a policy that bore a striking resemblance to the militarist nationalism of the Progressive party. In my reading, the rhetoric in *New Republic* editorials between 1914 and 1918 reflects a solid support for the Progressive party's domestic and foreign policy initiatives, i.e., for a vastly increased role of the state—supporting rather than merely supervising the relations between large, organized interests and the government—and for the role of an activist state as a major actor in the world order.

27. James Harvey Robinson, "A Journal of Opinion," *New Republic* 3 (May 8, 1915): 9–11.

28. Amos Pinchot, "A Communication," *New Republic* 3 (May 29, 1915): 95.

29. See John Dewey, *Characters and Events,* ed. Joseph Ratner (New York: Henry Holt, 1929), p. 91.

30. See, for instance, John Dewey, "Timid Neutrality," *New Republic* 1 (November 14, 1914): 7; Dewey, "Pacifism vs. Passivism," *New Republic* 1 (December 12, 1914): 7; and Dewey, "Aggressive Pacifism," *New Republic* 5 (January 15, 1916): 263–65.

31. Walter Lippmann, "Uneasy America," *New Republic* 5 (December 25, 1915): 195–96.

32. See, for instance, John Dewey, "War at Any Price," *New Republic* 5 (November 27, 1915): 84–85.

33. John Dewey, "In a Time of National Hesitation," *Seven Arts* 2 (May 1917): 6.

34. John Dewey, "What Are We Fighting For?" *Independent* 94 (June 22, 1918): 474, 481.

35. Westbrook suggests that Dewey initially gave his support to the war because he took seriously the idea of an international democracy, thinking the war might be the way to spread democracy, and because he was opposed to German absolutism, which he considered to be hostile to pragmatism (*Dewey and American Democracy,* pp. 197–202). Dewey's *New Republic* writings on the war are reprinted in *Characters and Events,* ed. Joseph Ratner (New York: Henry Holt, 1929), vols. 1, 2. Bourne objected specifically to Dewey's "Conscience and Compulsion," "The Future of Pacifism," "What America Will Fight For," and "Conscription of Thought" (reprinted in Ratner).

36. John Dewey, "The Future of Pacifism," *New Republic* 11 (July 28, 1917): 359.

37. John Dewey, "The Social Possibilities of War," reprinted in Ratner, ed., *Characters,* 2: 558. Dewey suggests that this arrangement is a form of democratic socialism, temporarily requiring the intervention and administration of the state, but it appears to be a form of corporatism.

38. John Dewey, "Conscience and Compulsion," *New Republic* 11 (July 14, 1917): 298; "Conscription of Thought," *New Republic* 12 (September 1, 1917): 128–30; "In Explanation of Our Lapse," *New Republic* 13 (November 3, 1917): 17. Westbrook notes that Dewey made a distinction between force (energy) and violence to evaluate pragmatically which was the more efficient means of accomplishing a certain end and argues that only when war became the most efficient means was Dewey willing to support it (*Dewey and American Democracy,* pp. 201–2, quoting from "Force and Coersion," *New Republic* [1916]). Cf. Daniel Levine, "Randolph Bourne, John Dewey and the Legacy of Liberalism," *Antioch Review* 29 (Summer 1969: 234–44), who suggests that Dewey thought force and violence were morally neutral, thus enabling him to be ethically uncompromised in his support for war.

39. Walter Lippmann, "Morale," *New Republic* 10 (April 21, 1917): 337–38.

40. [Unsigned], "Who Willed American Participation?" *New Republic* 10 (April 14, 1917): 308–10.

41. Randolph S. Bourne, "The War and the Intellectuals," *Seven Arts* 2 (June 1917): 133–46, reprinted in Resek, ed., *War and the Intellectuals,* pp. 3–14.

42. Bourne, "Twilight of Idols," pp. 59–60.

43. Michel Foucault, *Discipline and Punish* (1977; rpt., New York: Vintage Books, 1979).

44. Randolph S. Bourne to Prudence Winterrowd, February 5, 1913, Bourne Papers, reprinted in Sandeen, ed., *Letters,* p. 71.

45. Bourne, "Twilight of Idols," pp. 60–61.

46. Ibid., pp. 61, 63.

47. See Casey Blake, *Beloved Community* (Chapel Hill: University of North Carolina Press, 1990), on Bourne's own instrumentalism (pp. 97–98).

48. The author thanks Michael Weinstein for this argument.

49. For an indication of the range of political values (not to say "private utopias") to which pragmatism has been applied, see *Pragmatism in Law and Society,* ed. Michael Brint and William Weaver (Boulder, Colo.: Westview Press, 1991).

50. Bourne, "Twilight of Idols," p. 55.

51. Levine, "Bourne, Dewey," pp. 238–39; Rick Tilman, *C. Wright Mills: A Native Radical and His American Intellectual Roots* (University Park: Pennsylvania State University, 1984), p. 150. Cf. Bullert, *Politics of Dewey,* who

reduced Bourne's critique of Dewey's wartime pragmatism to a personal vendetta and a "demonic quest for notoriety" (pp. 60–64). Bullert thoroughly misunderstands Bourne's position claiming that he wanted a German victory and thereby misunderstood Dewey's arguments on political grounds.

52. Mills, *Sociological Imagination,* pp. 111–41. See also R. Jeffrey Lustig, *Corporate Liberalism* (Berkeley: University of California Press, 1982), pp. 150–94.

53. Bourne, "A War Diary," p. 43, and "The War and the Intellectuals," p. 64.

54. Friedrich Nietzsche, *On the Genealogy of Morals,* trans. Walter Kaufmann (1887; rpt., New York: Modern Library, 1968), Third Essay. For an interpretation stressing the temporarily salutary influences of the ascetic priest as "physician" and "healer," see Tracy B. Strong, *Friedrich Nietzsche and the Politics of Transfiguration* (Berkeley: University of California Press, 1975), pp. 254–59.

55. William James, *The Letters of William James,* ed. Henry James (Boston: Atlantic Monthly, 1920), 2: 100–101, quoted in Diggins, *American Left,* p. 28; see also William James, "The Social Value of the College-Bred," *McClure's* 3 (1908): 419–22.

56. John Dewey, *Ethics* (New York, 1908), p. 26, quoted in Sidney Kaplan, "Social Engineers as Saviors," *Journal of the History of Ideas* 17 (June 1956): 349; Karl Mannheim, *Ideology and Utopia: An Introduction to the Sociology of Knowledge,* trans. Louis Wirth and Edward Shils (New York: Harcourt, Brace and World, 1936), pp. 153–71. See also Alvin W. Gouldner's revisionist application of a Mannheimian intellectual in *The Future of Intellectuals and the Rise of the New Class* (New York: Seabury Press, 1979).

57. See, for instance, [Unsigned], "What Is Opinion?," *New Republic* 4 (September 18, 1915): 171–72; cf. Bourke, "Status of Politics," on Bourne's advocacy of disengagement from contemporary and partisan affairs (pp. 188–89).

58. Julien Benda, *The Treason of the Intellectuals* (*La Traison des Clercs*), trans. Richard Aldington (Boston: Beacon, 1955).

59. Randolph S. Bourne to Van Wyck Brooks, March 27, 1918, Van Wyck Brook Papers, Van Pelt Library, University of Pennsylvania, reprinted in Sandeen, ed., *Letters,* pp. 410–14.

60. See, for instance, Casey Blake, "'Below the Battle,'" *Nation* (February 25, 1991): 239–41.

61. Randolph S. Bourne, "Old Tyrannies," in *The Radical Will,* ed. Olaf Hansen (New York: Urizen Books, 1977), p. 171.

62. Bourne, "The War and the Intellectuals," p. 11.

63. [Unsigned], "American Independence and the War," *Seven Arts* 1

(April 1917): 1. Cf. Forcey, *Crossroads,* on the liberals' gravitation toward power like "moths" to a flame.

64. Karl Marx, "On the Jewish Question," in *The Marx-Engels Reader,* ed. Robert C. Tucker (New York: W. W. Norton, 1972); Randolph Bourne, "The State," in *Untimely Papers,* ed. James Oppenheim (New York: B. W. Huebsch, 1919), reprinted in Resek, ed., *War and the Intellectuals,* pp. 65–104.

65. Bourne, "A War Diary," p. 36.

66. See, for instance, "Old Tyrannies": "So you have never overtaken the given. Actually you have fallen farther and farther behind. You have not affected the world you live in; you have been molded and shaped by it yourself. Your moral responsibility has been a myth, for you were never free enough to have any responsibility. While you thought you were making headway, you were really being devoured" (p. 170).

67. Posnock, "Politics," 51–52.

68. The phrase appears in Randolph S. Bourne, "The Cult of Convention," *Liberator* 1 (June 1918): 38–39, review of *On Contemporary Literature* by Stuart P. Sherman.

69. See Bob Jessop, *The Capitalist State* (New York: 1982; rpt., New York University Press, 1983), especially pp. 145–62, for the view of the state as an agent of social cohesion; cf. Max Lerner, "Randolph Bourne and Two Generations," in *Ideas for the Ice Age* (New York: Viking Press, 1941), pp. 116–42, who views Bourne's theory of the state as strictly an instrument of class domination (p. 72).

70. Randolph S. Bourne, "The New Revolution," *Columbia Monthly* 10 (May 1913): 221–27. It should be noted that the concept of the state was not solely the province of the left. In 1889 Woodrow Wilson aimed to revive a Jeffersonian model of a gentlemen's state rather than a state run by politicians, in his treatise "The State," in *The Papers of Woodrow Wilson,* ed. Arthur S. Link (Princeton: Princeton University Press, 1969), vol. 6 (1888–1890), pp. 244–396. Herbert Croly's *Promise of American Life* (New York: Macmillan, 1909) argued for a Hamiltonian state regulating corporations in the public interest. The state, in other words, was a viable concept in the latter half of the nineteenth century, an entity that reflected at least theoretically the blurring of the lines between public and private that was taking place under an ascendant corporate liberalism.

71. Bourne, "The State," in Resek, ed., *War and the Intellectuals,* pp. 80–81.

72. Ibid., pp. 68–69.

73. Jean-Jacques Rousseau, "The Social Contract," in *Social Contract,* ed. Ernest Barker (New York: Oxford University Press), pp. 175–76.

74. Bourne, "The State," pp. 79–80, 72.

75. For an illuminating discussion of the promises of universality in

the liberal state, see Michael A. Mosher, "Civic Identity in the Juridical Society: On Hegelianism as Discipline for the Romantic Mind," *Political Theory* 11(1) (1983): 117–32.

76. Bourne, "The State," pp. 69, 74–75.

77. Ibid., pp. 100–101, 103.

78. Ibid., pp. 77–79.

79. Ibid., pp. 76–78.

80. Ibid., pp. 75–76. See also "A War Diary,", pp. 36–47, where the disproportionate impact of the war on different classes is discussed.

81. Randolph S. Bourne to Van Wyck Brooks, March 27, 1918, Brooks Papers, reprinted in Sandeen, ed., *Letters,* pp. 413–14; Bourne, "The State," pp. 76–77.

82. Bourne, "Twilight of Idols," p. 60.

83. Bourne, "The State," pp. 78, 89.

84. See Randolph S. Bourne to Prudence Winterrowd, March 2, 1913, Bourne Papers, reprinted in Sandeen, ed., *Letters,* p. 76. "You tease me by misrepresenting James; he was very far from being a defender of existing conditions; indeed he wrote one of the most effective and practicable Utopias that has been suggested—'The Moral Equivalent of War.'" Cf. Bourne, "A Moral Equivalent for Universal Military Service," *New Republic* 7 (July 1,1916): 217–19, reprinted in Resek, ed., *War and the Intellectuals,* pp. 142–47, where he argued the idea was no longer utopic. See Blake, *Beloved Community,* on Bourne accepting the military equivalence thesis (pp. 97–99). For Bourne's own pragmatic analysis of the ends and means of military involvement and the idea of a limited military engagement, see "The Collapse of American Strategy," *Seven Arts* 2 (August 1917): 409–24.

85. Randolph S. Bourne to Van Wyck Brooks, March 27, 1918, Brooks Papers, reprinted in Sandeen, ed., *Letters,* p. 412.

CHAPTER 7. "TRANS-NATIONAL AMERICA"

1. Robert Frost to Louis Untermeyer, November 3, 1917, in *The Letters of Robert Frost to Louis Untermeyer,* ed. Louis Untermeyer (New York: Holt, Rinehart and Winston, 1963), p. 60. For a history of the short-lived *Seven Arts,* see Waldo Frank, "The Tragedy of the *Seven Arts,*" in *Memoirs of Waldo Frank,* ed. Alan Trachtenberg (Amherst: University of Massachusetts Press, 1973), pp. 83–95, and James Oppenheim, "The Story of the *Seven Arts,*" *American Mercury* 20 (June 1930): 156–64.

2. *Masses Publishing Company v. Patten,* 244 Fed. 535 (So. Dist., N.Y., 1917). The history of the suspension of civil liberties during World War

I has been extensively documented. See, for example, Harry N. Scheiber, *The Wilson Administration and Civil Liberties, 1917–21* (Ithaca, N.Y.: Cornell University Press, 1960); H. C. Peterson and Gilbert Fite, *Opponents of War, 1917–1918* (Seattle: University of Washington Press, 1968), chap. 5; James Weinstein, *The Decline of American Socialism in America* (New York: Vintage, 1969), chap. 3; Carol S. Gruber, *Mars and Minerva* (Baton Rouge: Louisiana State University Press, 1975); Paul L. Murphy, *World War I and the Origin of Civil Liberties in the United States* (New York: W. W. Norton, 1979); and David Kennedy, *Over Here* (New York: Oxford University Press, 1980), chap. 1.

3. Randolph S. Bourne to Van Wyck Brooks, March 27, 1918, Brooks Papers, reprinted in *Letters of Randolph Bourne,* ed. Eric Sandeen (Troy, N.Y.: Whitston, 1981), p. 412.

4. The familiar epigram, the "aestheticization of politics," is Walter Benjamin's, constructing the process of Fascist domination. See Walter Benjamin, "The Work of Art in the Age of Mechanical Reproduction," in *Illuminations,* ed. Hannah Arendt (New York: Schocken Books, 1968), p. 242. For a brilliant comparison of fascist and modern forms of aesthetic politics, see Linda Shulte-Sasse, "Leni Riefenstahl's Feature Films and the Question of a Fascist Aesthetic," *Cultural Critique* 18 (Spring 1991): 123–48.

5. Randolph S. Bourne to Everett Benjamin, November 26, 1917, Bourne Papers, reprinted in Sandeen, ed., *Letters,* p. 404.

6. See Michael Lind, *The Next American Nation: The New Nationalism and the Fourth American Revolution* (New York: Free Press, 1995), on the efforts of the "second republic" to create a common American identity on the basis of nativist assimilationism (chaps. 2 and 6); cf. Eldon J. Eisenach, *The Lost Promise of Progressivism* (Lawrence: University Press of Kansas, 1994), who is strangely silent on anti-immigration campaigns during the Progressive Era.

7. See, for instance, Michael Rogin, *Fathers and Children, Andrew Jackson and the Subjugation of the American Indian* (New York: Vintage Books, 1976), and *Ronald Reagan, The Movie and Other Episodes in Political Demonology* (Berkeley: University of California Press, 1987), and Ronald Takaki, *A Different Mirror: A History of Multicultural America* (Boston: Little, Brown, 1993).

8. The term was first used in 1924 by Horace Kallen.

9. To be sure, the question of American identity has been inseparably related to questions of its ethnic origins, according to Norman Jacobson, from the very beginning. Depending partly on when one dates its founding, America's national identity has been determined either to be

ethnically pure, a mixed amalgam of different races and nationalities, or a mixed and fundamentally unmeltable entity. The question of American identity and the meaning of America itself are complicated further by the fact that the "idea of America" preceded its "discovery" by European settlers. As early as 1519, European intellectuals began to refer to America as a once and future idea, part fantasy and part reality. A possession of the European imagination, and a term over which the European mind battled in its efforts to come to grips with its own failures and disappointments, America became a repository of European expectations and illusions. It symbolized at once the absence of European culture and an emblem of what could be, the potentiality and testing ground of their noblest ideals. Even today, the word "America" is ambiguous, denoting the name of an entire hemisphere and connoting at the same time a place, unspecified and indefinite.

10. Randolph Bourne, "A War Diary," in *War and the Intellectuals,* ed. Carl Resek (New York: Harper and Row, 1964), p. 46.

11. Randolph S. Bourne, "Our Cultural Humility," *Atlantic Monthly* 114 (October 1914): 503–7, reprinted in *History of a Literary Radical and Other Essays,* ed. Van Wyck Brooks (New York: B. W. Huebsch, 1920), p. 41. The original plans for the show, nearly two years in the making, were for a strictly American exhibit with the theme of the New Spirit, but they were set aside for the more ambitious plan of an international retrospective of modern art, tracing its origins from its nineteenth-century roots. It was a huge display of over 1,600 paintings, drawings, prints, and pieces of sculpture. Although American art dominated the exhibit in actual number of contributions, it was generally dwarfed by the public's reaction to the bold colors and shapes of the antirealism of the Europeans. For studies of the Armory Show and its impact, see Milton W. Brown, *The Story of the Armory Show* (New York: New York Graphic Society, 1963); B. L. Reid, *The Man from New York, John Quinn and His Friends* (New York: Oxford University Press, 1968); and Meyer Schapiro, "Rebellion in Art," in *America in Crisis,* ed. Daniel Aaron (New York: Alfred A. Knopf, 1952), pp. 203–42.

12. Randolph Bourne, "Trans-National America," in Resek, ed., *War and the Intellectuals,* p. 123.

13. The etymology of "culture" can be said to fall into three traditions. The first views culture as the intellectual, spiritual, and aesthetic development of a civilization. It focuses on the ideal of "cultivation" as the standard of a nation's progress. The second defines culture as a way of life of a people or group or as a form of life peculiar to a specific period of time. This tradition begins with Johann Herder (and implicitly with Hegel) and informs Thomas Jefferson's and de Tocqueville's studies of American

political culture; it is influential in the work of Charles Beard and Franz Boas in the 1910s. The third tradition refers to the works and practices of intellectual and artistic production. This conception focuses on the aesthetic processes, relations, and artifacts that constitute a nation's ideational identity. The first and third sense of the term are closely related, and in the case of Matthew Arnold, virtually identical. Bourne's conception of culture, and "national culture" in particular, falls in the second tradition primarily, as did the cultural nationalism of the writers on the *Seven Arts*. But he also wrote of culture in the third sense, in terms of the literature and art of a people (see chapter 8). This hybrid sense of culture, the convergence of the second and third definitions, finds its contemporary expression in the works of the Manchester school, among its members the cultural critics Raymond Williams and E. P. Thompson, who understand culture to be a collective creation, not a fixed symbol system but a continuously constituted structure of meanings created by family, community, and work. In my analysis, the hybrid sense of culture will be assumed.

14. Michael Paul Rogin, "Political Suppression, Intimidation and Control," *American Encyclopedia of Political History,* ed. Jack P. Greene (New York: Scribners, 1984), pp. 392–416.

15. The psychology is even more complicated, as Slavoj Zizek outlines, for the Other is part of the Self, and the hatred of the Other becomes hatred of our own excesses of enjoyment (see Slavoj Zizek, "Eastern Europe's Republics of Gilead," in *Dimensions of Radical Democracy,* ed. Chantal Mouffe [New York: Verso Press, 1992], pp. 193–207).

16. Ibid. See also Michael Rogin, *Black Face, White Nöise* (Berkeley: University of California Press, 1996), p. 25.

17. Ronald Fernandez, "Getting Germans to Fight Germans: The Americanizers of World War I," *Journal of Ethnic Studies* 9 (Summer 1981): 52–56.

18. George E. Pozzetta, "The Italian Immigrant Press of New York City: The Early Years 1880–1915," *Journal of Ethnic Studies* 1 (Fall 1983): 3. For insider views of the urban immigrant experience, see also Uri D. Herscher, "The Metropolis of Ghettos," *Journal of Ethnic Studies* 4 (Summer 1976): 2, 33–47.

19. Nativism is well entrenched in American political history, its theories of national culture, and its immigration policies, beginning as early as 1609. See William S. Bernard, "Immigration: History of U.S. Policy," *Harvard Encyclopedia of American Ethnic Groups,* ed. Stephen Thernstrom, Ann Orlov, and Oscar Handlin (Cambridge: Harvard University Press, 1980), pp. 486–95. For the definitive history of nativism at the turn of the

century, see John Higham, *Strangers in the Land* (New Brunswick N.J.: Rutgers University Press, 1955).

20. Theodore Roosevelt, quoted in Michael Kazin, "The New Historians," *New York Times Book Review,* July 2, 1989, p. 18.

21. Woodrow Wilson, quoted in Kennedy, *Over Here,* pp. 24, 87.

22. Woodrow Wilson, quoted in Irving Howe, *World of Our Fathers* (New York: Touchstone, 1976), p. 411.

23. Higham usefully sorted out the competing theories of American national identity and its ethnic origins that came to prominence between 1880 and 1920 in "Immigration and the Redefinition of America in the Early Twentieth Century," a speech delivered at the New York Public Library, July 1, 1986. He pointed out that in the nineteenth century Anglo-conformity and the melting pot theses frequently overlapped in an often-unrecognized and built-in contradiction, but by the twentieth century, the split became apparent. The divergence, he suggested, was due to a generational change in the intellectual community, as individuals of the genteel tradition were replaced by the "young intellectuals" of progressive and pragmatist inclinations. My emphasis is on the role of preparedness imperatives, as they affected both generations, creating a schism not only *between* generations but *within* them as well. Bourne, in particular, differed from his progressive and pragmatist counterparts on issues of military participation, nationalism, social reform, and so forth.

24. Werner Sollors, *Beyond Ethnicity: Consent and Descent in American Culture* (New York: Oxford University Press, 1986), pp. 4–6.

25. Sollors offers a fascinating etymology of the terms "ethnic" and "ethnicity," which reveals, in his telling, a progressive transformation from its earliest usage as a conception connoting a deficit or a quality or status lacking in certain persons to one that is prized as an asset or mark of distinction. The root *ethnikos,* meaning "gentile" or "heathen," carried with it the connotation of being foreign or not one of "the people" (i.e., non-Greek), and its noun form *ethnos* denoted "other-ness" as well. English usage based on the Greek shifted from referring to non-Israelites to non-Christians, and in fourteenth- to nineteenth-century usages, the term generally held the meaning of being "heathen." By the mid-nineteenth century in Christian usage, "ethnicity" came to carry the meaning commonly associated with it today, as something "peculiar to a race or nation." Ethnicity had a sense of the "pagan" about it, as "other" or "non-people," and in the United States as "non-Americans." Even American natives referred to themselves as "the people" and to all others as strangers (pp. 20–39). Though ethnicity has become a source of pride for many people and the basis of a grassroots politics associated with the idea of cultural

diversity, it nevertheless still retains its sense of illegitimacy (as non-American) or deviancy (as disloyal), which can be a political liability.

26. For an alternative understanding of recognizing strangers—not as foreigners, but as ourselves—see Julia Kristeva, *Nations Without Nationalism,* trans. Leon S. Roudiez (1990; rpt., New York: Columbia University Press, 1993).

27. Cf. Sollors, *Beyond Ethnicity,* whose consent adaptations are indistinct from assimilation.

28. Madison Grant, *The Passing of the Great Race, or, the Racial Basis of European History* (New York: C. Scribner's Sons, 1918), quoted in Bruce Clayton, *Forgotten Prophet* (Baton Rouge: Louisiana State University Press, 1984), pp. 190–91. See also Edward A. Ross, *The Old World in the New: The Significance of Past and Present Immigration to the American People* (New York: Century, 1914).

29. [Hector St. John] de Crevecoeur, *Letters from an American Farmer* (1782; New York: Fox, Duffield Company, 1904), pp. 54–55.

30. An excellent study of the melting pot thesis is Philip Gleason's "The Melting Pot: Symbol of Fusion or Confusion?" *American Quarterly* 16 (Spring 1964): 20–46.

31. Kennedy, *Over Here,* pp. 17–18.

32. James Madison, *The Federalist,* No. 10. For a discussion of the varieties of cultural and ethnic pluralism in the twentieth century, see John Higham, "Ethnic Pluralism in American Thought," in *Send These to Me: Jews and Other Immigrants in Urban America* (Baltimore: Johns Hopkins University Press, 1984), pp. 196–230.

33. Horace Meyer Kallen, "Democracy versus the Melting Pot," *Nation* 100 (February 18–25, 1915): 190–94, 217–20. See also Kallen, "Zionism and the Struggle Towards Democracy," *Nation* 101 (September 23, 1915): 379–80, and *The Structure of Lasting Peace* (1918), quoted in Sollors, *Beyond Ethnicity,* p. 151. For informative analyses of Kallen's thought and its influences on Bourne, see Sollors, *Beyond Ethnicity,* pp. 97, 99, 151, 181–83, 186, and Higham, *Send These to Me,* pp. 204–11, 213, 220.

34. The point is further developed by Sollors, *Beyond Ethnicity,* pp. 151, 182–83, 231, 254, and Higham, *Send These to Me,* pp. 212, 207; see also Higham's conclusion that ethnic diversity is incompatible with democratic ideals (pp. 225–30).

35. Howe, *World of Our Fathers,* p. 413.

36. G. W. F. Hegel, *Hegel's Philosophy of Mind,* trans. William Wallace and A. V. Miller (1971; rpt., New York: Oxford University Press, 1984), pp. 255–68.

37. Randolph S. Bourne, "The Jew and Trans-National America," *Meno-*

rah Journal 2 (December 1916): 277–84, reprinted in Resek, ed., *War and the Intellectuals,* pp. 124–33.

38. Brandeis's turn to Zionism was not out of religious conviction but out of his own insecurity as an American, according to Lewis J. Paper, *Brandeis* (Englewood Cliffs, N.J.: Prentice Hall, 1983). Brandeis's late support (after the age of fifty) of Jewish pioneers in Palestine was a way of demonstrating his American patriotism, for he had convinced himself they were the modern incarnation of his Puritan ancestors. And indeed, partly through his efforts at philanthropic organizing, American Zionism was credentialed as an affirmation of American patriotism. See also Philippa Strum, *Brandeis: Beyond Progressivism* (Lawrence: University Press of Kansas, 1993), chap. 5.

39. Bourne, "The Jew and Trans-National America," p. 128.

40. Chaim Potok, quoted in Richard F. Shepard, "Chaim Potok, Man of Contrasts," *New York Times,* November 2, 1986, p. 71.

41. Bourne, "The Jew and Trans-National America," pp. 129–30.

42. Thorstein Veblen, "The Intellectual Pre-eminence of Jews in Western Europe" (1919), reprinted in Max Lerner, ed., *The Portable Veblen* (New York: Viking Press, 1948), pp. 467–79. Veblen's significant essay regarding Jewish "exceptionalism" was written three years after Bourne's study of Zionism, and they share the same spirit.

43. The benefits of a double citizenship applied equally to Afro-Americans. W. E. B. DuBois, whose *Souls of Black Folk* (New York: New American Library, 1969) Bourne had read, told of his own struggles to reconcile his racial and national identities, "two warring ideals in one dark body." "Am I an American or am I a Negro?" he asked in another book. "Can I be both? Or is it my duty to cease to be a Negro as soon as possible and be an American?" DuBois understood that assimilation would have to occur within the terms of an Anglo-Saxon hegemony, requiring a sacrifice of one part of his self, a price he was unwilling to pay.

44. For the importance of cosmopolitanism for American intellectuals, see David A. Hollinger, "Ethnic Diversity, Cosmopolitanism, and the Emergence of the American Liberal Intelligentsia," *American Quarterly* 27 (May 1975): 133–51, and Terry A. Cooney, *The Rise of the New York Intellectuals: Partisan Review and Its Circle, 1934–1945* (Madison: University of Wisconsin Press, 1986), chap. 1. For the decline of cosmopolitanism, see Higham, *Strangers in the Land,* pp. 250–54.

45. Cf. Michael M. J. Fischer, "Ethnicity and the Post-Modern Arts of Memory," in *Writing Culture,* ed. James Clifford and George Marcus (Berkeley: University of California Press, 1986), pp. 194–233.

46. Bourne, "The Jew and Trans-National America," pp. 130–31

(emphasis added). For the dangers of an atrophied cultural identity, see, for instance, Maxine Hong Kingston's *Tripster Monkey: His Fake Book* (New York: Alfred A. Knopf, 1989).

47. Cf. David M. Potter, "The Historian's Use of Nationalism," in *History and American Society: Essays* (New York: Oxford University Press, 1966), p. 75. Potter argues that nationalism itself can provide the social glue necessary to hold together disparate groups into a "mutually supportive relation." Potter's conception of nationalism is close to Bourne's notion of dual citizenship or transnationalism in finding no contradiction in having multiple loyalties or identifications. But Bourne recognizes the very real possibility of discord and dissension in attaining common ends, and Potter presumes a preexisting harmony underlying the social order that is enhanced by differences and the protection of them. Thus he restates the Roycean position.

48. As Philip Gleason argues, critics of the melting pot theory have often presented confused analyses seeking to challenge the thesis, not always distinguishing clearly between its failure as reality (as unattained and never existing, and therefore a myth) and a reprehensible reality that ought never to be. Bourne's confusion is slightly different from the others, but he shared the same contradictory approach, aiming to discredit the melting pot thesis as a "mere" myth and a reprehensible one as well as declaring it to be a failed reality (unworkable and unsuccessful in accomplishing its ends). It was, thus, neither adequate as a description of American society nor desirable as a prescription. See Gleason, "The Melting Pot, pp. 20–46, and "Confusion Compounded: The Melting Pot in the 1960s and 1970s, *Ethnicity* 6(1) (March 1979): 10–20.

49. Bourne, "Trans-National America," pp. 107–8.

50. Ibid., pp. 108–9, 112–14, and "The Jew and Trans-National America," p. 124. See also Randolph S. Bourne, "Americans in the Making," *New Republic* 14 (February 2, 1918): 30–32, review of *An American in the Making* by M. E. Ravage and *The Rise of David Levinsky* by Abraham Cahan.

51. Bourne, "Trans-National America," pp. 109, 111.

52. Alan Wald, "The Culture of 'Internal Colonialism': A Marxist Perspective," MELUS 8(3) (Fall 1981): 18–27.

53. See, for instance, E. San Juan, Jr., "The Cult of Ethnicity and the Fetish of Pluralism: A Counterhegemonic Critique," *Cultural Critique* 18 (Spring 1991): 215–29, and Sollors, *Beyond Ethnicity,* p. 36. San Juan is also critical of the mechanistic treatment of ethnicity in Sollors's descent/consent binary. In my view, what is missing in the schema is a classification of identity as constructed by others. Sollors uses the terms to characterize how ethnicity is symbolized in American literature; the construction of identity by others is thereby built in.

54. San Juan, "Cult of Ethnicity," p. 222.

55. Slavoj Zizek, "Ideology Between Fiction and Fantasy," *Cardozo Law Review* 16 (1995): 1530–32.

56. Randolph S. Bourne to Elizabeth Shepley Sergeant, December 21, 1916, Elizabeth Shepley Sergeant Papers, Beinecke Library, Yale University, reprinted in Sandeen, ed., *Letters,* pp. 391–92. See also [Unsigned], "The Will to Lynch," *New Republic* 8 (October 14, 1916): 261–62.

57. Bourne, "The Jew and Trans-National America," p. 130.

58. William James's idea of a pluralistic universe was fleshed out in *A Pluralistic Universe* (New York: Longman's Green, 1909), but its initial outline was hinted at in *The Will to Believe* (New York: Longman's Green, 1897).

59. Bourne, "Trans-National America," pp. 110, 114, 121. See also Randolph S. Bourne, "Emerald Lake," *New Republic* 9 (January 6, 1917): 267–68.

60. Cf. Kathy Peiss, *Cheap Amusements: Working Women and Leisure in Turn-of-the-Century New York* (Philadelphia: Temple University Press, 1986).

61. Randolph S. Bourne, "Pageantry and Social Art," [n.d.], Bourne Papers, first published in *The Radical Will,* ed. Olaf Hansen (New York: Urizen Books, 1977), pp. 515–19.

62. George F. Roederer, Jr., "What Have Modernists Looked At? Experiential Roots of Twentieth-Century American Painting," *American Quarterly* 39 (Spring 1987): 56–83, and Wanda Corn, "The Artist's New York," typescript. The entire issue of *American Quarterly* (Spring 1987) is devoted to modernist culture in America.

63. Randolph S. Bourne, "A Sociological Poet," [n.d.], Bourne Papers, first published in Hansen, ed., *Radical Will,* pp. 521–22. The city's magnetism had a negative impact, reducing surrounding towns to skeletons as their residents commuted to the city and left political administration in the hands of the town elders. In his master's essay, written under Dewey's supervision, Bourne examined his hometown, a suburb of Newark, which was on the periphery of New York. In Bloomfield, an Italian working-class community resided in the northern part of town, providing the skilled labor for the town's clothing factory. As first generation immigrants, they spoke little English, attended parochial schools and the Catholic church, shopped in separate stores, and benefited little from the improvements in public schooling, made possible by the increased tax base of the commuters. The essay is notable for its analysis of the impact of the "suburbanization" of the town on various social classes—the workers, the commuters, and the town gentry—who, though living in three separate worlds, were all affected by the larger social process. See

Randolph S. Bourne, "A Study of the 'Suburbanizing' of a Town and the Effects of the Process upon Its Social Life" (Master's thesis, Department of Political Science, Columbia University, 1913), pp. 1–72, and a version of the study, published as "The Social Order in an American Town," *Atlantic Monthly* 111 (February 1913): pp. 227–36. See also "Emerald Lake," pp. 267–68, reprinted in Hansen, ed., *Radical Will,* pp. 271–74.

64. See Daniel Joseph Singal, "Towards a Definition of American Modernism," *American Quarterly* 39 (Spring 1987): 7–26, for its careful attention to the contradictions in American modernism (the rational and the irrational, the orderly and the disorderly); cf. David A. Hollinger, "The Knower and the Artificer," in *In the American Province* (Bloomington: Indiana University Press, 1985), pp. 37–55.

65. Casey Blake, "'The Cosmopolitan Note': Randolph Bourne and the Challenge of 'Trans-National America,'" *Culturefront* (Winter 1995–1996): 28.

66. Aldon D. Morris, *The Origins of the Civil Rights Movement: Black Communities Organizing for Change* (New York: Free Press, 1984), pp. 139–73. I am grateful to Don Culverson for this reference and for discussions on the nature and possibilities of prefigurative politics.

67. Winni Breines, *Community and Organization in the New Left, 1962–1968* (New Brunswick, N.J.: Rutgers University Press, 1989).

68. George Lipsitz, "Land of a Thousand Dances: Youth, Minorities, and the Rise of Rock and Roll," in *Recasting America: Culture and Politics in the Age of Cold War,* ed. Lary May (Chicago: University of Chicago Press, 1989), pp. 267–84.

69. Kristie McClure makes a related argument for decentering the state as the privileged site of political agency and augmenting notions of citizenship to include new subjects. See Kristie McClure, "On the Subject of Rights: Pluralism, Plurality and Political Identity," in Mouffe, ed., *Dimensions of Radical Democracy,* pp. 108–27.

CHAPTER 8. "CREATIVE DESIRE"

1. Lewis Mumford, "The Image of Randolph Bourne," *New Republic* 64 (September 24, 1930): 151–52.

2. See Van Wyck Brooks, *America's Coming of Age* (New York: B. W. Huebsch, 1915), p. 120. For his assessment of Bourne's healing potential for American culture, see Van Wyck Brooks, "Introduction," in *History of a Literary Radical and Other Essays,* ed. Van Wyck Brooks (New York: B. W. Huebsch, 1920), pp. xxxi–xxxv. The terms "highbrow" and "lowbrow"

originated with George Santayana, but Brooks was responsible for giving them currency.

3. Charles Forcey, *Crossroads of Liberalism* (New York: Oxford University Press, 1961), pp. 307, 300, 284.

4. Paul F. Bourke, "The Status of Politics, 1909–1919: *The New Republic,* Randolph Bourne and Van Wyck Brooks," *American Studies,* 8(2) (August 1974): 200–202; and "Culture and the Status of Politics, 1909–1917: Studies in the Social Criticism of Herbert Croly, Walter Lippmann, Randolph Bourne, and Van Wyck Brooks" (Ph.D. diss., University of Wisconsin, 1967). Bourke's conclusion rests on the persuasive claim that "Bourne was not simply rejecting the performance of liberals during the war; he was offering an historical judgment on the very nature of liberalism" (Bourne, "Status of Politics"). See also Michael D. True, "The Social and Literary Criticism of Randolph Bourne: A Study of His Development as a Writer" (Ph.D. diss., Duke University, 1964).

5. Christopher Lasch, *The New Radicalism in America, 1889–1963* (New York: Vintage Books, 1965), pp. xiv, 163, 329, and Lewis Mumford, quoted in Gary Bullert, *The Politics of John Dewey* (Buffalo, N.Y.: Prometheus Books, 1983), p. 64; Casey Blake, *Beloved Community: The Cultural Criticism of Randolph Bourne, Van Wyck Brooks, Waldo Frank, and Lewis Mumford* (Chapel Hill: University of North Carolina Press, 1990), pp. 169, 180; cf. p. 322. See also Bourke, "The Status of Politics," pp. 171–202, who also argues that the new intelligentsia was fundamentally naive about politics.

6. Cf. James W. Tuttleton, "American Literary Radicalism in the Twenties," *New Criterion* (March 1985): 16–30, for the view that Bourne's cultural radicalism was "Leninist," and James Hoopes, "The Culture of Progressivism: Croly, Lippmann, Brooks, Bourne, and the Idea of American Artistic Decadence," *Clio* 7 (1977): 91–111, for the related conclusion that Bourne's cultural theory was "proto-fascist." Neither Tuttleton nor Hoopes adequately distinguishes between Bourne's cultural criticism and that of the progressives at the *New Republic,* the cultural nationalists of the *Seven Arts,* or the writers at the *Masses.*

7. Randolph S. Bourne to Van Wyck Brooks, March 27, 1918, Brooks Papers, reprinted in *Letters of Randolph Bourne,* ed., Eric Sandeen (Troy, N.Y.: Whitston, 1981), p. 410.

8. Randolph Bourne, "A War Diary," in *War and the Intellectuals,* ed. Carl Resek (New York: Harper and Row, 1964), p. 45.

9. Ibid., pp. 45–46.

10. Ibid., pp. 43–44.

11. Randolph S. Bourne to Van Wyck Brooks, March 27, 1918, Brooks Papers, reprinted in Sandeen, ed., *Letters,* p. 410.

12. Resek, ed., "Introduction," *War and the Intellectuals,* p. xii; see also Casey Blake, " 'The Cosmopolitan Note': Randolph Bourne and the Challenge of 'Trans-National America,' " *Culturefront* (Winter 1995–1996): 28.

13. James Oppenheim, "Editorial," *Seven Arts* 1 (November 1916): 52.

14. Waldo Frank, *Our America* (New York: Boni and Liveright, 1919), p. 19. For historical appreciations of Bourne's work as deliberately uniting avant-garde ideas with revolutionary politics, see also Floyd Dell, *Homecoming* (New York: Farrar and Rinehart, 1933); Resek, ed., "Introduction"; James Burkhart Gilbert, *Writers and Partisans* (New York: John Wiley, 1968), pp. 1–4, 7, 34–39; Daniel Aaron, *Writers on the Left* (New York: Oxford University Press, 1977), pp. 45–49; Alan Trachtenberg, "Introduction: The Genteel Tradition and Its Critics," in *Critics of Culture: Literature and Society in the Early Twentieth Century,* ed. Nan Trachtenberg (New York: John Wiley and Sons, 1976), pp. 7, 9, 12; and Edward Abrahams, *The Lyrical Left: Randolph Bourne, Alfred Stieglitz, and the Origins of Cultural Radicalism in America* (Charlottesville: University Press of Virginia, 1986), pp. 18–20, 38–45, 63–64, 90–91.

15. Randolph S. Bourne, "The Suicide of Criticism," *Columbia Monthly* 8 (March 1911): 188–92. Spingarn later become the first director of the NAACP.

16. Randolph S. Bourne, "The Cult of the Best," *New Republic* 5 (January 15, 1916): 275–76. See also Bourne's "Education in Taste," *New Republic* 6 (March 4, 1916): 122–24, and "A Stronghold of Obscurantism," *Dial* 62 (April 5, 1917): 303–5.

17. Bourne, "The Cult of the Best," p. 276.

18. Jean-Jacques Rousseau, *Letter to M. D'Alembert on the Theatre* (1758), trans. and with notes and introduction by Allan Bloom (Ithaca, N.Y.: Cornell University Press, 1978).

19. Randolph S. Bourne to Carl Zigrosser, November 3, 1913, Zigrosser Papers, reprinted in Sandeen, ed., *Letters,* p. 167.

20. Randolph S. Bourne, "Our Unplanned Cities," *New Republic* 3 (June 26, 1915): 202–3. See also "Guiding the City," *New Republic* 7 (May 13, 1916): 47–48. Review of *City Planning,* ed. John Nolen.

21. See Randolph S. Bourne, "A Little Thing of Brunelleschi's," [n.d.], Bourne Papers, first published in *The Radical Will,* ed. Olaf Hansen (New York: Urizen Books, 1977), pp. 528–31, in which he is critical of the professionalization of architecture and architectural education in America. Cf. [Juvenis], "The Architect," *New Republic* 5 (January 1, 1916): 222–23, reprinted in Hansen, ed., *Radical Will,* pp. 279–81, where he argues that architecture must be judged in terms of art and not engineering but insists at the same time that architecture be functional and democratic,

that is, concerned with the dailiness of ordinary men and women. For a defense of town planning, see "Our Unplanned Cities," pp. 202–3 (reprinted in Hansen, ed., *Radical Will,* pp. 275–78).

22. See Randolph S. Bourne to Elizabeth Shepley Sergeant, October 10, 1915, Sergeant Papers, reprinted in Sandeen, ed., *Letters,* pp. 339–40: "Denunciations of my recent articles continue to come in. I have become an impious, ungrateful, pro-German, venomous viper. This sums up my college, *Atlantic* and German articles, and gives me a Byronic reputation that I shall have work living down, even if I wanted to."

23. Randolph S. Bourne, "American Use for German Ideals," *New Republic* 4 (September 4, 1915): 117–19, reprinted in Resek, ed., *War and the Intellectuals,* pp. 47–48. See also "Impressions of Europe, 1913–14," *Columbia University Quarterly* 17 (March 1915): 109–26, reprinted in Brooks, ed., *History of a Literary Radical,* pp. 259–63.

24. Randolph S. Bourne to Carl Zigrosser, November 3, 1913, Zigrosser Papers, reprinted in Sandeen, ed., *Letters,* p. 167. See also Randolph S. Bourne to Alyse Gregory, July 30, 1914, Gregory Papers, reprinted in Sandeen, ed., *Letters,* pp. 262–63.

25. Cf. Hoopes, "Culture of Progressivism," for the view that Bourne's cultural theory, like that of Croly, Lippmann, and Brooks, maintained that art led to spiritual uplift and moral regeneration, a view strongly influenced by the nineteenth-century notion of art as an expression of the spiritual, even as they rebelled against it. Cf. Tuttleton, "American Literary Radicalism," who considered the cultural radicalism of writers on the *Seven Arts,* including Bourne, and those on the *Masses* (primarily John Reed and Max Eastman) to be heirs to a "progressive" tradition with a functionalist view of art as an instrument for social change (p. 29). Cf. Resek, ed., *War and the Intellectuals,* and Trachtenburg, "Introduction," in *Critics of Culture,* pp. 3–13.

26. This perspective can be seen today in the criticism of Timothy J. Clark, *The Absolute Bourgeois* (New York: New York Graphic Society, 1973). This interpretation is not to suggest that Bourne was or would have become a Marxist cultural critic, a conclusion that is impossible to draw, given the limitations in his literary criticism and the fact that it was closely tied to the contemporary debates in the teens, specifically the debates among the realists, influenced by W. D. Howells, the humanists, and the expressionists. For a summary of the debates within New York's cultural communities, see Arthur Frank Wertheim, *The New York Little Renaissance: Iconoclasm, Modernism, and Nationalism in American Culture, 1908–1917* (New York: New York University Press, 1976), especially pp. 99–184.

27. Randolph S. Bourne, "A Sociological Poet," [n.d.], first published

in Hansen, ed., *Radical Will,* pp. 521–22. The probable date of the essay was 1914, written during his travels to Europe or just after his return to the United States.

28. Randolph S. Bourne to Alyse Gregory, [n.d.] October 1916, Gregory Papers, reprinted in Sandeen, ed., *Letters,* pp. 376–77. Bourne also dismissed the efforts of writers on the *Masses* for failing to achieve artistic "form" or "expressive beauty"; see his "History of a Literary Radical," *Yale Review* 8 (April 1919): 468–84, reprinted in Brooks, ed., *History of a Literary Radical,* p. 30.

29. Randolph S. Bourne, "Paul Elmer More," *New Republic* 6 (April 1, 1916): 245–47, reprinted in Resek, ed., *War and the Intellectuals,* p. 169.

30. Bourne, "History of a Literary Radical," in Brooks, ed., *History of a Literary Radical,* p. 26.

31. Randolph Bourne, "Trans-National America," in Resek, ed., *War and the Intellectuals,* p. 113.

32. Randolph S. Bourne, "Traps for the Unwary," *Dial* 64 (March 28, 1918): 277–79, reprinted in Resek, ed., *War and the Intellectuals,* pp. 182–83.

33. Randolph S. Bourne, "The Heart of the People" *New Republic* 3 (July 3, 1915): 233, reprinted in Resek, ed., *War and the Intellectuals,* pp. 173–74.

34. Randolph S. Bourne, "H. L. Mencken," *New Republic* 13 (November 24, 1917): 102–3. Review of *A Book of Prefaces,* by H. L. Mencken, reprinted in Resek, ed., *War and the Intellectuals,* p. 164.

35. Randolph S. Bourne, "The Artist in Wartime," [n.d.], manuscript, Bourne Papers, first published in Hansen, ed., *Radical Will,* pp. 408–13.

36. Bourne, "History of a Literary Radical," in Brooks, ed., *History of a Literary Radical,* p. 27.

37. Randolph S. Bourne and Van Wyck Brooks, "The Retort Courteous," *Poetry* 12 (September 1918): 341–44, reprinted in Resek, ed., *War and the Intellectuals,* p. 324.

38. Bourne, "Traps for the Unwary," p. 182.

39. Randolph S. Bourne to Van Wyck Brooks, March 27, 1918, Brooks Papers, reprinted in Sandeen, ed., *Letters,* pp. 410–14.

40. Bourne, "Traps for the Unwary," p. 181.

41. See Randolph S. Bourne, "Seeing It Through," *Dial* 61 (December 28, 1916): 563–65. Review of *Mr. Britling Sees It Through* by H. G. Wells, and "The Relegation of God," *Dial* 65 (September 19, 1918): 215–16. Review of *Joan and Peter* by H. G. Wells.

42. Bourne, "The Retort Courteous," p. 343. See also Randolph S. Bourne, "Sincerity in the Making," *New Republic* 1 (December 5, 1914):

26–27. Review of *The Congo, General William Booth Enters into Heaven,* and *Adventures While Preaching the Gospel of Beauty* by Vachel Lindsay.

43. Bourne, "Traps for the Unwary," p. 181. Bourne's appreciation of imagist poetry and modernist stream-of-consciousness novels can be seen in "A Sociological Poet" and "An Imagist Novel," *Dial* 64 (May 9, 1918): 451–52. Review of *Honeycomb* by Dorothy M. Richardson.

44. Bourne, "A Sociological Poet," pp. 520–23.

45. Randolph S. Bourne, "Theodore Dreiser," *New Republic* 2 (April 17, 1915): Supp., 7–8, reprinted in Hansen, ed., *Radical Will,* pp. 457–61. Bourne wrote three essays on Dreiser's work, among the best of his literary criticism.

46. Randolph S. Bourne, "Desire as Hero," *New Republic* 5 (November 20, 1915): Supp. 5–6. Review of *The 'Genius'* by Theodore Dreiser.

47. Randolph S. Bourne, "The Art of Theodore Dreiser," *Dial* 62 (June 14, 1917): 507–9. In this essay, Bourne calls Dreiser a "true hyphenate, a product of that conglomerate Americanism that springs from other roots than the English tradition" (p. 509).

48. Randolph S. Bourne, "Sociologic Fiction," *New Republic* 12 (October 27, 1917): 359–60. Review of *King Coal* by Upton Sinclair, reprinted in Resek, ed., *War and the Intellectuals,* pp. 175–78.

49. Randolph S. Bourne, "The Immanence of Dostoyevsky," *Dial* 62 (June 28, 1917): 24–25. Review of *The Eternal Husband* by Fyodor Dostoyevsky. Cf. [Unsigned], "Dostoyevsky's Stories," *New Republic* 16 (September 28, 1918): 267. Review of *The Gambler* by Fyodor Dostoyevsky. See also "From an Older Time," *Dial* 65 (November 2, 1918): 363–65. Review of *Lovers of Louisiana* by George Washington Cable.

50. Randolph S. Bourne, "Morals and Art from the West," *Dial* 65 (December 14, 1918): 556–57. Review of *In the Heart of a Fool* by William Allen White and *My Antonia* by Willa Cather. See also [Unsigned], "Diminuendo," *New Republic* 5 (December 11, 1915): 153–55. Review of *The Song of the Lark* by Willa Cather. For a scathingly critical assessment of the irreducibly middle-class character of the culture of the American Middle West, see "A Mirror of the Middle West," *Dial* 65 (November 30, 1918): 480–82. Review of *The Valley of Democracy* by Meredith Nicholson.

51. Bourne, "Sociologic Fiction," pp. 176–77.

52. Bourne, "History of a Literary Radical," p. 190.

53. Randolph S. Bourne, "The Brevity School in Fiction," *Dial* 64 (April 25, 1918): 405–7. Review of *On the Stairs* by Henry B. Fuller.

54. Bourne, "History of a Literary Radical," pp. 192–94, 196.

55. Carol Gruber, *Mars and Minerva* (Baton Rouge: Louisiana State University Press, 1975), pp. 242–44.

56. Bourne, "History of a Literary Radical," p. 196.

57. Ibid., pp. 193–94, 197.

58. Randolph S. Bourne to Van Wyck Brooks, March 27, 1918, reprinted in Sandeen, ed., *Letters,* p. 413; Bourne, "Twilight of Idols," in Resek, ed., *War and the Intellectuals,* p. 63.

CHAPTER 9. EPILOGUE

1. For this interpretation of Nietzsche's aesthetic impulse, see Hayden White, *Metahistory: The Historical Imagination in Nineteenth-Century Europe* (Baltimore: Johns Hopkins University Press, 1973), p. 332.

2. James Oppenheim, "R. B.," in *History of a Literary Radical and Other Essays,* ed. Van Wyck Brooks (New York: B. W. Huebsch, 1920), p. viii.

3. See Louis Filler, *Randolph Bourne* (Washington, D.C.: American Council on Public Affairs, 1943); Max Lerner, "Introduction" in ibid.; and "Randolph Bourne: Some Pre-War Letters (1912–1914)," *Twice-a-Year* 2 (Spring–Summer 1939): 79–102; "Randolph Bourne: Letters (1913–1914)" and "Randolph Bourne: Diary for 1901," *Twice-a-Year* 5–6 (Fall–Winter 1940; Spring–Summer 1941): 79–88, 89–98.

4. For biographies of Bourne, see Filler, *Randolph Bourne;* John Moreau, *Randolph Bourne* (Washington, D.C.: Public Affairs Press, 1966); James Vitelli, *Randolph Bourne* (Boston: Twayne, 1981); Bruce Clayton, *Forgotten Prophet* (Baton Rouge: Louisiana State University Press, 1984); Christopher Lasch, *The New Radicalism in America, 1889–1963: The Intellectual as a Social Type* (New York: Vintage Books, 1965), chap. 3 and passim; Wilson Carey McWilliams, *The Idea of Fraternity in America* (Berkeley: University of California Press, 1973), pp. 505–8; Thomas Bender, *New York Intellect* (New York: Alfred A. Knopf, 1987), pp. 228–48; and Robert Westbrook, *John Dewey and American Democracy* (Ithaca, N.Y.: Cornell University Press, 1991), pp. 195–240.

5. Lerner, *Bourne,* pp. 347–69; Charles Forcey, *Crossroads of Liberalism* (New York: Oxford University Press, 1961), pp. 221–315; Sidney Kaplan, "Social Engineers as Saviors," *Journal of the History of Ideas* 17 (June 1956): 347–69; Harold Laski, "The Liberalism of Randolph Bourne," *Freeman* 1 (May 19, 1920): 237; Sheldon S. Wolin, "The New Conservatives," *New York Review of Books,* February 5, 1975, pp. 6–11; and Casey Blake, *Beloved Community* (Chapel Hill: University of North Carolina Press, 1990), chap. 3 and passim.

6. Blake, *Beloved Community,* chap. 1. For his analysis of the "feminine ideal," conceived by the Young Americans as a substitute for both the mas-

culine world of business and the feminine world of the household, see pp. 24, 32–53, 62, 178, 230, 232, 307n. For a sympathetic treatment of Addams's personal politics, see Jean Bethke Elshtain, "Self/Other, Citizen/State: G. W. F. Hegel and Jane Addams," in *Meditations on Modern Political Thought: Masculine/Feminine Themes from Luther to Arendt* (New York: Praeger, 1986), pp. 71–84.

7. Lasch, *The New Radicalism in America,* p. 76. See also Christopher Lasch, *Haven in a Heartless World* (New York: Basic Books, 1977), pp. 3–43, on the absence of the father and the dislocation of women from the center of household production, which led to a lack of discipline and the overnurturance of children. For a critique of his analysis of the crisis of capitalism and of the inadequacy of solutions to it, see Michael Fischer, "Criticizing Capitalist America," in *A Symposium: Christopher Lasch and the Culture of Narcissism, Salmagundi* 46 (Fall 1979): 166–73; see Fischer also for the antifeminist implications of his thesis and Berenise M. Fisher, "The Old Wise Men and the New Women: Christopher Lasch Besieged," *History of Education Quarterly* 19(1) (Spring 1979): 125–41.

8. See Christopher Lasch, *The Culture of Narcissism: American Life in an Age of Diminishing Expectations* (New York: W. W. Norton, 1979), and *The Minimal Self* (New York: W. W. Norton, 1984). For a critique of his psychology of the intact (masculine) self and the self-absorbed feminine self, see Janice Doane and Devon Leigh Hodes, "Mobilizing the Ranks of Reality," in *A Symposium,* pp. 185–93.

9. Randolph S. Bourne to Paul Strand, August 16, 1917, Paul Strand Papers, Center for Creative Photography, University of Arizona.

10. See Michael Walzer, *The Company of Critics* (New York: Baisic Books, 1988), chap. 3, for his assessment of Bourne's unsuccessful accommodation of the demands of detachment and engagement. Walzer's underlying, and somewhat contradictory, purpose is to outline a prophetic role for leftist intellectuals, and in these terms Bourne failed, according to Walzer, by retreating in his final essays into "distance" and "despair." See Randolph S. Bourne to Van Wyck Brooks, March 27, 1918, in *Letters of Randolph Bourne,* ed. Eric Sandeen (Troy, N.Y.: Whitson, 1981), p. 412.

11. Friedrich Nietzsche, *Thus Spake Zarathustra,* in *The Portable Nietzsche,* trans. and ed. Walter Kaufmann (New York: Modern Library, 1966), p. 137.

12. See Paul F. Bourke, "The Status of Politics, 1909–1919," *American Studies* 8(2) (August 1974): 187–94.

13. Randolph Bourne, "A War Diary," in *War and the Intellectuals,* ed. Carl Resek (New York: Harper and Row, 1964), pp. 46–47.

14. Ibid., p. 46.

15. Irving Kristol, in his early *Partisan Review* days, cited Bourne favorably as an "irreconcilable" in his review of Saul Bellow's *Dangling Man,* suggesting that Bourne was a precursor to Bellow's hero, demonstrating "restraint, dignity and insight" in bracing against the war and fighting "below the battle" and in holding onto, or searching for, alternative standards of value. See Irving Kristol review of *Dangling Man,* by Saul Bellow *Politics* 1 (June 1944): 156.

16. Randolph Bourne, "Twilight of Idols," in Resek, ed., *War and the Intellectuals,* p. 64.

SELECTED BIBLIOGRAPHY

Primary Sources

Manuscripts and Unpublished Writings

Randolph S. Bourne. Papers. Butler Library, Rare Books and Manuscript Collections, Columbia University, New York.

Holdings include correspondence, college notes and essays, travel notes and diaries, unpublished manuscripts, clippings and books. Unpublished writings include "Battle Call" (poem); "The Breakers" (poem); "Comparison of Romeo and Juliet" (college theme); "Doctrine" (poem); "Doubts About Enforcing Peace"; "The Fallen" (poem); "The Justice of the Story" (college theme); *The Major Chord* (play); "Man" (poem); "A Modern College"; "New Love and New Religion" (essay); "Outline of a Proposed Autobiographical Novel"; [Untitled] "Progressive Educators"; "Sex and Ferryboats"; "Sketches" (poems); "Song for a Little Boy" (poem); "A Spring Song" (poem); "A Study of the 'Suburbanizing' of a Town and the Effects of the Process upon Its Social Life" (Master's thesis); "Twilight" (poem); "Two Sonnets on Youth"; "The War of Cultures"; "What Plato Means to Me" (college theme).

John Erskine. Papers. Butler Library, Rare Books and Manuscript Collections, Columbia University, New York.

Alyse Gregory. Papers. Beinecke Library, Yale University, New Haven.

Elsie Clews Parsons. Papers. American Philosophical Society Library, Philadelphia.

Elizabeth Shepley Sergeant. Papers. Beinecke Library, Yale University, New Haven.

Paul Strand. Papers. Center for Creative Photography, University of Arizona, Tucson.

Bourne's Published Works

"Some Aspects of Good Talk." *Columbia Monthly* 7 (January 1910): 92–97.
"Chesterton's 'Orthodoxy.'" *Columbia Monthly* 7 (March 1910): 170–72.
["Aurelius."] "Prof. Peck's 'Studies.'" *Columbia Monthly* 7 (March 1910): 176. Review of *Studies in Several Literatures* by Harry Thurston Peck.
"On Hero-Making." *Columbia Monthly* 7 (April 1910): 178–81.
"The Function of a College Literary Magazine." *Columbia Monthly* 8 (November 1910): 3–7.
"The Blue Bird for Happiness," *Columbia Monthly* 8 (December 1910): 61–64.
"On Playing at Five Hundred," *Columbia Monthly* 8 (January 1911): 105–10.
["Aurelius Bloomfield."] "The Prayer of a Materialist." *Columbia Monthly* 8 (February 1911): 165–67.
Review. *Columbia Monthly* 8 (February 1911): 183–85. Review of *Socialism and Christianity* by Percy S. Grant.
"The Suicide of Criticism." *Columbia Monthly* 8 (March 1911): 188–92.
Review. *Columbia Monthly* 8 (April 1911): 269–70. Review of *The Social Basis of Religion* by Simon S. Patten.
Review. *Columbia Monthly* 8 (May 1911): 313–15. Review of *A Defense of Prejudice and Other Essays* by John Grier Hibben.
"The Two Generations." *Atlantic Monthly* 108 (May 1911): 591–98.
"The Editor on Examinations—with Apologies to F. Bacon." *Columbia Monthly* 8 (June 1911): 344–46.
"Over the Quadrangle." *Columbia Monthly* 8 (August 1911): 401–3.
"The Handicapped." *Atlantic Monthly* 108 (September 1911): 320–29.
"The College: An Undergraduate View." *Atlantic Monthly* 108 (November 1911): 667–74.
Review. *Columbia Monthly* 9 (November 1911): 31–32. Review of *The Mind of Primitive Man* by Franz Boaz.
"A Letter to Mr. John Galsworthy." *Columbia Monthly* 9 (December 1911): 36–43.
"Individuality and Education." *Columbia Monthly* 9 (January 1912): 88–90.
"The Mystic Turned Radical." *Atlantic Monthly* 109 (February 1912): 236–38.
"Seeing, We See Not." *Columbia Monthly* 9 (February 1912): 133–35.
"Law and Order." *Masses* 3 (March 1912): 12.

"Poker and Veronica." *Columbia Monthly* 9 (April 1912): 175–79.
"Youth." *Atlantic Monthly* 109 (April 1912): 433–41.
"Some Thoughts on Religion." *Columbia Monthly* 9 (May 1912): 229–32.
Review. *Journal of Philosophy, Psychology and Scientific Methods* 9 (May 9, 1912): 277. Review of *The Moral Life* by W. R. Sorley.
"Student Life." *Columbia Monthly* 14 (June 1912): 341–42.
Review. *Journal of Philosophy, Psychology and Scientific Methods* 9 (August 15, 1912): 471–73. Review of *Nietzsche* by Paul Elmer More.
"College Life Today." *North American Review* 196 (September 12, 1912): 365–72.
Review. *Journal of Philosophy, Psychology and Scientific Methods* 9 (September 12, 1912): 530–31. Review of *The Desire for Qualities* by Stanley M. Bligh.
"Socialism and the Catholic Ideal." *Columbia Monthly* 10 (November 1912): 11–19.
"The Excitement of Friendship." *Atlantic Monthly* 90 (December 1912): 795–800.
"Social Order in an American Town." *Atlantic Monthly* 111 (February 1913): 227–36.
Letter to Editor. *Columbia Spectator* (February 24, 1913). Re: Columbia University's hiring of "scrubwomen" to clean student dormitories and lecture halls.
"The Life of Irony." *Atlantic Monthly* 111 (March 1913): 357–67.
Youth and Life. Boston: Houghton Mifflin Company, [March] 1913; Edinburgh: Constable, [May] 1913.
Contents: "Youth"; "The Two Generations"; "The Virtues and Seasons of Life"; "The Life of Irony"; "The Excitement of Friendship"; "The Adventure of Life"; "Some Thoughts on Religion"; "The Dodging of Pressures"; "For Radicals"; "The College: An Inner View"; "A Philosophy of Handicap."
Letter to Editor. *Columbia Spectator* (March 1, 1913). Re: the "scrubwomen" controversy.
"The New Revolution." *Columbia Monthly* 10 (May 1913): 221–27.
The College Lecture Course as the Student Sees It." *Educational Review* 46 (June 1913): 66–70.
"Stoicism." *The Open Court* 27 (June 1913): 364–71.
"Arbitration and International Politics." No. 70. New York: American Association for International Conciliation, September 1913. A pamphlet.
"Sabotage." *Columbia Monthly* 10 (November 1913): 1–2. A poem.
Review. *Journal of Philosophy, Psychology and Scientific Methods* 10 (November 6, 1913): 641–42. Review of *History of Past Ethics: An Introduction to the History of Morals* by Philip Van Ness Myers.
"In the Mind of the Worker." *Atlantic Monthly* 113 (March 1914): 375–82.

"An Experiment in Cooperative Living." *Atlantic Monthly* 113 (June 1914): 813–31.

"The Tradition of War." No. 79. New York: American Association for International Conciliation, June 1914. A pamphlet.

Review. *Journal of Philosophy, Psychology and Scientific Methods* 11 (June 4, 1914): 332–33. Review of *The Making of Character: Some Educational Aspects of Ethics* by John MacCunn.

"An Hour in Chartres." *Atlantic Monthly* 11 (August 1914): 214–17.

"Maurice Barres and the Youth of France." *Atlantic Monthly* 114 (September 1914): 394–99.

"Our Cultural Humility." *Atlantic Monthly* 114 (October 1914): 503–7.

"Berlin in Wartime." *Travel* 24 (November 1914): 9–12, 58–59.

"In a Schoolroom." *New Republic* 1 (November 7, 1914): 23–24.

"Holy Poverty." *New Republic* 1 (November 14, 1914): 25. Review of *The Ragged-Trousered Philanthropists* by Robert Wessall.

"Maeterlinck and the Unknown." *New Republic* 1 (November 21, 1914): 26. Review of *The Unknown Guest* by Maurice Maeterlinck and *The New Philosophy of Henri Bergson* by Edouard LeRoy.

"Sincerity in the Making." *New Republic* 1 (December 5, 1914): 26–27. Review of *The Congo, General William Booth Enters into Heaven,* and *Adventures While Preaching the Gospel of Beauty* by Vachel Lindsay.

[Unsigned.] "A Danish Epic." *New Republic* 1 (December 19, 1914): 28. Review of *Pelle the Conqueror* by Martin A. Nexo.

[Unsigned.] "Paul Claudel's East." *New Republic* 1 (December 19, 1914): 27–28. Review of *The East I Know* by Paul Claudel.

"Town Planning and the Law." *New Republic* 1 (December 19, 1914): 27–28. Review of *Carrying Out the City Plan* by Flavel Shurtleff.

"Bumptious Psychology." *New Republic* 1 (December 21, 1914): 26. Review of *The War and America* by Hugo Muensterberg.

[Unsigned.] "Puzzle Education." *New Republic* 1 (January 2, 1915): 10–11.

[Unsigned.] "What Might Be in Education." *New Republic* 1 (January 2, 1915): 28. Review of *What Is and What Might Be* by Edmond Holmes.

"Continental Cultures." *New Republic* 1 (January 16, 1915): 14–16.

[Unsigned.] "The Schools from the Outside." *New Republic* 1 (January 30, 1915): 10–11.

"A Glance at German 'Kultur.'" *Lippincott's Monthly* 95 (February 1915): 22–27.

"A Substitute for Schools." *New Republic* 2 (February 6, 1915): 25–26.

"When We Went to School." *New Republic* 2 (February 27, 1915): 101–3.

"Impressions of Europe, 1913–14." *Columbia University Quarterly* 17 (March 1915): 109–26.

"Mon Amie." *Atlantic Monthly* 115 (March 1915): 354–59.
"Class Struggle in Education." *New Republic* 2 (March 6, 1915): 135. Review of *School Discipline* by William Chandler Bagby.
"John Dewey's Philosophy." *New Republic* 2 (March 13, 1915): 154–56.
"Schools in Gary." *New Republic* 2 (March 27, 1915): 198–99.
"Communities for Children." *New Republic* 2 (April 3, 1915): 233–34.
"Really Public Schools." *New Republic* 2 (April 10, 1915): 259–61.
"A Map of the Public." *New Republic* 2 (April 17, 1915): Supp., 11–12. Review of *Problems of Community Life* by Seba Eldridge.
"Theodore Dreiser." *New Republic* 2 (April 17, 1915): Supp., 7–8.
"Apprentices to the School." *New Republic* 2 (April 24, 1915): 302–3.
"Democracy and University Administration." *Educational Review* (May 1915): 455–59.
"The Natural School." *New Republic* 2 (May 1, 1915): 326–28.
[Unsigned.] "The School Room." *New Republic* 2 (May 1, 1915): 333. Review of *School Hygiene* by Leo Burgerstein.
"The Failing Church." *New Republic* 3 (May 15, 1915): 49. Review of *The Reconstruction of the Church* by Paul Moore Strayer.
"Fergus—A Portrait." *New Republic* 3 (May 22, 1915): 62–64.
[Unsigned.] "The Inside of a Settlement." *New Republic* 3(May 29, 1915): 87–89.
"The Wasted Years." *New Republic* 3 (June 5, 1915): 120–22.
"Schools Overwhelmed." *New York Times,* June 15, 1915, p. 12. Letter.
"Platitude." *New Republic* 3 (June 19, 1915): 183–84. Review of *Play in Education* by Joseph Lee and *Education Through Play* by Henry S. Curtis.
[Unsigned.] "The Issue in Vocational Education." *New Republic* 3 (June 26, 1915): 191–92.
[Unsigned.] "Our Educational Prospect." *New Republic* 3 (June 26, 1915): 210–11. Review of *Schools of Tomorrow* by John Dewey and Evelyn Dewey.
"Our Unplanned Cities." *New Republic* 3 (June 26, 1915): 202–3.
"The Heart of the People." *New Republic* 3 (July 3, 1915): 233. Review of *The White Terror* (movie).
[Unsigned.] "Educating the Educators." *New Republic* 3 (July 10, 1915): 263–64. Review of *The Hygiene of the School Child* by Louis M. Terman.
"The Professor." *New Republic* 3 (July 10, 1915): 257–58.
"Who Owns the Universities?" *New Republic* 3 (July 17, 1915): 269–70.
"A French Glimpse at America." *New Republic* 3 (July 24, 1915): 318. Review of *America and Her Problems* by Paul H. B. d'Estournelle.
"Studies in Tone Poetry." *New Republic* 4 (August 7, 1915): 26–27. Review of *Nature in Music* by Lawrence Gilman.
[Unsigned.] "The Organic School." *New Republic* 4 (August 21, 1915): 64.

"Medievalism in the Colleges." *New Republic* 4 (August 28, 1915): 87–88.
[Unsigned.] "Social Workmanship." *New Republic* 4 (August 28, 1915): 108. Review of *The Field of Social Service,* edited by Philip Davis.
"This Older Generation." *Atlantic Monthly* 116 (September 1915): 385–91.
"American Use for German Ideals." *New Republic* 4 (September 4, 1915): 117–19.
["Juvenis."] "One of Our Conquerors." *New Republic* 4 (September 4, 1915): 121–23.
"To Make Undergraduates Think." *New Republic* 4 (September 4, 1915): 134–35. Review of *The College and the Future* by Richard Rice, Jr.
[Unsigned.] "Mental Unpreparedness." *New Republic* 4 (September 11, 1915): 143–44.
[Unsigned.] "What Is Opinion?" *New Republic* 4 (September 18, 1915): 171–72.
"The Undergraduate." *New Republic* 4 (September 25, 1915): 197–98.
"The Fortress of Belief." *New Republic* 4 (October 16, 1915): 283–84.
[Unsigned.] "The Democratic School." *New Republic* 4 (October 23, 1915): 297–99.
[Unsigned.] "The Reality of Peace." *New Republic* 4 (October 30, 1915): 322–23.
[Unsigned.] "Religion in Public Schools." *New Republic* 5 (November 13, 1915): 33–34.
"Sophronisba." *New Republic* 5 (November 13, 1915): 41–43.
[Unsigned.] "American Heights." *New Republic* 5 (November 20, 1915): Supp., 24. Review of *Letters to a Friend* by John Muir.
[Unsigned.] "Anna Howard Shaw." *New Republic* 5 (November 20, 1915): Supp., 24. Review of *The Story of a Pioneer* by Anna Howard Shaw.
"Desire as Hero." *New Republic* 5 (November 20, 1915): Supp., 5–6. Review of *The 'Genius'* by Theodore Dreiser.
"What Is College For?" *New Republic* 5 (December 4, 1915): 127–28. Review of *College Sons and College Fathers* by Henry Seidel Canby and *Through College on Nothing a Year* by Christian Gauss.
"The Basis of the Gary Plan of Teaching." *New York Times,* December 11, 1915, p. 12. Letter.
[Unsigned.] Review. "Diminuendo." *New Republic* 5 (December 11, 1915): 153–55. Review of *The Song of the Lark* by Willa Cather.
The Gary Schools. Introduction by William Wirt. Boston: Houghton Mifflin Company, 1916.
Contents: "The Community Setting"; "The School Plant: Educating the Whole Child"; "Work, Study, and Play"; "The School as a Community"; "Programs: The School as a Public Utility"; "Organization"; "Curricu-

lum: Learning by Doing"; "Discipline: The Natural School"; "Criticisms and Evaluations"; "Appendix."

"New York and the Gary School System." *Education Administration and Supervision* 2 (1916): 284–89.

[Edited.] *Towards an Enduring Peace: A Symposium of Peace Proposals and Programs, 1914–1916.* Introduction by Franklin N. Giddings. New York: American Association for International Conciliation, 1916.

["Juvenis."] "The Architect." *New Republic* 5 (January 1, 1916): 222–23.

[Unsigned.] "The Portland School Survey." *New Republic* 5 (January 8, 1916): 238–39.

"The Cult of the Best." *New Republic* 5 (January 15, 1916): 275–77.

[Unsigned.] "The School Situation in New York. *New Republic* 6 (February 5, 1916): 6–8.

[Unsigned.] "Politics Against the Schools." *New Republic* 6 (February 12, 1916): 32–33.

"Parents and Children." *New Republic* 6 (February 19, 1916): 81–82. Review of *How to Know Your Child* by Miriam Finn Scott.

[Unsigned.] "Real Estate and the City Plan." *New Republic* 6 (February 19, 1916): 60–61.

[Unsigned.] "House Keeping for Men." *Atlantic Monthly* 117 (March 1916): 430–32.

"Education in Taste." *New Republic* 6 (March 4, 1916): 122–24.

[Unsigned.] "Education for Work." *New Republic* 6 (March 11, 1916): 145–46.

"The Price of Radicalism." *New Republic* 6 (March 11, 1916): 161.

[Unsigned.] "Smoking." *Atlantic Monthly* 117 (April 1916): 573–75.

"Paul Elmer More." *New Republic* 6 (April 1, 1916): 245–47. Review of *Aristocracy and Justice* by Paul Elmer More.

"The Self-Conscious School." *New Republic* 6 (April 8, 1916): 260–61.

"Learning to Write." *New Republic* 6 (April 22, 1916): 326. Review of *How the French Boy Learns to Write* by Rollo Walter Brown.

[Unsigned.] "Organized Labor on Education." *New Republic* 7 (May 6, 1916): 8–9.

[Unsigned.] "Guiding the City." *New Republic* 7 (May 13, 1916): 47–48. Review of *City Planning,* edited by John Nolen.

"On Discussion." *New Republic* 7 (May 27, 1916): 87–89.

"Continuation Schools." *New Republic* 7 (June 10, 1916): 143–45.

"The World's Second Worse Failure." *New Republic* 7 (June 17, 1916): 177–78. Review of *The American College* (multiple authors): introduction by William H. Crawford.

"Trans-National America." *Atlantic Monthly* 118 (July 1916): 86–97.

"A Moral Equivalent for Universal Military Service." *New Republic* 7 (July 1, 1916): 217–19.

"Training for Public Service." *New Republic* 7 (July 8, 1916): 140–41.

[Unsigned.] "The Business Man in Office." *New Republic* 7 (July 15, 1916): 267–68.

"Very Long and Sunny." *New Republic* 7 (July 15, 1916): 282–83.

"Education as Living." *New Republic* 8 (August 5, 1916): 10–12.

["Max Coe."] "Making One's Own Contribution." *New Republic* 8 (August 26, 1916): 91–92.

"The Gary Public Schools." *Scribner's* 60 (September 1916): 371–80.

"Americanism." *New Republic* 8 (September 23, 1916): 197. Review of *Straight America* by Frances A. Kellor.

["Max Coe."] "Karen: A Portrait." *New Republic* 8 (September 23, 1916): 187–88.

"Heroics." *New Republic* 8 (October 7, 1916): 249. Review of *Americanization* by Royal Dixon.

"Perishable Books." *New Republic* 8 (October 14, 1916): 258–59.

[Unsigned.] "The Will to Lynch." *New Republic* 8 (October 14, 1916): 261–62.

"What Is Exploitation?" *New Republic* 9 (November 4, 1916): 12–14.

"The Jew and Trans-National America." *Menorah Journal* 2 (December 1916): 277–84.

"Magic and Scorn." *New Republic* 9 (December 2, 1916): 130–31. Review of *Industrial Preparedness* by C. N. Knoeppel and *Inviting War to America* by Allen R. Benson.

"France of Yesterday." *New Republic* 9 (December 9, 1916): 156, 158. Review of *French Perspectives* by Elizabeth Shepley Sergeant.

"Seeing It Through." *Dial* 61 (December 28, 1916): 563–65. Review of *Mr. Britling Sees It Through* by H. G. Wells.

Education and Living. New York: Century Company, 1917.

Contents: Preface. "Education and Living"; "The Self-Conscious School"; "The Wasted Years"; "Puzzle Education"; "Learning Out of School"; "In a Schoolroom"; "The Cult of the Best"; "Education in Taste"; "The Portland School Survey"; "What Is Experimental Education?"; "The Organic School"; "Communities for Children"; "Really Public Schools"; "Apprentices to the School"; "The Natural School;" "The Democratic School"; "The Trained Mind"; "Class and School"; "A Policy in Vocational Education"; "An Issue in Vocational Education"; "Organized Labor on Education"; "Education for Work"; "Continuation Schools"; "Who Owns the Universities?"; "The Undergraduate"; Medievalism in the Colleges."

"Emerald Lake." *New Republic* 9 (January 6, 1917): 267–68.

"Extending the University." *New Republic* 9 (January 6, 1917): 259–60.

"Joseph Fels." *New Republic* 10 (February 3, 1917): 28–29. Review of *Joseph Fels: His Life-Work* by Mary Fels.

[Unsigned.] "The Reply." *New Republic* 10 (February 10, 1917): 46–47. Answer to "Interesting Schools" by Edith Hamilton.

"1917—American Rights—1798." *New Republic* 10 (February 17, 1917): 82. Letter advertisement signed by Bourne, Max Eastman, Amos Pinchot, and Winthrop Lane of the Committee for Democratic Control, in reply to "American Rights League" by Agnes Repplier and Lyman Abbott.

[Unsigned.] "A Policy in Vocational Education." *New Republic* 10 (February 17, 1917): 63–65.

"New Ideals in Business." *Dial* 62 (February 22, 1917): 133–34. Review of *America and the New Epoch* by Charles P. Steinmet and *An Approach to Business Problems* by A. W. Shaw.

"Do the People Want War?" *New Republic* 10 (March 3, 1917): 145. Advertisement signed by Bourne, Max Eastman, Amos Pinchot, and Winthrop Lane of the Committee for Democratic Control.

"The Charm of Distance." *New Republic* 10 (March 10, 1917): 170–73. Review of *The Emperor of Portugallia* by Selma Lagerlof.

"The Inquisition at Columbia." *New York Tribune,* March 16, 1917. Letter.

"A Modern Mind." *Dial* 62 (March 22, 1917): 239–40. Review of *Social Rule* by Elsie Clews Parsons.

"American Independence and the War." *Seven Arts* 1 (April 1917): Supp., 1–9.

"The Puritan's Will to Power." *Seven Arts* 1 (April 1917): 631–37.

"Experimental Education." *New Republic* 10 (April 5, 1917): 345–47.

"A Stronghold of Obscurantism." *Dial* 62 (April 5, 1917): 303–5. Review of *Problems of Secondary Education* by David Snedden.

"An Epic of Labor." *New Republic* 10 (April 21, 1917): Supp., 8–10. Review of *Pelle the Conqueror: Daybreak* by Martin Nexo.

"Two Amateur Philosophers." *New Republic* 10 (April 28, 1917): 383–84. Review of *The Amateur Philosophers* by Carol H. Grabo and *Philosophy: An Autobiographical Fragment* by Henrie Waste.

"International Dubieties." *Dial* 62 (May 3, 1917): 387–88. Review of *League to Enforce Peace* by Robert Goldsmith and *American World Policies* by Walter E. Weyl.

"A Reverberation of War." *New Republic* 11 (May 17, 1917): 86–87. Review of *A Soldier of Life* by Hugh de Selincourt.

"Ernest: or Parent for a Day." *Atlantic Monthly* 119 (June 1917): 778–86.

"The Vampire." *Masses* 9 (June 1917): 35–36. Review of *Regiment of Women* by Clemence Dane.

"The War and the Intellectuals." *Seven Arts* 2 (June 1917): 133–46.
"The Art of Theodore Dreiser." *Dial* 62 (June 14, 1917): 507–9.
"The Immanence of Dostoyevsky." *Dial* 62 (June 28, 1917): 24–25. Review of *The Eternal Husband* by Fyodor Dostoyevsky.
"Below the Battle." *Seven Arts* 2 (July 1917): 270–77.
"The Collapse of American Strategy." *Seven Arts* 2 (August 1917): 409–24.
"Conspirators." *Seven Arts* 2 (August 1917): 528–30.
"Thinking at Seventy-Six." *New Republic* 12 (August 15, 1917): 111–13. Review of *The New Reservation of Time* by William Jewett Tucker.
"The Later Feminism." *Dial* 63 (August 16, 1917): 103–4. Review of *Towards a Sane Feminism* by William Meikle and *Motherhood* by C. Gascquoine Hartley.
"An American Humanist." *Dial* 63 (August 30, 1917): 148–50.
"A War Diary." *Seven Arts* 2 (September 1917): 535–47.
"Conscience and Intelligence in War." *Dial* 63 (September 13, 1917): 193–95.
"The Belgian Carthage." *Dial* 63 (October 1917): 343–44. Review of *The New Carthage* by Georges Eekhoud.
"Twilight of Idols." *Seven Arts* 2 (October 1917): 688–702.
"The American Adventure." *New Republic* 12 (October 20, 1917): 333–34. Review of *A Son of the Middle Border* by Hamlin Garland.
"Those Columbia Trustees." *New Republic* 12 (October 20, 1917): 328–29.
"Denatured Nietzsche." *Dial* 63 (October 25, 1917): 389–91. Review of *The Will to Freedom* by John Neville Figgis.
"Mr. Hillquit for Mayor." *New Republic* 12 (October 27, 1917): 356–57. Letter by Bourne and others.
"Sociologic Fiction." *New Republic* 12 (October 27, 1917): 359–60. Review of *King Coal* by Upton Sinclair.
"Gorky's Youth." *New Republic* 13 (November 3, 1917): 26–27. Review of *In the World* by Maxim Gorky.
"The Idea of a University." *Dial* 63 (November 22, 1917): 509–10.
"H. L. Mencken." *New Republic* 13 (November 24, 1917): 102–3. Review of *A Book of Prefaces* by H. L. Mencken.
"Mr. Huneker's Zoo." *New Republic* 13 (December 1, 1917): 130–31. Review of *Unicorns* by James Huneker.
"The Industrial Revolution." *Dial* 63 (December 20, 1917): 642. Review of *The Town Laborer, 1760–1832* by J. L. and Barbara Hammond.
[Unsigned.] Review. *New Republic* 13 (January 12, 1918): 323. Review of *Applied Psychology* by H. L. Hollingsworth and A. T. Poffenberger.
"A Primer of Revolutionary Idealism." *Dial* 64 (January 17, 1918): 69. Review of *Political Ideas* by Bertrand Russell.

[Unsigned.] Review. *New Republic* 13 (January 19, 1918): 355. Review of *Suggestions of Modern Science Concerning Education* by H. S. Jennings et al.

[Unsigned.] Review. *New Republic* 13 (January 26, 1918): 387. Review of *Housemates* by J. D. Beresford.

"Americans in the Making." *New Republic* 14 (February 2, 1918): 30–32. Review of *An American in the Making* by M. E. Ravage and *The Rise of David Levinsky* by Abraham Cahan.

"Quadrangles Paved with Good Intentions." *Dial* 64 (February 14, 1918): 151–52. Review of *The Undergraduate and His College* by Frederick P. Keppel.

"The Guild Idyl." *New Republic* 14 (March 2, 1918): 151–52. Review of *Old World for New* by Arthur J. Penty.

"Adventures in Miniature." *New Republic* 14 (March 9, 1918): 180–82. Review of *Persian Miniatures* by H. G. Dwight.

"A Vanishing World of Gentility." *Dial* 64 (March 14, 1918): 234–35. Review of *These Many Years* by Brander Matthews.

"Clipped Wings." *Dial* 64 (April 11, 1918): 358–59. Review of *The House of Conrad* by Elias Tobenkin.

"Traps for the Unwary." *Dial* 64 (March 28, 1918): 277–79.

"The Brevity School in Fiction." *Dial* 64 (April 25, 1918): 405–7. Review of *On the Stairs* by Henry B. Fuller.

"Making Over the Body." *New Republic* 15 (May 4, 1918): 28–29. Review of *Man's Supreme Inheritance* by F. Matthias Alexander.

"An Imagist Novel." *Dial* 64 (May 9, 1918): 451–52. Review of *Honeycomb* by Dorothy M. Richardson.

"Our Enemy Speaks." *Dial* 64 (May 23, 1918): 486–87. Review of *Men in War* by Andreas Latzko.

"Other Messiahs." *New Republic* 15 (May 25, 1918): 117. Letter.

"The Cult of Convention." *Liberator* 1 (June 1918): 38–39. Review of *On Contemporary Literature* by Stuart P. Sherman.

"Purpose and Flippancy." *Dial* 64 (June 6, 1918): 540–41. Review of *His Second Wife* by Ernest Poole and *The Boardman Family* by Mary S. Watts.

[Unsigned.] "Oxford Ideas." *New Republic* 15 (June 15, 1918): 214. Review of *The Oxford Stamp* by Frank Aydelotte.

"Mr. Bennett Is Disturbed." *Dial* 65 (July 18, 1918): 72. Review of *The Pretty Lady* by Arnold Bennett.

"The Retort Courteous." *Poetry* 12 (September 1918): 341–44. Letter with Van Wyck Brooks.

"Two Scandinavian Novelists." *Dial* 65 (September 5, 1918): 167–68. Review of *The Holy City* by Selma Lagerlof and *Marie Grubbe* by Jens Peter Jacobsen.

"The Relegation of God." *Dial* 65 (September 19, 1918): 215–16. Review of *Joan and Peter* by H. G. Wells.

[Unsigned.] "Dostoyevsky Stories." *New Republic* 16 (September 28, 1918): 267. Review of *The Gambler* by Fyodor Dostoyevsky.

"The Morality of Sacrifice." *Dial* 65 (October 19, 1918): 309–10. Review of *Three French Moralists* by Edmund Gosse.

"From an Older Time." *Dial* 65 (November 2, 1918): 363–65. Review of *Lovers of Louisiana* by George Washington Cable.

"The Light Essay." *Dial* 65 (November 16, 1918): 419–20. Review of *Walking Stick Papers* by Robert Cortes Holliday and *The Merry-Go-Round* by Carl Van Vechten.

"A Mirror of the Middle West." *Dial* 65 (November 30, 1918): 480–82. Review of *The Valley of Democracy* by Meredith Nicholson.

"Morals and Art from the West." *Dial* 65 (December 14, 1918): 556–57. Review of *In the Heart of a Fool* by William Allen White and *My Antonia* by Willa Cather.

"An Examination of Eminences." *Dial* 65 (December 28, 1918): 603–4. Review of *Eminent Victorians* by Lytton Strachey.

Bourne's Posthumous Publications and Reprints

"The War and the Intellectuals." *Mother Earth* (June 1917). Reprint.

Untimely Papers. New York: B. W. Huebsch, 1919. Edited and with a foreword by James Oppenheim.
Four essays, previously published, and first publication of "Old Tyrannies" (fragment) and "The State" (fragment published in incorrect sequence).

[Translation.] *Vagabonds of the Sea* by Maurice Larrouy. New York: E. P. Dutton, 1919.

"History of a Literary Radical." *Yale Review* 8 (April 1919): 468–84.

History of a Literary Radical and Other Essays. Edited and with an introduction by Van Wyck Brooks. New York: B. W. Huebsch, 1920.
Nineteen essays, previously published.

"An Autobiographical Chapter." *Dial* 68 (January 1920): 1–21.

"The War and the Intellectuals" and "Randolph Bourne: A Letter to Van Wyck Brooks." *Twice-a-Year* 1 (Fall–Winter 1938): 37–49, 50–55.
Letter of March 27, 1918.

"Randolph Bourne: Some Pre-War Letters (1912–1914)." *Twice-a-Year* 2 (Spring–Summer 1939): 79–102.
Thirteen letters, not all complete.

"Randolph Bourne: Letters (1913–1914)" and "Randolph Bourne: Diary for 1901." *Twice-a-Year* 5–6 (Fall–Winter 1940; Spring–Summer 1941): 79–88, 89–98.

Nine letters, not all complete.

"Randolph Bourne: Letters (1913–1916)." *Twice-a-Year* 7 (Fall–Winter 1941): 76–90.

Ten letters, not all complete.

The History of a Literary Radical and Other Papers. Introduction by Van Wyck Brooks. New York: S. A. Russell, 1956.

Nineteen essays, previously published.

War and the Intellectuals: Essays by Randolph S. Bourne, 1915–1919. Edited and with an introduction by Carl Resek. New York: Harper and Row, 1964.

Twenty-one essays, previously published.

The World of Randolph Bourne: An Anthology of Essays and Letters. Edited and with an introduction by Lillian Schlissel. New York: E. P. Dutton and Company, 1965.

Twenty-four essays and four letters, previously published, and first publication of fourteen letters, not all complete.

The Gary Schools. Introduction by Adeline and Murray Levine, epilogue by Abraham Flexner and Frank P. Backman. Cambridge: M.I.T. Press, 1970.

The Radical Will: Randolph Bourne, Selected Writings, 1911–1918. Edited and with an introduction by Olaf Hansen; preface by Christopher Lasch. New York: Urizen Books, 1977.

Fifty-six essays and poems, previously published, and first publication of "The Doctrine of the Rights of Man as Formulated by Thomas Paine"; "The 'Scientific' Manager"; "Practice vs. Product"; "Law and Order"; "The Disillusionment"; "The Artist in Wartime"; "Suffrage and Josella"; "Chivalry and Sin"; "Pageantry and Social Art"; "A Sociological Poet"; "A Little Thing of Brunelleschi's"; "The Night Court."

The Letters of Randolph Bourne: A Comprehensive Edition. Edited and with an introduction by Eric J. Sandeen. Troy: Whitston Publishing Company, 1981.

Two hundred nineteen letters from manuscript collections and personal sources.

SECONDARY SOURCES

Manuscript Collections

Van Wyck Brooks. Papers. Van Pelt Library, University of Pennsylvania, Philadelphia.

Theodore Dreiser. Papers. Van Pelt Library, University of Pennsylvania, Philadelphia.

John Erskine. Papers. Butler Library, Rare Books and Manuscript Collections, Columbia University, New York.

Waldo Frank. Papers. Van Pelt Library, University of Pennsylvania, Philadelphia.

James Oppenheim. Papers. Manuscripts and Archives Division, New York Public Library.

Carl Zigrosser. Papers. Van Pelt Library, University of Pennsylvania, Philadelphia.

Unpublished Works

Bourke, Paul Francis. "Culture and the Status of Politics, 1909–1917: Studies in the Social Criticism of Herbert Croly, Walter Lippmann, Randolph Bourne, and Van Wyck Brooks." Ph.D. dissertation, University of Wisconsin, 1967.

Broderick, Vincent. "Randolph Bourne." History Department thesis. Princeton University, 1941.

Dunkel, William Paul. "Between Two Worlds: Max Eastman, Floyd Dell, John Reed, Randolph Bourne and the Revolt Against the Genteel Tradition." Ph.D. dissertation. Lehigh University, 1976.

Feeney, Joseph J., S. J. "American Anti-War Writers of World War I: A Literary Study of Randolph Bourne, Harriet Monroe, Carl Sandburg, John Dos Passos, E. E. Cummings, and Ernest Hemingway." Ph.D. dissertation. University of Pennsylvania, 1971.

Harris, Mark. "Randolph Bourne: A Study in Immiscibility." Ph.D. dissertation. University of Minnesota, 1956.

Jones, Ann Margret. "Three American Responses to World War I: Wharton, Empey, and Bourne." Ph.D. dissertation. University of Wisconsin, 1970.

Levine, Norman Sidney. "Randolph Bourne: His Thought and Its Sources." Master's thesis. New York University, 1948.

Mosher, Michael A. "Is Hegelianism an Appropriate Form of Discipline for a Romantic Mind in a Liberal State?" Paper presented at annual meeting of American Political Science Association, New York, September 1981.

Rosenthal, Melvyn. "The American Writer and His Society: The Response to Estrangement in the Works of Nathaniel Hawthorne, Randolph Bourne, Edmund Wilson, Norman Mailer, and Saul Bellow." Ph.D. dissertation. University of Connecticut, 1968.

Sacks, Clair. "The Seven Arts Critics: A Study of Cultural Nationalism in America, 1910–1930." Ph.D. dissertation. University of Wisconsin, 1955.

Test, George Austin. "The Vital Connection: A Study of the New Republic Magazine as a Literary Journal, 1914–1922." Ph.D. dissertation. University of Pennsylvania, 1960.

Tompkins, Mary. "Randolph Bourne: Majority of One." Ph.D. dissertation. University of Utah, 1964.

True, Michael D. "The Social and Literary Criticism of Randolph Bourne: A Study of His Development as a Writer." Ph.D. dissertation. Duke University, 1964.

Published Works

Aaron, Daniel. *Writers on the Left.* New York: Oxford University Press, 1977.

______. "American Prophet." *New York Review of Books* 25 (November 23, 1978): 36–40.

Abrahams, Edward. "Randolph Bourne on Feminism and Feminists." *Historian* 43 (May 1981): 365–77.

______. *The Lyrical Left: Randolph Bourne, Alfred Stieglitz, and the Origins of Cultural Radicalism in America.* Charlottesville: University Press of Virginia, 1986.

Adams, Henry. *The Education of Henry Adams.* With an introduction by D. W. Brogan. Boston: Houghton Mifflin, 1961. First published 1918.

Adler, Alfred. *Individual Psychology of Alfred Adler.* Edited by Heinz L. Ansbacher and Rowena Ansbacher. New York: Harper and Row, 1964. First published 1956.

Adorno, Theodor W. *Prisms.* Cambridge: MIT Press, 1990. First published 1967.

Aldridge, John. *After the Lost Generation: A Critical Study of the Writers of Two Wars.* New York: Farrar, Straus and Giroux, 1951.

Arnold, Matthew. *Culture and Anarchy.* New Haven: Yale University Press, 1995.

Bakhtin, Mikhail Mikhailovich. *The Dialogic Imagination: Four Essays.* Edited by Michael Holquist, translated by Carl Emerson and Michael Holquist. Austin: University of Texas Press, 1981.

Ballowe, James C. "The Last Puritan and the Failure in American Culture." *American Quarterly* 18 (Summer 1966): 123–35.

Barrow, Clyde W. *Universities and the Capitalist State: Corporate Liberalism and the Reconstruction of American Higher Education, 1894–1928.* Madison: University of Wisconsin Press, 1990.

Beard, Charles A. *American City Government: A Survey of Newer Tendencies.* New York: Arno Press, 1970. First published 1912.

Benda, Julien. *La Traison des Clercs* (The Treason of the Intellectuals). Translated by Richard Aldington. Boston: Beacon, 1955.

Bender, Thomas. *New York Intellect: A History of Intellectual Life in New York City, from 1750 to the Beginnings of Our Own Time.* New York: Alfred A. Knopf, 1987.

Bercovitch, Sacvan. *The Puritan Origins of the American Self.* New Haven: Yale University Press, 1975.

Bercovitch, Sacvan, ed. *Reconstructing American Literary History.* Cambridge: Harvard University Press, 1986.

Beringause, A. F. "The Double Martyrdom of Randolph Bourne." *Journal of the History of Ideas* 18 (October 1957): 594–603.

Berlowitz, Leslie, and Rick Beard, eds. *Greenwich Village: Culture and Counterculture.* New Brunswick, N.J.: Rutgers University Press, 1991.

Blake, Casey Nelson. "The Young Intellectuals and the Culture of Personality." *American Literary History* 1(3) (Fall 1989): 510–34.

______. *Beloved Community: The Cultural Criticism of Randolph Bourne, Van Wyck Brooks, Waldo Frank, and Lewis Mumford.* Chapel Hill: University of North Carolina Press, 1990.

______. " 'The Battle,'" *Nation* (February 25, 1991): 239–41.

______. " 'The Cosmopolitan Note': Randolph Bourne and the Challenge of 'Trans-national America.' " *Culturefront* (Winter 1995–1996): 25–28.

Bourke, Paul F. "The Social Critics and the End of American Innocence: 1907–1921." *Journal of American Studies* 3 (1969): 57–72.

______. "The Status of Politics, 1909–1919: The *New Republic,* Randolph Bourne and Van Wyck Brooks." *Journal of American Studies* 8(2) (August 1974): 171–202.

Branford, Victor. "RSB." *Political Science Quarterly* 30 (1915): 343–44.

Brantlinger, Patrick. *Bread and Circuses.* Ithaca, N.Y.: Cornell University Press, 1983.

Brittain, Vera. *Chronicle of Youth.* New York: Morrow, 1982.

Bromwich, David. "Literary Radicalism in America." *Dissent* (Winter 1985): 35–44.

Brooks, Van Wyck. *The Wine of the Puritans.* London: Sisley's, 1908.

______. *America's Coming of Age.* New York: B. W. Huebsch, 1915.

______. *Letters and Leadership.* New York: B. W. Huebsch, 1918.

______. "Introduction." In *History of a Literary Radical and Other Essays,* edited by Van Wyck Brooks. New York: B. W. Huebsch, 1920. Also in *The History of a Literary Radical and Other Papers.* New York: S. A. Russell, 1956.

______. "Randolph Bourne." *Encyclopedia of Social Sciences.* New York: Macmillan, 1930.

______. *The Confident Years, 1885–1915.* New York: E. P. Dutton, 1952.

______. "Randolph Bourne." In *Fenollosa and His Circle: With Other Essays in Biography,* 259–321. New York: E. P. Dutton, 1962.

______. *An Autobiography.* New York: E. P. Dutton, 1965.

Brown, Milton W. *American Painting from the Armory Show to the Depression.* Princeton: Princeton University Press, 1955.

______. *The Story of the Armory Show.* New York: New York Graphic Society, 1963.

Bullert, Gary. *The Politics of John Dewey.* Buffalo, N.Y.: Prometheus Books, 1983.

Cantor, Milton. "The Radical Confrontation with Foreign Policy: War and Revolution, 1914–1920." In *Dissent: Explorations in the History of American Radicalism,* ed. by Alfred F. Young, 217–49. DeKalb: Northern Illinois University Press, 1968.

Carlson, Robert A. "Americanization as an Early Twentieth Century Adult Education Movement." *History of Education Quarterly* 10 (Winter 1970): 440–64.

Chafee, Zechariah, Jr. *Free Speech in the United States.* Cambridge: Harvard University Press, 1941.

Chamberlain, John. *A Farewell to Reform.* Chicago: Quadrangle, 1965. First published 1932.

Chase, Richard. "The Fate of the Avant-Garde." *Partisan Review* 24(3) (Summer 1957): 363–75.

______. "Radicalism Today." *Partisan Review* 24(1) (Winter 1975): 45–54.

Chomsky, Noam."The Responsibility of Intellectuals." In *American Power and the New Mandarins,* 323–66. New York: Pantheon, 1969.

______. "Intellectuals and the State (1977)." In *Towards a New Cold War: Essays on the Current Crisis and How We Got There,* 60–85. New York: Pantheon, 1982.

Clayton, Bruce. *Forgotten Prophet: The Life of Randolph Bourne.* Baton Rouge: Louisiana State University Press, 1984.

Cohen, Sol. *Progressives and Urban School Reform.* New York: Teachers College of Columbia University, 1963.

Collins, Seward. "Criticism in America." *Bookman* (June 1930): 241–56, 353–64.

Commager, Henry Steele. *The American Mind: An Interpretation of American Thought and Character Since the 1880s.* New Haven: Yale University Press, 1950.

______. *The Search for a Usable Past and Other Essays in Historiography.* New York: Alfred A. Knopf, 1967.

Conn, Peter. *The Divided Mind: Ideology and Imagination in America, 1989–1917.* Cambridge: Cambridge University Press, 1983.

Cooney, Terry. *The Rise of the New York Intellectuals.* Madison: University of Wisconsin Press, 1986.

Cooperman, Stanley. *World War I and the American Novel.* Baltimore: Johns Hopkins University Press, 1967. First published 1970.

Cott, Nancy F. *The Grounding of Modern Feminism.* New Haven: Yale University Press, 1987.

Cowley, Malcolm. *After the Genteel Tradition: American Writers Since 1910.* New York: W. W. Norton, 1937.

______. *Exile's Return: A Literary Odyssey of the 1920s.* New York: Penguin, 1978. First published 1951.

Creel, George. *How We Advertised America.* New York: Harper, 1920.

Cremin, Lawrence. *The Transformation of the School.* New York: Vintage, 1961.

Croly, Herbert. *The Promise of American Life.* New York: Macmillan, 1909.

______. *Progressive Democracy.* New York: Macmillan, 1914.

Curtis, Tom. "Bourne, Macdonald, Chomsky, and the Rhetoric of Resistance." *Antioch Review* 29 (Summer 1969): 245–52.

Dahlberg, Edward. "Randolph Bourne: In the Saddle of Rosinante." In *Can These Bones Live,* 27–39. Rev. ed. New York: New Directions, 1960. First published 1941.

______. "Randolph Bourne." In *Alms for Oblivion,* 79–86. Minneapolis: University of Minnesota Press, 1964.

Damico, Alfonso J. *Individuality and Community: The Social and Political Thought of John Dewey.* Gainesville: University of Florida Press, 1978.

Dearborn, Mary V. "Anzia Yezierska and the Making of an Ethnic American Self." In *Inventing Ethnicity,* edited by Werner Sollors, 105–23. New York: Oxford University Press, 1989.

Dell, Floyd. "Randolph Bourne." *New Republic* 16 (January 4, 1919): 276.

______. *Intellectual Vagabondage.* New York: George H. Doran, 1926.

______. *Love in Greenwich Village.* New York: George H. Doran, 1926.

______. *Homecoming.* New York: Farrar and Rinehart, 1933.

Deutsch, Babbette. *A Brittle Heaven.* New York: Greenberg, 1926.

Dewey, John. *Democracy and Education.* New York: Macmillan, 1916.

______. *The School and Society.* Chicago: University of Chicago Press, 1916.

______. *Characters and Events.* Edited by Joseph Ratner. New York: Henry Holt, 1929.

Dewey, John, and Evelyn Dewey. *Schools of Tomorrow.* New York: E. P. Dutton, 1915.

Diggins, John Patrick. *The American Left in the Twentieth Century.* New York: Harcourt Brace Jovanovich, 1973.

______. "John Dewey in Peace and War." *American Scholar* 50 (Spring 1981): 213–30.

______. "The *New Republic* and Its Times, 1914–1984." *New Republic* 191 (December 10, 1984): 23–73.

______. "Republicanism and Progressivism." *American Quarterly* 84(4) (Fall 1985): 572–98.

______. *The Promise of Pragmatism: Modernism and the Crisis of Knowledge and Authority.* Chicago: University of Chicago Press, 1994.

Dos Passos, John. *Nineteen-Nineteen.* New York: Harcourt, Brace, 1932.

Dreiser, Theodore. "Appearance and Reality." In *American Spectator Year Book,* No. 11, 204–9. New York: Frederick A. Stokes, 1934.

DuBois, W. E. B. *The Souls of Black Folk.* New York: New American Library, 1969. First published 1903.

Eagan, Maurice Francis. "Five American Essayists." *Yale Review* 10 (October 1920): 186–89.

Eisenach, Eldon J. *The Lost Promise of Progressivism.* Lawrence: University Press of Kansas, 1994.

Erikson, Erik. *Childhood and Society.* 2d ed. New York: W. W. Norton, 1963.

______. *Youth: Change and Challenge.* New York: Basic Books, 1963.

______. *Identity, Youth, and Crisis.* New York: W. W. Norton, 1968.

Erskine, John. *The Memory of Certain Persons.* Boston: J. P. Lippincott, 1947.

Featherstone, Joseph. "Foreword." *Randolph Silliman Bourne: Education Through Radical Eyes,* by Thomas N. Walters. Kennebunkport, Maine: Mercer House, 1982.

Feuer, Lewis S. "The Political Linguistics of 'Intellectual': 1898–1918." *Survey* 16 (Winter 1971): 156–83.

Filler, Louis. *Randolph Bourne.* Washington, D.C.: American Council on Public Affairs, 1943.

______. *Vanguards and Followers: Youth in the American Tradition.* New York: Transaction Books, 1995. First published 1978.

Forcey, Charles. *Crossroads of Liberalism: Croly, Weyl, Lippmann, and the Progressive Era, 1900–1925.* New York: Oxford University Press, 1961.

Forum Exhibition Catalogue. Whitney Museum of American Art, 1983.

Fox, Richard Wightman. "Apostle of Personality." *New York Times Book Review,* January 13, 1985, p. 12.

Frank, Waldo. *Our America.* New York: Boni and Liveright, 1919.

______. *Discovery of America.* New York: Charles Scribners, 1929.

______. *In the American Jungle.* New York: Farrar and Rinehart, 1937.

______. *Memoirs of Waldo Frank.* Edited by Alan Trachtenberg. Amherst: University of Massachusetts Press, 1973.

Freeman, Joseph. *An American Testament: A Narrative of Rebels and Romantics.* New York: Farrar and Rinehart, 1936.

Fussell, Paul. *The Great War and Modern Memory*. New York: Oxford University Press, 1975.

______. "My War." In *Penguin Book of Contemporary Essays,* edited by Maureen Howard, 231–48. New York: Viking Press, 1985.

Gilbert, James Burkhart. *Writers and Partisans: A History of Literary Radicalism in America*. New York: John Wiley, 1968.

Gleason, Philip. "The Melting Pot: Symbol of Fusion or Confusion?" *American Quarterly* 16 (Spring 1964): 20–46.

Gold, Michael. "America Needs a Critic." *New Masses* 1 (October 1926): 7–9.

Goldman, Eric. *Rendezvous with Destiny*. New York: Vintage, 1956.

Goldstein, Robert Justin. *Political Repression in America, 1870–1970*. New York: Schenkman, 1978.

Golin, Steve. "The Paterson Strike Pageant: Success or Failure?" *Socialist Review* 69 (May–June 1983): 45–78.

______. *The Fragile Bridge: Paterson Silk Strike, 1913*. Philadelphia: Temple University Press, 1988.

Gouldner, Alvin. *The Future of Intellectuals and the Rise of the New Class*. New York: Seabury Press, 1979.

Gramsci, Antonio. *Selections from the Prison Notebooks*. Translated and edited by Quentin Hoare and G. Nowell Smith. New York: International Publishers, 1971.

Graves, Robert. *Goodbye to All That*. Garden City, N.Y.: Doubleday, 1957.

Gregory, Alyse. *The Day is Gone*. New York: E. P. Dutton, 1948.

Gregory, Horace. "Salvos for Randolph Bourne." In *Selected Poems of Horace Gregory*. New York: Viking Press, 1951.

Greenstone, J. David. *The Lincoln Persuasion: Remaking American Liberalism*. Princeton: Princeton University Press, 1993.

Gruber, Carol S. *Mars and Minerva: World War I and the Uses of the Higher Learning in America*. Baton Rouge: Louisiana State University Press, 1975.

Gunther, Gerald. "Learned Hand and the Origins of the Modern First Amendment Doctrine: Some Fragments of History." *Stanford Law Review* 27 (1975): 719–73.

Hansen, Olaf. "Affinity and Ambivalence." In *The Radical Will: Randolph Bourne, Selected Writings, 1911–1918,* edited by Olaf Hansen, 17–62. New York: Urizen Books, 1977.

______. *Bewusstseinsformen literarischer Intelligenz: Bourne, Croly, Eastman, Calverton, Gold*. Stuttgart: J. B. Metzlersche Verlagsbuchhandlung, 1977.

Heller, Erich. *Thomas Mann: The Ironic German*. South Bend, Ind.: Regnery/Gateway, 1958.

______. *The Disinherited Mind.* New York: Harcourt Brace Jovanovich, 1975.

______. *The Artist's Journey into the Interior and Other Essays.* New York: Harcourt Brace Jovanovich, 1976.

______. *The Importance of Nietzsche.* Chicago: University of Chicago Press, 1988.

Higham, John. *Strangers in the Land: Patterns of American Nativism, 1860–1925.* New Brunswick, N.J.: Rutgers University Press, 1955.

______. "The Reorientation of American Culture in the 1890s." In *Writing American History,* 73–108. Bloomington: Indiana University Press, 1970.

______. *Send These to Me.* New York: Atheneum, 1975.

Hilfer, Anthony Channel. *The Revolt from the Village, 1915–1930: The Literary Attack on Small Town Provincialism.* Chapel Hill: University of North Carolina Press, 1969.

Hobsbawm, Eric. *The Age of Empire, 1875–1914.* New York: Pantheon, 1987.

Hoffman, Frederick J. *The Twenties: American Writing in the Post War Decade.* New York: Viking Press, 1949. First published 1955.

Hoffman, Frederick J., Charles Allen, and Carolyn F. Ulrich. *The Little Magazine.* Princeton: Princeton University Press, 1946.

Hofstadter, Richard. *Age of Reform.* New York: Vintage, 1955.

______. *Anti-Intellectualism in American Life.* New York: Alfred A. Knopf, 1963.

______. *The Progressive Historians.* New York: Alfred A. Knopf, 1968.

Hofstadter, Richard, and Walter P. Metzer. *The Development of Academic Freedom in the United States.* New York: Columbia University Press, 1955.

Hollinger, David A. *In the American Province.* Bloomington: Indiana University Press, 1985.

Hoopes, James. "The Culture of Progressivism: Croly, Lippmann, Brooks, Bourne, and the Idea of American Artistic Decadence." *Clio* 7(1) (1977): 91–111.

Horowitz, Helen L. *Campus Life.* New York: Alfred A. Knopf, 1987.

Howe, Irving. "The Culture of Modernism." *Commentary* 44 (November 1967): 48–59.

______. *World of Our Fathers.* New York: Touchstone, 1976.

______. *Celebrations and Attacks.* New York: Harcourt Brace Jovanovich, 1979.

Hughes, H. Stuart. *Consciousness and Society.* New York: Vintage, 1961. First published 1958.

Huyssen, Andreas. *After the Great Divide: Modernism, Mass Culture, Postmodernism.* Bloomington: Indiana University Press, 1986.

Hyman, Stanley E. *The Armed Vision.* New York: Alfred A. Knopf, 1947.

Jacoby, Russell. *The Last Intellectuals: American Culture in the Age of Academe.* New York: Basic Books, 1987.

James, William. *The Varieties of Religious Experience.* New York: Longmans, Green, 1902.

———. *Essays in Pragmatism.* Edited by Alburey Castell. New York: Hafner, 1948.

———. *Talks to Teachers.* New York: W. W. Norton, 1958.

———. *Pragmatism and Other Essays.* New York: Washington Square Press, 1963.

———. *The Moral Equivalent of War and Other Essays.* Edited by John K. Roth. New York: Harper and Row, 1971.

Jencks, Christopher, and David Reisman. *The Academic Revolution.* Garden City, N.Y.: Doubleday, 1968.

Jessop, Bob. *The Capitalist State.* New York: New York University Press, 1982.

Jones, Margaret C. *Heretics and Hellraisers: Women Contributors to "the Masses," 1911–1917.* Austin: University Press of Texas, 1993.

Joost, Nicholas. *Scofield Thayer and the Dial—An Illustrated History.* Carbondale: Southern Illinois University Press, 1964.

———. *Years of Transition: The Dial.* Barre, Mass.: Barre Publishers, 1967.

———. "Culture vs. Power: Randolph Bourne, John Dewey, and the *Dial." Midwest Quarterly* (April 1968): 245–58.

Kalaidjian, Walter. *American Culture Between the Wars: Revisionary Modernism and Postmodern Critique.* New York: Columbia University Press, 1993.

Kallen, Horace. *Culture and Democracy in the United States.* New York: Arno, 1970. First published 1924.

Kaplan, Sidney. "Social Engineers as Saviors: Effects of World War I on Some American Liberals." *Journal of the History of Ideas* 17 (June 1956): 347–69.

Kazin, Alfred. *On Native Grounds.* New York: Harcourt Brace Jovanovich, 1982.

Kelly, Florence. "Randolph Bourne." *Intercollegiate Socialist* 6 (February–March 1919): 8.

Kennedy, David M. *Over Here: The First World War and American Society.* New York: Oxford University Press, 1980.

Kerr, Clark. *The Uses of the University.* Cambridge: Harvard University Press, 1982.

Kirchwey, Freda. "Randolph Bourne." *Nation* 3 (December 1, 1920): 619.

Klein, Marcus. *After Alienation.* New York: World, 1964. First published 1962.

Kolko, Gabriel. *The Triumph of Conservatism, 1900–1916.* New York: Free Press, 1977. First published 1963.

Kristeva, Julia. *Nations Without Nationalism.* Translated by Leon S. Roudiez. New York: Columbia University Press, 1993.

Kristol, Irving. [Untitled], a review of *Dangling Man,* by Saul Bellow. *Politics* 1 (June 1944): 156.

LaMonte, Robert Rives. "The New Intellectuals." *New Review* (January 1914): 45–53.

Lasch, Christopher. *The New Radicalism in America, 1889–1963: The Intellectual as a Social Type.* New York: Vintage Books, 1967.

______. *Haven in a Heartless World: The Family Besieged.* New York: Basic Books, 1977.

______. "Preface." In *Radical Will: Randolph Bourne, Selected Writings, 1911–1918,* edited by Olaf Hansen. New York: Urizen Books, 1977.

______. *The Culture of Narcissism: American Life in an Age of Diminishing Expectations.* New York: W. W. Norton, 1979.

Lasch, Christopher, ed. *The Social Thought of Jane Addams.* Indianapolis: Bobbs Merrill, 1965.

Laski, Harold. "The Liberalism of Randolph Bourne." *Freeman* 1 (May 19, 1920): 237–38.

Leach, William R. *Land of Desire: Merchants, Power and the Rise of a New American Culture.* New York: Vintage Books, 1993.

Lears, T. J. Jackson. *No Place of Grace.* New York: Pantheon, 1981.

Lentriccia, Frank. *Criticism and Social Change.* Chicago: University of Chicago Press, 1983.

Lerner, Max. "Randolph Bourne and Two Generations." In *Ideas for the Ice Age,* 116–42. New York: Viking Press, 1941.

______. "Introduction." *Randolph Bourne,* by Louis Filler. Washington, D.C.: American Council on Public Affairs, 1943.

Leuchtenberg, William E. "Progressivism and Imperialism: The Progressive Movement and American Foreign Policy, 1898–1916." *Mississippi Valley Historical Review* 39(3) (December 1952): 483–504.

______. *Perils of Prosperity.* Chicago: University of Chicago Press, 1958.

______. "Introduction." *Drift and Mastery,* by Walter Lippmann. Englewood Cliffs, N.J.: Prentice-Hall, 1961. First published 1914. Also "Revised Introduction." *Drift and Mastery.* Madison: University of Wisconsin Press, 1985.

Levenberg, Diane. "Paul Rosenfeld and the Erotics of Art." *Book Forum,* 5(4) (1981): 525–33.

Levine, Daniel. "Randolph Bourne, John Dewey and the Legacy of Liberalism." *Antioch Review* 29 (Summer 1969): 234–44.

Levine, Murray, and Adeline Levine. "The Gary Schools: A Socio-Historical Analysis of the Process of Change." *California Elementary Administrator* (Spring 1970).

Levy, David. *Herbert Croly and the New Republic.* Princeton: Princeton University Press, 1985.

Lind, Michael. *The New American Nation: The New Nationalism and the Fourth American Revolution.* New York: Free Press, 1995.

Lippmann, Walter. *A Preface to Politics.* New York: Mitchell Kennerley, 1913.

______. *Drift and Mastery.* New York: Mitchell Kennerley, 1914.

Livingston, James. *Pragmatism and the Political Economy of Cultural Revolution, 1850–1940.* Chapel Hill: University of North Carolina Press, 1994.

Luhan, Mabel Dodge. *Intimate Memories.* New York: Kraus Reprints, 1971. First published 1933.

Lustig, R. Jeffrey. *Corporate Liberalism: The Origins of Modern American Political Theory, 1890–1920.* Berkeley: University of California Press, 1982.

Lynn, Kenneth S. "The Rebels of Greenwich Village." No. 8, *Perspectives in American History.* Cambridge: Harvard University Press, 1974.

Lyons, Paul. "Teaching the Sixties." *Socialist Review* 15(1) (January–February 1985): 71–91.

McClymer, John. *War and Welfare: Social Engineering in America, 1890–1925.* Westport, Conn.: Greenwood Press, 1980.

MacDonald, Dwight. "War and the Intellectuals: Act II." *Partisan Review* 6 (Spring 1939): 3–20.

______. "Randolph Bourne." *Politics* 1 (March 1944): 35–36.

McNaught, Kenneth. "Socialism and the Progressives: Was Failure Inevitable?" *Dissent: Explorations in the History of American Radicalism,* edited by Alfred F. Young, 253–71. DeKalb: Northern Illinois University Press, 1968.

McWilliams, Wilson Carey. *The Idea of Fraternity in America.* Berkeley: University of California Press, 1973.

Madison, Charles. "Randolph Bourne: The History of a Literary Radical." In *Critics and Crusaders: A Century of American Protest,* 419–42. New York: Henry Holt, 1947.

Mann, Thomas. *Reflections of a Non-Political Man.* New York: Frederick Ungar, 1983. First published 1918.

Mannheim, Karl. *Ideology and Utopia.* Translated by Louis Wirth and Edward Shils. New York: Harcourt, Brace, and World, 1936.

Marcell, David. *Progress and Pragmatism: James, Dewey, Beard, and the American Idea of Progress.* Westport, Conn.: Greenwood Press, 1974.

May, Henry F. *The End of American Innocence: A Study of the First Years of Our Own Time, 1912–1917.* New York: Oxford University Press, 1959.

______. *Discontent of the Intellectuals. Berkeley Series in American History.* New York: Rand McNally, 1963.

Mayer, Arno. *The Persistence of the Old Regime.* New York: Pantheon, 1981.

Meltzer, Milton. *Bread and Roses: The Struggle of American Labor, 1865–1915.* New York: Vintage, 1967.

Merod, Jim. *The Political Responsibility of the Critic.* Ithaca, N.Y.: Cornell University Press, 1987.

Mills, C. Wright. "The Powerless People: The Role of the Intellectual in Society." *Politics* 1 (April 1944): 68–74.

______. *The Sociological Imagination.* New York: Oxford University Press, 1958.

Monroe, Harriet. "Mr. Bourne on Traps." *Poetry* 12 (May 1918): 91–94.

______. *A Poet's Life.* New York: Macmillan, 1938.

Moreau, John Adam. *Randolph Bourne: Legend and Reality.* Washington, D.C.: Public Affairs Press, 1966.

Morton, H. W. "Randolph Bourne vs. the State." *Anarchy* 31 (September 1963): 265–69.

Mumford, Lewis. "The Image of Randolph Bourne." *New Republic* 64 (September 24, 1930): 151–52.

______. "The Corruption of Liberalism." *New Republic* 102 (April 29, 1940): 568–73.

Munson, Gorham. *Awakening Twenties: A Memoir-History of the Literary Period.* Baton Rouge: Louisiana State University Press, 1985.

Murphy, Paul L. *World War I and the Origin of Civil Liberties in the United States.* New York: W. W. Norton, 1979.

Nashaw, David. *Children of the City: At Work and at Play.* Garden City, N.Y.: Anchor Press, 1985.

Nearing, Scott. *The Making of a Radical: A Political Autobiography.* New York: Harper and Row, 1972.

Nelson, Cary. *Repression and Recovery: Modern American Poetry and the Politics of Cultural Memory, 1910–1945.* Madison: University of Wisconsin Press, 1989.

Nelson, Raymond. *Van Wyck Brooks: A Writer's Life.* New York: E. P. Dutton, 1981.

Nietzsche, Friedrich W. *The Use and Abuse of History.* Translated by Adrian Collins. Indianapolis: Liberal Arts Press 1957. First published 1949.

______. *Basic Writings of Nietzsche.* Translated and edited by Walter Kaufmann. New York: Modern Library, 1966.

______. *The Portable Nietzsche.* Translated and edited by Walter Kaufmann. New York: Penguin Books, 1968. First published 1954.

Noble, David W. "The *New Republic* and the Idea of Progress, 1914–20." *Mississippi Valley Historical Review* 38 (1951): 387–402.

______. *The Paradox of Progressive Thought.* Minneapolis: University of Minnesota Press, 1958.

Nochlin, Linda. "The Paterson Pageant." *Art in America* 52 (May–June 1974): 67.

Oppenheim, James. "Foreword." In *Untimely Papers,* edited by James Oppenheim. New York: B. W. Huebsch, 1919.

______. "Randolph Bourne: Died December 22 [*sic*], 1918." *Dial* 66 (January 11, 1919): 7.

______. "Randolph Bourne: Died December 22 [*sic*], 1918." *Liberator* 1 (February 1919): 14–15 (different verses).

______. "The Story of the *Seven Arts.*" *American Mercury* 20 (June 1930): 156–64.

Oppenheimer, Franz. *The State.* Translated by John M. Gitterman. Indianapolis: Bobbs-Merrill, 1923. First published 1914.

Parrington, Vernon. *Main Currents in American Thought.* New York: Harcourt Brace, 1930. First published 1927.

Parsons, Elsie Clews. "A Pacifist Patriot." *Dial* 68 (March 1920): 367–70.

Paul, Sherman. *Randolph Bourne.* Minneapolis: University of Minnesota Press, 1966.

Peiss, Kathy. *Cheap Amusements: Working Women and Leisure in Turn-of-the-Century New York.* Philadelphia: Temple University Press, 1986.

Pells, Richard H. *Radical Visions and American Dreams: Culture and Social Thought in the Depression Years.* Middletown, Conn.: Wesleyan University Press, 1987. First published 1973.

Peterson, H. C., and Gilbert C. Fite. *Opponents of War, 1917–1918.* Seattle: University of Washington, 1968. First published 1957.

Pitkin, Hannah. *The Concept of Representation.* Berkeley: University of California Press, 1972.

Porter, Carolyn. *Seeing and Being.* Middletown, Conn.: Wesleyan University Press, 1981.

Posnock, Ross. "The Politics of Nonidentity: A Genealogy." *boundary 2* 19(1) (Spring 1992): 34–68.

Preston, William, Jr. *Aliens and Dissenters: Federal Suppression of Radicals, 1903–1933.* New York: Harper and Row, 1963.

Quandt, Jean B. *From Small Town to the Great Community: The Social Thought of Progressive Intellectuals.* Princeton: Princeton University Press, 1970.

Reed, John. *The Education of John Reed: Selected Writings.* New York: International, 1955.

Remarque, Erich Maria. *All Quiet on the Western Front.* Greenwich, Conn.: Fawcett, 1968.

Resek, Carl. "Introduction." In *War and the Intellectuals: Randolph S. Bourne, Collected Essays, 1915–1919.* New York: Harper and Row, 1964.

______. "Prodigal Sons and the Lyrical Left." *Wilson Quarterly* 11(1) (January 1987): 150–52.

Ricci, David M. *The Tragedy of Political Science.* New Haven: Yale University Press, 1984.

Rideout, Walter. *The Radical Novel in the United States, 1900–1954.* Cambridge: Harvard University Press, 1956.

Rodgers, Daniel T. "In Search of Progressivism." *Reviews in American History* 10 (December 1982): 113–31.

Rogin, Michael. "In Defense of the New Left." *Democracy* 3(4) (Fall 1983): 106–16.

______. *Ronald Reagan, the Movie and Other Episodes in Political Demonology.* Berkeley: University of California Press, 1987.

______. "The Great Mother Domesticated: Sexual Difference and Sexual Indifference in D. W. Griffith's Intolerance." *Critical Inquiry* 15 (Spring 1989): 510–55.

Roosevelt, Jinx. "Randolph Bourne: The Education of a Critic, an Interpretation." *History of Education Quarterly* 17(3) (Fall 1977): 257–75.

Rosenfeld, Paul. "Randolph Bourne." In *Port of New York: Essays on Fourteen American Moderns,* 211–36. New York: Harcourt, Brace, 1924.

Rugg, Harold. *Culture and Education.* New York: Harcourt, Brace, 1931.

Rutkoff, Peter M., and William B. Scott. *New School: A History of the New School for Social Research.* New York: Free Press, 1986.

Ryan, Alan. *John Dewey and the High Tide of American Liberalism.* New York: W. W. Norton, 1995.

Salmagundi. (Spring–Summer 1986): Nos. 70–71. "Intellectuals."

Sandeen, Eric J. "Introduction." In *The Letters of Randolph Bourne: A Comprehensive Edition,* edited by Eric J. Sandeen. Troy, N.Y.: Whitston, 1981.

______. "Bourne Again: The Correspondence Between Randolph Bourne and Elsie Clews Parsons." *American Literary History* 1(3) (Fall 1989): 489–509.

Santayana, George. *The Letters of George Santayana.* Edited by Daniel Cory. New York: Scribners, 1955.

______. *The Genteel Tradition: Nine Essays.* Edited by Douglas L. Wilson. Cambridge: Harvard University Press, 1967.

Schapiro, Meyer. "Rebellion in Art." In *America in Crisis,* edited by Daniel Aaron, 203–42. New York: Alfred A. Knopf, 1952.

Schieber, Harry N. *The Wilson Administration and Civil Liberties, 1917–1921.* Ithaca, N.Y.: Cornell University Press, 1960.

Schlissel, Lillian. "Introduction." In *The World of Randolph Bourne.* New York: E. P. Dutton, 1965.

Schutte, Ofelia. *Beyond Nihilism: Nietzsche Without Masks.* Chicago: University of Chicago Press, 1984.

Scialabba, George. "Bourne in Flames." *Voice Literary Supplement* (February 1985): 6.

Sedgwick, Ellery. *The Happy Profession.* Boston: Little, Brown, 1946.

Seidelman, Raymond. *Disenchanted Realists: Political Science and the Amer-*

ican Crisis, 1884–1984. Albany: State University of New York Press, 1985.

Seideman, David. *The New Republic.* New York: Praeger, 1986.

Shannon, David A. *The Socialist Party of America.* Chicago: Quadrangle, 1967.

Shapiro, Michael J. "Introduction: The Problem of Ideology: Locating the Political Analyst/Writer." In *The Politics of Representation: Writing Practices in Biography, Photography and Policy Analysis,* 3–54. Madison: University of Wisconsin Press, 1988.

Shulte-Sasse, Linda. "Leni Riefenstahl's Feature Films and the Question of the Fascist Aesthetic." *Cultural Critique* 18 (Spring 1991): 123–48.

Sillen, Samuel. "The Challenge of Randolph Bourne." *Masses and Mainstream* 6 (December 1953): 24–32.

Sklar, Martin. "Woodrow Wilson and the Political Economy of Modern Liberalism." *Studies on the Left* 1(3) (1960): 17–47.

Smith-Rosenberg, Carroll. *Disorderly Conduct: Visions of Gender in Victorian America.* New York: Alfred A. Knopf, 1995.

Sochen, June. *The New Woman in Greenwich Village, 1910–1920.* New York: Quadrangle Books, 1972.

Sollors, Werner. "Theory of American Ethnicity, Or: "? S Ethnic?/Ti and American/Ti, de or United (W) States S S1 and Theor?" *American Quarterly* 33(3) (1981): 257–83.

______. *Beyond Ethnicity: Consent and Descent in American Culture.* New York: Oxford University Press, 1986.

______. "A Critique of Pure Pluralism." In *Reconstructing American Literary History,* edited by Sacvan Bercovitch, 250–79. Cambridge: Harvard University Press, 1986.

Sollors, Werner, ed. "Introduction." In *The Invention of Ethnicity.* New York: Oxford University Press, 1989.

Sorel, Georges. *Reflections on Violence.* Translated by T. E. Hulme. New York: Collier, 1961. First published 1908.

Spiller, Robert E., ed. *Literary History of the United States,* 3d ed. New York: Macmillan, 1963.

Spingarn, J. E. *Creative Criticism: Essay on the Unity of Genius and Taste.* New York: Henry Holt, 1917. First published 1911.

Stearns, Harold E. *Liberalism in America: Its Origin, Its Temporary Collapse, Its Future.* New York: Boni Liveright, 1919.

Stearns, Harold E., ed. *Civilization in the United States.* New York: Harcourt, Brace, 1922.

Steele, Ronald. *Walter Lippmann and the American Century.* Boston: Little, Brown, 1980.

Stettner, Edward A. *Shaping Modern Liberalism: Herbert Croly and Progressive Thought.* Lawrence: University Press of Kansas, 1993.

Strong, Tracy. *Friedrich Nietzsche and the Politics of Transfiguration.* Berkeley: University of California Press, 1975.

Strout, Cushing. "William James and the Twice-Born Sick Soul." *Daedalus* 117 (Summer 1968): 1062–82.

______. *The Veracious Imagination.* Middletown, Conn.: Wesleyan University Press, 1981.

Strum, Philippa. *Brandeis: Beyond Progressivism.* Lawrence: University Press of Kansas, 1993.

Sullivan, Mark. *Our Times: The United States, 1900–1925.* New York: Scribner's, 1926–1935.

Susman, Warren I. *Culture as History: The Transformation of American Society in the Twentieth Century.* New York: Pantheon, 1985. First published 1973.

Symes, Lillian, and Travers Clement. *Rebel America.* New York: Harper and Row, 1934.

Taylor, Frederick Winslow. *The Principles of Scientific Management.* New York: W. W. Norton, 1967. First published 1911.

Teall, Dorothy. "Bourne into Myth." *Bookman* 75 (October 1932): 590–99.

Trachtenberg, Alan. "Introduction: The Genteel Tradition and Its Critics." In *Critics of Culture: Literature and Society in the Early Twentieth Century,* edited by Alan Trachtenberg, 3–13. New York: John Wiley and Sons, 1976.

______. *Incorporation of America: Culture and Society in the Gilded Age.* New York: Hill and Wang, 1982.

Trotter, Wilfred. *Instincts of the Herd in Peace and War.* London: T. F. Unwin, 1920.

True, Michael D. "The Achievement of an American Literary Radical: A Bibliography of Randolph Silliman Bourne (1889–1918)." *Bulletin of the New York Public Library* 69 (October 1965): 523–36.

Tuttleton, James W. "American Literary Radicalism in the Twenties." *New Criterion* (March 1985): 16–30.

Untermeyer, Louis. *From Another World.* New York: Harcourt Brace, 1939.

Utley, Phillip Lee. "Radical Youth: Generational Conflict in the *Anfang* Movement, 1912–January 1914." *History of Education Quarterly* 19(2) (Summer 1979): 207–28.

Van Doren, Carl. *Three Worlds.* New York: Harper, 1936.

Veblen, Thorstein. *The Theory of the Leisure Class.* Edited by Max Lerner. New York: Mentor, 1953. First published 1899.

Vitelli, James R. *Randolph Bourne.* Boston: Twayne Publishers, 1981.

Walters, Thomas N. *Randolph Silliman Bourne: Education Through Radical Eyes*. Kennebunkport, Maine: Mercer House Press, 1982.

Walzer, Michael. "The War and Randolph Bourne." In *The Company of Critics: Social Criticism and Political Commitment in the Twentieth Century*, 45–63. New York: Basic Books, 1988.

Wasserstrom, William. *The Times of the Dial*. Syracuse, N.Y.: Syracuse University Press, 1963.

Wasserstrom, William. ed. *A Dial Miscellany*. Syracuse, N.Y.: Syracuse University Press, 1963.

Weinberg, Arthur, and Lila Weinberg, eds. *The Muckrakers*. New York: G. P. Putnam, 1964. First published 1961.

Weinstein, James. *The Corporate Ideal in the Liberal State, 1900–1918*. Boston: Beacon Press, 1968.

Weinstein, Michael. *The Wilderness and the City*. Amherst: University of Massachusetts Press, 1982.

______. "The Dark Night of the Liberal Spirit and the Dawn of the Savage." *Canadian Journal of Political and Social Theory* 12(1–2) (1988): 165–79.

Wertheim, Arthur Frank. *The New York Little Renaissance: Iconoclasm, Modernism, and Nationalism in American Culture, 1908–1917*. New York: New York University Press, 1976.

West, Cornel. *The American Evasion of Philosophy: A Genealogy of Pragmatism*. Madison: University of Wisconsin Press, 1989.

Westbrook, Robert B. *John Dewey and American Democracy*. Ithaca, N.Y.: Cornell University Press, 1989.

Weyl, Walter. *The New Democracy*. New York: Harper and Row, 1964 . First published 1912.

White, Hayden. *Metahistory: The Historical Imagination in Nineteenth-Century Europe*. Baltimore: Johns Hopkins University Press, 1973.

Whitman, Walt. *Leaves of Grass*. Edited by Malcolm Cowley. New York: Penguin, 1959. First published 1885.

Wiebe, Robert H. *The Search for Order, 1877–1920*. New York: Hill and Wang, 1967.

Wohl, Robert. *The Generation of 1914*. Cambridge: Harvard University Press, 1979.

Wolin, Sheldon S. "The New Conservatives." *New York Review of Books*, February 5, 1976, pp. 6–11.

Zigrosser, Carl. "Randolph Bourne and the Gary Schools." *Modern School* 6(4) (October 1917): 155–57.

______. *My Own Shall Come to Me*. Philadelphia: Casa Laura, 1971.

______. *A World of Art and Museums*. Philadelphia: Art Alliance Press, 1974.

Zizek, Slavoj. "Eastern Europe's Republics of Gilead." In *Dimensions of Radical Democracy: Pluralism, Citizenship, Community,* edited by Chantal Mouffe, 193–207. New York: Verso Press, 1992.

______. "Introduction: The Spectre of Ideology." In *Mapping Ideology,* edited by Slavoj Zizek, 1–33. New York: Verso Press, 1994.

INDEX